REALITY, RELIGION,
AND THE MIND

THE FACTS ON FILE GUIDE TO PHILOSOPHY

Reality, Religion, and the Mind

David Boersema
Kari Middleton

☑ Facts On File
An Infobase Learning Company

The Facts On File Guide to Philosophy: Reality, Religion, and the Mind

Facts On File, Inc.
An imprint of Infobase Learning
132 West 31st Street
New York NY 10001

Library of Congress Cataloging-in-Publication Data
Boersema, David.
   The Facts on File guide to philosophy. Reality, religion, and the mind / David Boersema, Kari Middleton.
       p. cm.
   Includes bibliographical references (p.   ) and index.
   ISBN 978-0-8160-8159-2 (alk. paper)
   1. Reality. 2. Metaphysics. 3. Religion—Philosophy. 4. Philosophy of mind.
I. Middleton, Kari. II. Title. III. Title: Reality, religion, and the mind.
   BD331.B5925 2012
   110—dc23   2011029437

Facts On File books are available at special discounts when purchased in bulk quantities for businesses, associations, institutions, or sales promotions. Please call our Special Sales Department in New York at (212) 967-8800 or (800) 322-8755.

You can find Facts On File on the World Wide Web at
http://www.infobaselearning.com

Text design by Erik Lindstrom
Composition by Julie Adams
Cover printed by Yurchak Printing, Inc., Landisville, Pa.
Book printed and bound by Yurchak Printing, Inc., Landisville, Pa.
Date printed: March 2012
Printed in the United States of America

This book is printed on acid-free paper.

Table of Contents

Introduction   ix

Part I: Metaphysics   1

Introductory Discussion Questions   3

Introduction to Metaphysics   5

Categories of Reality   16

Universals and Particulars   27

Causality and Knowledge of the World   40

The Rejection of Metaphysics   53

Emergentism   57

Images of the World   61

Consciousness and Freedom   70

Modality and Possible Worlds   78

Concluding Discussion Questions   86

    Further Reading   87

    Glossary   88

    Key People   91

Part II: Philosophy of Religion   105

Introductory Discussion Questions   107

What Is Philosophy of Religion?   109

Faith and Philosophy   117

Religious Epistemology and the Ontological Argument   121

The Cosmological Argument   129

Argument from Design   134

Natural versus Revealed Religion   143

The Nature of God's Perfection   147

Theodicy and the Problem of Evil   152

Modern Science and Ethics   157

Twentieth-Century Philosophy   177

Concluding Discussion Questions   178

    Further Reading   179

    Glossary   180

    Key People   182

Part III: Philosophy of Mind   195

Introductory Discussion Questions   197

What Is Philosophy of Mind?   199

The Mind/Body Problem, Dualism, and Monism   204

Solipsism and the Problem of Other Minds   212

Mental Causation and Parallelism   216

Epiphenomenalism and Emergentism   219

Idealism, Behaviorism, and Identity Theory   224

Consciousness, Qualia, and Materialism   239

Anomalous Monism and Functionalism   246

Cognition, Artificial Intelligence, and the Chinese Room
Argument   255

Mysterianism and Extended Mind   267
Animal Minds   272
Concluding Discussion Questions   276
    Further Reading   278
    Glossary   279
    Key People   282

    Index   291

Introduction

Albert Einstein is said to have remarked, "Reality is merely an illusion, albeit a persistent one." Think about the page before you right now. Which is more real: the page itself, the atoms that make up the page, or the sensation you have looking at the page? We have all had experiences that seem real, only later to be uncertain they were. Also, we have all had dreams that certainly seemed very real while we were dreaming, until we woke up and realized they were just dreams.

What is reality? This seemingly very abstract question is one we all have asked at some point. We may have asked it about some particular aspect of reality: Is this feeling I have for that person love or just a fleeting fancy? Did I really see my sister at the mall or was that someone who only looked like her? Or we might well have asked these questions about very broad aspects of reality: Is there really a God? Is there life on other planets? Do we really know that other people feel the same sensations that we do?

The philosophical study of reality is called metaphysics. Consider the following list: cats, shadows, wind, weighing three pounds, being a mother, the number two, information, a sneeze, dropping a ball onto the floor. The list's components all seem to be real, but they are quite different. Cats are physical objects; a sneeze is an event, not an object; being a mother is neither an object nor an event but a relation between two objects (a woman and her child). One very basic question, then, is what kinds of things (where "things" might include events or relations or abstract objects such as numbers) are real? This question might seem to be very abstract, but it can easily be made more practical, such as when we ask whether or not a fetus is a person, or whether a person who has lost all memory or consciousness is the same person he or she used to be.

Metaphysics is the basic, broad study of reality. One subarea within metaphysics is what is called the philosophy of mind. We take it for granted that people (and perhaps other animals) have minds, but what does that mean? Is the mind the same thing as the brain? Are people really made up of at least two very different things: minds and bodies? Another subarea within metaphysics, or at least related to metaphysics, is philosophy of religion. What, or who, is God? Are there souls? What, exactly, does *soul* refer to? Are there aspects of reality that relate to religion but not to science? Can science and religion contradict each other? Is there a religious reality that is different than a scientific one?

This book, then, is about the philosophical study of reality, first from the perspective of metaphysics broadly, then the philosophy of religion, and finally the philosophy of mind. It is one volume in the Facts On File Guide to Philosophy set, which is designed to provide an accessible and engaging introduction to philosophy for students.

Note that, because major ideas can be important in different contexts and because certain thinkers made important contributions in more than one area, material within the set is occasionally repeated, with the intention of providing full context for each discussion.

David Boersema
Kari Middleton

PART I
Metaphysics

Introductory Discussion Questions

1. What does it mean to say that something is real or not real? How would we know?
2. Are there questions about reality that, even in principle, science could not answer? What would such a question be?
3. What is more real, the chair someone sits on or the atoms that make up that chair or the person's belief that there is a chair there?
4. Does white exist independently of particular white things that exist?
5. Could the world be some way that we could never possibly know about? If not, what does it mean to say that we discover how things are? If so, how could we ever know that this is true?
6. What does it mean to say that something is possible? Necessary?

Introduction to Metaphysics

Metaphysics is the study of the ultimate nature of reality. It is considered one of the major overall branches of philosophy, along with epistemology (the study of knowledge) and axiology (the study of value). The word *metaphysics* comes from a Greek expression, *meta ta phusika,* meaning "after the things of nature." In turn, this expression refers to select writings of Aristotle (384–322 B.C.E.) that dealt with topics about what is real but that were not covered in his writings on physics (or natural science).

By speaking of the ultimate nature of reality, philosophers include various topics. One broad set of metaphysical topics has to do with beings (that is, things that exist) and even the very concept of Being. This broad set of metaphysical topics is often called ontology (from the Greek word *ontos,* meaning "being"). These topics are not directly about everyday things, such as trees and tables (although those kinds of things are talked about by metaphysicians), but broad kinds of things. For example, one ontological issue is about the nature of events. An event is not a physical object. Events include a person sneezing, two people shaking hands, and the landing of astronauts on the Moon. An astronaut is an object, and the Moon is an object (that is, they are physical things that exist in certain times and spaces), but the astronauts and the Moon are not events. So, if someone were to try to describe the world in terms of what is real, that description would include objects, such as the astronaut and the Moon, but it would also need to include events, such as astronauts landing on the Moon. Ultimate reality, then, would include both objects and events. Metaphysics investigates the nature of events, generally speaking (that is, not just particular events, but the very nature of what events are). This is something that no science does; it is a metaphysical issue.

Besides events (and objects), there are other broad kinds of components of reality that metaphysics is concerned with. For example, a cat is an object. But a cat has many features, or properties. Cats (usually) have ears and tails and claws and particular genetic structures; they purr and meow and walk; they have certain colored fur, etc. These various properties are themselves not necessarily objects; the ability to purr is not a physical object (even though having that ability requires having certain physical objects present, namely, whatever it is that allows cats to purr). Or weighing a certain amount is not in itself a physical object. So, properties seem to be another basic kind of reality, along with objects and events.

In addition, there are certain aspects of things that seem not to be events or objects or properties. For instance, cats are smaller than elephants. So, "being smaller than elephants" is true of cats. This is said to be a relation between cats and elephants. "Smaller than" is a relation, but "smaller than" is not an object or event or even a property. At least, it is not a property like having ears or being able to purr, since "smaller than" requires at least two things to be related, where "having ears" does not.

Another ontological issue is about abstract objects. Usually when we think or speak of objects, we mean physical objects, such as trees or tables. But we also think and speak of things such as numbers or money or families. These are not physical things that we can touch or taste or smell, etc. Although we might think of money as being physical, such as coins or dollar bills, those physical things are simply convenient tools that we use to exchange money. A dollar is an abstract thing, even though a particular dollar bill is a physical thing. Metaphysicians have argued for centuries about abstract objects, whether they exist, what they are, what properties or relations they might have, etc.

Finally, there are ontological questions about particular things or kinds of things. For instance, the issue of whether God exists, or what God's nature could be, is an ontological issue. Also, the questions within science of fundamental types of things that are real—for example, quarks or other subatomic things—are among the basic theoretical parts of science that blend over into metaphysics.

Besides the broad set of ontological topics that are part of metaphysics, there are also metaphysical topics that are not directly about kinds of beings or things. For example, a long-standing metaphysical topic is the nature of time. Another is the nature of cause. Yet another is what is called modality. Modality refers to the notions of necessity and possibility. For example, what does it mean to say that it is possible that George Washington might never have been born or that it is necessary that two plus two equals four? Is it possible that you (a particular person) could have had different parents? Metaphysicians do not address simply these particular questions (although they do that) but the broader question of what is the nature of necessity and possibility.

Yet another broad sort of topic that metaphysics deals with is the study, not directly of things themselves, but of how things are categorized or grouped together or classified. We think and speak of particular things in the world as being grouped in various ways. Are those ways natural or are they imposed by us onto the world? That is, do we discover that things are naturally grouped together or do we construct the groupings and classifications of them? This type of issue—about categories and classifications—also includes the metaphysical concern about persistence and identity over time. That is, what makes something the same thing over time (or what is it that persists over time with respect to something)? An acorn becomes an oak tree; is the oak tree the same thing as the acorn? A person gets amnesia and cannot remember anything at all about her childhood; is she the same person as that child?

All of the topics and issues noted so far have been about the content of metaphysics. Philosophers also are concerned with the methods and processes of metaphysical investigations. That is to say, there are epistemological questions about metaphysics. If metaphysics is the study of the nature of ultimate reality, then what type of study is it? How can and should metaphysics be done? Science investigates the world through observation and experimentation; it is said to be empirical. If metaphysics is not the same thing as science, then does that mean that metaphysics is, or must be, nonempirical (that is, must it be different than science)? If metaphysical topics and issues can be addressed empirically, then are they really scientific topics and issues—and, if so, would science not investigate them better than philosophers? On the other hand, if metaphysical topics and issues cannot be addressed empirically, then how can and should it be done? What standards are relevant to understanding and evaluating metaphysical claims? That is, how can and should metaphysics be conducted? If there are no scientific observations or experiments that will answer metaphysical questions, then what would count as having a good answer? For instance, if the question is about the nature of necessity, how would metaphysicians know if they had a good answer? Many philosophers have argued that they perform thought experiments, not physical experiments. Others have said that intuition or even common sense serves as a proper standard, just as commonsense observation does for science. Because it is difficult to say how one would know if a metaphysical question has been answered well, many philosophers have been critical of metaphysics. For instance, the 18th-century British philosopher David Hume said that much of metaphysics was nonsense. A 20th-century school of philosophical thought called logical positivism also rejected metaphysics as being nonsense. Nonetheless, many philosophers have seen metaphysical questions as basic and important.

One reason they have argued that metaphysics is important is because they claim that there are some very practical results and consequences of it, even if it does seem very abstract and removed from everyday concerns. An example of a metaphysical issue that many philosophers say is important is the issue of personal identity. The issue of personal identity involves two questions: (1) What is a person? and (2) What makes someone the same person over time (that is, what is the nature of someone's identity)? First, what is a person? By this question, we mean what is a person as opposed to being something else (the emphasis is on *person*). Being a human is a biological concept and fact; it is a matter of having a certain genetic structure. But are genes what make something a person? Many people claim that being a person is more an issue about social nature and having rights or dignity. In any case, one broad view about being a person is one that focuses on biology, which is about material bodies. A different view about being a person is one that focuses on mentality, or having basic mental capacities or abilities. So, it is mind more than body that determines being a person. These two views also speak to what makes someone the same person over time. The body view says that it is the fact of having the same body over time that makes someone the same person, while the mind view says that it is the fact of having the same mind over time. Of course, by having the *same* body or mind over time, this does not mean that there are no changes in the body or mind.

One's body constantly undergoes changes (we lose cells and gain new ones all the time), and so does one's mind (we forget things and learn new things all the time). Because both body and mind change all the time, some philosophers have argued that there is no such thing as persons or of personal identity; the notion of a person is simply a convenient way for us to interact in some predictable way. (If we did not think of particular people as being the same person over time, then every time someone left his house and came back, it would be a stranger returning, or every time someone got a haircut, it would be a different person who sat down than the person who had to pay the bill!)

Where the issue of personal identity becomes practical and important is in terms of holding someone responsible for something that was done in the past. If someone committed a crime, normally it would be unfair and unreasonable to hold someone else responsible for that crime (and perhaps even punish that other person). But what about a person who commits a crime and is arrested but genuinely cannot remember having done it? Is the person who committed the crime the same person who is arrested? Given the body view of personal identity, yes, they are the same person. However, given the mind view, they are not necessarily the same person. But to hold anyone responsible for his actions presupposes that it is the same person. The important practical matter of responsibility also shows the significance of another metaphysical topic, cause. Normally, we would hold only the person who caused some harm to be responsible for that harm. (Normally, it would be unfair and unreasonable to hold someone else responsible, someone who did not cause the harm. However, there are cases, such as neglect, in which we might hold someone responsible for not having done something.) But what exactly does it mean to say that someone caused some event (in this case, some harmful event or result)? This is a metaphysical question, but one that clearly has important social and legal consequences, as well as more philosophical and academic consequences. As with much of philosophy, and in spite of its abstract nature, metaphysics actually has practical implications, consequences, and value.

Pre-Socratic Philosophers

The term *pre-Socratic philosophy* refers to thinkers in the Mediterranean area, stretching from modern-day Italy to modern-day Turkey, roughly between 600 and 400 B.C.E. They are grouped together for two major reasons. First, because they focused largely on the same sorts of conceptual and philosophical concerns, and, second, because Socrates had such a significant influence on subsequent philosophical thought that he is seen as a turning point between those who preceded him and those who followed him. The concerns of the pre-Socratic philosophers were fundamentally metaphysical, being about the basic, underlying nature of the world.

Pre-Socratic philosophy is characterized by four overlapping fundamental themes: (1) appearance versus reality, (2) change versus permanence, (3) accident versus essence, and (4) the many versus the one. The theme of appearance versus reality has to do with questioning whether or not the way things appear to be to us is, in fact, the way they really are. Is the real nature of trees or water or anything in the world the same as how we experience it? Today, for example, we would say that water is composed of two gases, and even those gases are composed of molecules and atoms and subatomic particles. So, what we experience on an everyday basis—a wet liquid—is not what we would take to be an experience of gases or atoms. If everyday knowledge of things as we experience them is not necessarily the same thing as knowledge of things as they really are (knowledge of an underlying reality), then it is important, said the pre-Socratics, to go beyond or beneath everyday experience—that is, beyond appearances—to come to know reality. This relates directly to the theme of change versus permanence. In our everyday experience, we note that things often change, or at least they appear to change: Acorns become oak trees, kittens become cats, bananas ripen and change color and texture, things come into being and go out of existence. Is there, asked the pre-Socratics, anything that is permanent, that does not change or that remains the same beneath the apparent change? This was asking whether there is a permanent substance, or thing, that stands under the changes we experience.

The third theme of accident and essence gets at much of the same concern. Things have different properties or features. For example, a cat has physical properties, such as fur and eyes, as well as behavioral properties, such as purring and running. Some properties are said to be essential, meaning that if those properties changed or were different, then the thing itself that had those properties would be different. If a particular cat lost an ear, it would not necessarily be a different cat but would be the same cat with fewer ears. But if a given cat had a different set of genes, then it might well be taken as a different cat, not the same cat that had somehow changed. Essential properties, then, are taken as properties that are defining of what something is. Accidental properties, however, are taken as features of something that happen to be characteristic of that thing but are not necessary for that thing to be what it is. Having certain length claws can be a feature of some cat, but if those claws are trimmed, it is still the same cat; having a certain set of genes, however, can be necessary for some cat to be that particular cat. Pre-Socratic philosophers saw essential features as the underlying permanent reality of things in the world.

Finally, the theme of the many versus the one also connects with issues of what is real and permanent and essential. The question here is: Are the things that are real (as opposed to mere appearances) constituted by many basic kinds of things or are they ultimately constituted by one kind of thing? At the level of appearance, the answer seems to be: many kinds of things. Cats are not the same things, or kind of things, as oak trees, and neither is the same kind of thing as water. But, the question is whether at the level of what is real there are many fundamental kinds of things or just one?

The focus on this last theme in particular led to several basic schools of thought among the pre-Socratic philosophers. One school of thought is called monism, because it holds the view that all things are ultimately constituted by one kind of thing. The other school of thought is called pluralism, because it holds the view that there is more than one ultimate kind of thing that constitutes things in the world. The pre-Socratic philosophers understood things in the world to be composed of four basic elements: earth, water, air, and fire. These four elements were associated with two basic characteristics: heat and moisture. Earth was said to be cold and dry; water, cold and wet; air, hot and wet; and fire, hot and dry. The monists argued that ultimately things could be understood as being composed of one of these basic elements, while the pluralists argued that all four were necessary, and no element could be accounted for in terms of any of the other three.

Earliest among the monists was Thales (fl. 580 B.C.E.). Thales argued that water was the source of all things. Commonsense observation shows that living organisms require water to survive. In addition, the natural landscape itself is shaped by water, or at least moisture. Even the air contains water. This view, however, was immediately criticized by Anaximander (610–546 B.C.E.), who argued that no element could generate its opposite. Since fire is the opposite of water (fire is dry and hot, water is wet and cold), it could not be generated by or composed of water. Furthermore, Anaximander argued, no basic element could be generated by another. Rather, there is an even more basic reality, which he labeled the *apeiron,* meaning boundless or unlimited. The world, for Anaximander, is a "war of opposites" in which the basic elements are separated from the apeiron by a whirling motion. A third pre-Socratic monist was Anaximenes (fl. 545 B.C.E.), who claimed that air was the fundamental element and source of all things. Anaximenes thought that Anaximander's notion of the apeiron did not resolve the problem of opposites, or how one element could be generated by another with opposite features. Rather, he said, the apeiron ignores the problem and simply offers a label to explain it away. Like Thales, Anaximenes thought that one of the material elements was basic and only a material explanation would suffice to resolve the problem of opposites. As a result, he offered such an explanation by saying that air was basic and the other elements were generated by air being condensed or rarefied. As air condensed, clouds could form and eventually moisture/water would be created. If this were condensed even further, silt and mud—that is, earth—would be generated. On the other hand, by rarefying air, fire would be produced. This process could be demonstrated, he claimed, by blowing air out of one's mouth. If the opening in one's lips is small (that is, condensed), then the air coming out feels cool to the touch, but if one opens one's mouth wide (that is, rarefied) and blows air out, then the air coming out feels warm. The important conceptual point is that qualitative features (that is, features of things that we experience every day, such as heat or color) are accounted for in terms of quantity and nothing extra-material, such as the apeiron, is needed.

Other pre-Socratic monists were not convinced of the fundamental nature of the four material elements of earth, water, air, and fire. Pythagoras (571–497 B.C.E.) claimed that what was basic and most real is quantity itself, number. The world is ultimately accounted for in terms of quantity and proportion. Besides his famous work on mathematics and musical harmony, Pythagoras argued for the basic essence of reality less in terms of some material content, such as water, but in terms of quantitative form or structure. Another monist was Heraclitus (fl. 500 B.C.E.), who spoke of fire as the basic element. Even more important,

Bust of Pythagoras at the Capitoline Museum in Rome

Heraclitus viewed the basic underlying reality and unity as a unity of pattern, rather than of things. Change itself is the most basic reality. Heraclitus is famous for having said that one cannot step into the same river twice, because whatever constitutes the river is in constant motion and change. Parmenides (fl. 485 B.C.E.), with the opposite view of Heraclitus, claimed that Being was the one underlying permanent reality. We cannot even think of or speak of nonbeing, because to think or speak of something is to think or speak of some *thing*. There must be something—even if it is not a material thing—that is being referred to even when we deny that it exists; otherwise, for Parmenides, what we say is simply nonsense. Change is impossible, even inconceivable, he argued. In addition, whatever is—whatever exists—must be uncreated (otherwise, there was a time when a thing was nothing) and indestructible (otherwise, there will come a time when a thing is nothing). Likewise, Being is One, since if two separate things existed, both would Be, but they would both be Being, which is one unity. So, all change and motion is mere appearance, not actual reality, for Parmenides.

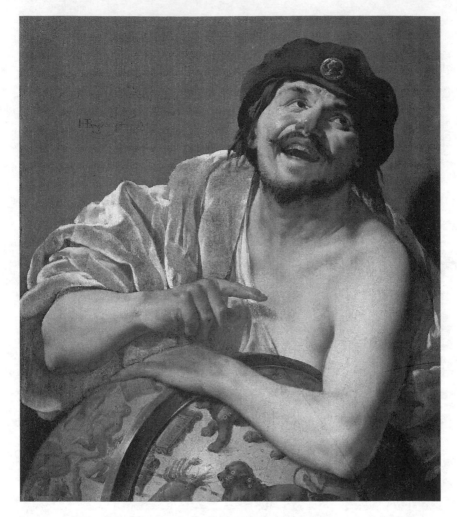

Painting of Democritus *(Painting by Hendrick ter Brugghen)*

His student Zeno of Elea (fl. 465 B.C.E.) presented various arguments to show that motion and change and plurality were mere illusions and not really possible. One such argument was offered to show that motion was impossible. It is called the flying arrow paradox. At any instant in time, Zeno claimed, an arrow occupies an exact set of points in space. At that instant, there is no motion, or movement through space. However, time is just a collection of instants. For any and every given instant, the arrow is not moving (it occupies just an exact set of points in space). So, there is zero motion at any instant in time. But to add up a collection of zeroes—that is, a collection of instants in time—is still to come up with zero. Motion, then, is only apparent, not real.

The pre-Socratic pluralists included Empedocles (484–424 B.C.E.), Anaxagoras (500–428 B.C.E.), and the atomists Democritus (460–370 B.C.E.) and Leucippus (fl. 440 B.C.E.). Empedocles claimed that what Parmenides showed was only that monism and motion were incompatible, not that monism was true. Instead, Empedocles rejected monism and accepted the four material elements of earth, water, air, and fire. The different things that we experience in the world are the result of varying proportions of those elements. In addition, he claimed, while Anaximenes spoke of material causes for change in the world, via condensation and rarefaction, he did not provide any explanation for them. Empedocles claimed that Love and Strife (or attraction and separation) were fundamental forces in nature, just as basic and ultimate as the four material elements. Change and appearance, for him, were the result of these forces acting on the basic material elements. Anaxagoras agreed with Empedocles that the four basic elements were indeed basic, and he argued that those elements were eternal: They could not be created or destroyed. Instead, the varying mixtures and proportions of those elements that accounted for different things in the world could alter. Common things, then, could be created or destroyed, but the elements that made them up could not. An additional fundamental component of the world was Mind (or *nous*). Finally, the atomists argued that all things are composed of countless atoms. The Greek word *atomos* meant "that which could not be cut or divided." The atomists argued that there must be some smallest material entity, which takes up some amount of space, no matter how small. Whatever this smallest thing was could not be divided any further, hence was *atomos*. The variation we experience in the world, such as cats and trees and water, are the result of the different combinations of atoms. While this sounds modern, it must be remembered that this pre-Socratic notion of atoms is strictly conceptual and not the result of physical observation or experimentation.

Categories of Reality

Idealism

Idealism in philosophy is not the same as idealism as it is usually understood outside philosophy. In a nonphilosophical sense, idealism regards having or working toward high ideals, as when a person seeks perfect justice or beauty. However, in philosophy, idealism is the view that reality is in some way dependent on the mind. Idealism is often contrasted with realism about the objects of ordinary, everyday experience (such as trees and computers), which holds that these objects are not dependent on the mind. Sometimes idealism is also used to refer to views according to which what is most real is not physical. In this sense, Plato (ca. 428–348 B.C.E.) is an idealist: He believed that what is most real are nonphysical things called Ideas (or Forms). However, Plato held that ideas exist independently of the mind. So, he was not an idealist in the first philosophical sense of the term described here. The modern philosopher George Berkeley (1685–1753) was the first major idealist in this sense. According to Berkeley, *all* the qualities of the objects we perceive—qualities such as shape, size, solidity, taste, smell, and so on—are mind-dependent. As the ordinary objects we perceive are collections of ideas, their reality is essentially mental. "*Esse est percipi,*" Berkeley wrote (Latin for "to be is to be perceived"). Objects continue to exist even when no particular person perceives them, according to Berkeley, because God perceives them: They are ideas in God's mind, and it is God who causes humans to have the ideas.

Immanuel Kant (1724–1804) gave a different account of idealism, calling his view transcendental idealism. Kant considered what made it possible for us to experience the objects of perception in the first place. How is it we experience a world of clocks, tables, chairs, and trees? His answer is that the mind organizes experience, rather than passively receiving ideas. That the mind organizes experience is what makes it possible for us to experience to begin with. For example, Kant argued that space does not exist absolutely and independently of the mind. Rather, we experience objects in time and in space because the mind organizes experience that way: In this way, space is something the mind itself brings to experience rather than something the mind encounters in experience. Kant's view is transcendental in the sense that it transcends, or goes beyond, particular experiences to consider instead what makes experience in general possible. His view is an idealist one in the sense that he argued that the objects of our knowledge are dependent on the mind. They are dependent on the mind in the sense that we can experience these objects only because the mind organizes experience by applying particular concepts. However, our knowledge of things is limited to how they appear to us; we cannot have knowledge of things themselves. In Kant's terms, we know the phenomena (the appearances of things), but we cannot know the noumena (the things in themselves).

After Kant, among the most significant versions of idealism in philosophy are found in German Idealism, in the absolute idealism expressed by F. W. J. von Schelling (1775–1854), Johann Gottlieb Fichte (1762–1814), and Georg W. F. Hegel (1770–1831). Although the German idealists were much influenced by Kant, they expressed notably different views. The most important of the German idealists, Hegel, rejected Kant's view that there are things in themselves, as well as the view that there is some aspect of reality that is unknowable. Hegel regarded reality as essentially rational, and for him what is most real is Mind, an absolute Mind (Hegel's German term for this is also translated as Absolute Spirit). All that is real must be understood in relation to this Mind, not independently of it: Again, what is fundamentally real is mental.

Once prominent, idealism finds less favor in philosophy today. However, idealism is not dead. Few philosophers deny with Berkeley that matter exists, but it is more common to agree, à la Kant, that the mind somehow organizes experience. What we know of reality would seem to depend in part on how the mind works; it is difficult to make sense of the reality of anything that is wholly beyond our ability to grasp mentally.

George Berkeley

George Berkeley (1685–1753) was an empiricist philosopher best known today for his metaphysical idealism. A devout Christian, Berkeley disliked the contemporary view of his time that the physical world operated mechanistically, as though the physical world and the physical objects within it were complex machines. He also rejected skepticism and was eager to defend belief in God and in an immaterial soul from atheism. Together with the influence of John Locke (1632–1704) on Berkeley, these were factors in Berkeley's views about the nature of reality and about the nature of knowledge. To understand Berkeley, it is necessary to understand something about Locke's views. According to Locke, we have no innate ideas. Instead, all our ideas are ultimately based on experience. Experience, in turn, Locke understood as including not only what one experiences through the five senses but one's awareness of the operations of one's own mind (such as thinking and remembering). Like other philosophers of his time, Locke also thought that we experience only our own ideas. The word *ideas* is used here in a broad, special sense, including not only thoughts but also things such as sensations, memories, and images. When Locke wrote that we experience only our own ideas, he meant in particular that we do not experience things in the world directly. For example, a person does not see a pine tree directly. Instead, the tree produces in a person certain ideas, such as the idea of green pine needles and brown bark. What one is directly aware of are those ideas—not the tree itself. Locke also distinguished between primary and secondary qualities. Primary qualities are qualities of an object that are in the object itself—for example, the solidity of a tree really is in the tree, not just in one's mind. Secondary qualities are qualities that are not in an object itself. The scent of pine needles, for instance, is not in the tree itself, although the tree produces in a person the idea of that scent.

Berkeley agreed with Locke that all our ideas are derived from experience; moreover, for Berkeley all knowledge is based on experience. Berkeley also agreed that we experience only ideas directly.

However, Berkeley thought that Locke's claim that there are material objects that exist independently of being perceived leads to skepticism: After all, if we never experience anything but our own ideas, how do we know that our ideas in any way match up with an independently existing reality? It appears that we *cannot* know. And that suggests that what we seem to know of ordinary, existing things—that apples are red, that pine needles smell a certain way, that mountains are tall, and so on—we do not actually know at all. Berkeley rejected this conclusion.

Portrait of George Berkeley, 1730 *(Painting by John Smibert)*

His solution was simply to deny that matter exists at all: There are no material objects, Berkeley argued. According to Berkeley, all that exists are minds and the ideas they perceive. What we ordinarily take to be material objects are collections of ideas. A pine tree, for example, is a collection of ideas such as the color green, rough bark, and pine needles of a certain size and shape. That is *all* apparently material objects are—collections of ideas in the mind. This does not mean that sensible objects (objects perceived through the senses) are not real; it just means that their existence is mind-dependent. Now the question of how it is possible to know that our ideas match up with independently existing objects does not arise. That is because there are no such independently existing objects. Moreover, knowledge of what we experience can count as genuine knowledge because we experience all that there is to experience: our ideas. The view that what is real are ideas, not material objects, is idealism. Berkeley himself called his view immaterialism.

It might sound strange to believe that only ideas and minds exist and material objects do not. Berkeley believed, however, that his view was actually consistent with common sense, because what we ordinarily talk about and have beliefs about are objects of experience. Berkeley gave specific arguments for his idealism. As noted, we experience only our ideas; sensible objects are collections of ideas. But ideas can exist only in a mind; they cannot exist independently of a mind. If they exist, therefore, they exist because they are perceived by a mind. To be, Berkeley wrote, is to be perceived (in Latin, *esse est percipi*)—or, in the case of minds, to be is to perceive. Berkeley also rejected the primary/secondary qualities distinction. Secondary qualities are not in the objects themselves and therefore depend on a perceiver. But, Berkeley argued, it was impossible to conceive of a sensible object without thinking of it as having secondary qualities. So, if secondary qualities depend for their existence on the perceiver, so, too, do primary qualities.

Our ideas do have a cause, Berkeley believed: The cause is God. To see why this is so, Berkeley noted that some of our ideas are involuntary; it is not up to us whether we have them (for instance, one cannot decide to see an apple just because one wants to). Yet they must have a cause, and for Berkeley, that cause must be another mind, the mind of God. God's existence also explains why objects continue to exist even when an individual mind no longer sees them. They continue to exist because God perceives them. In general, sensible ideas are ideas in the mind of God.

Materialism

Materialism is the view that everything that is real is material, or physical. (The term *physicalism* is often used today rather than the term *materialism*; although there are some subtle differences between the two terms, they are very often used interchangeably.) This view goes back as far as the beginnings of philosophy. For example, among the pre-Socratic philosophers, Thales claimed that all things come from water. Although throughout the history of philosophy there have been disputes over materialism, it is the prominent view among contemporary philosophers. In large part, this is because most philosophers today think that science, which they take to be a purely material enterprise, seems to explain more and more things, including things and events and processes that previously were thought to be nonmaterial. For example, the more that scientists understand about how the brain (a material object) works, the more they claim to understand mentality (which had been seen as being nonmaterial). Likewise, purely material explanations have been given for phenomena that were not obviously material. For instance, today scientists explain that light is a form of electromagnetic radiation, a purely material thing.

Besides the fact that material explanations seem to be available to account for things and events and processes, materialism seems to fit in with the notion that the world is something we discover by investigating its material features and properties. If some event occurs, the assumption by most people, say materialists, is that there must have been a cause or set of causes for that to have occurred; the only kind of causes that we could possibly investigate are material causes. Of course, we might not know what caused something to occur, but we assume it did not happen by magic! A technical term that philosophers and scientists use for this assumption is the *causal closure of the physical.* This simply means that the assumption is that any event or thing has a physical cause or set of causes; the explanation is not open to other kinds of causes, since we could not investigate those and also because nonmaterial causes would violate fundamental laws of physics. Materialism, then, is not a view that is said to be proven; rather it is a view that is said to be assumed, in order for investigation to be possible and reliable.

There have been a number of issues involving materialism that have interested philosophers and others. One such issue is whether or not life itself could be explained in purely material ways. Living organisms, of course, are physical, biological objects, but what is it that makes them living? What is the difference between a living person and the corpse or body of that person? Can life be accounted for (meaning two things: can it be explained as and is it nothing more than) in purely material ways? For centuries, many people have claimed that for a person to be alive it must mean that there is something above and beyond the collection of material features and components (such as blood and bones) of that person; otherwise there is no metaphysical difference between a living person and a human body. Materialists, of course, claim that there is no additional component or thing that makes a person alive versus dead; rather, the difference can be explained by material, physical causes.

Besides the issue of the nature of life, where the view of materialism has been the most controversial for philosophers is in explaining human behavior, especially human mental capabilities and consciousness. Materialist philosophers claim that human mental capabilities can be fully explained (at least, in principle) simply on the basis of material causes, because the mind is not something more, or substantially different than, certain material objects and interactions. When speaking of the mind, the brain (a material object) is what is key. Does anyone truly believe, asks the materialist, that a person with no brain could have thoughts?

There are various views about the relationship between the mind and the brain, one of the most prominent being what is called identity theory. According to identity theory, mental states are identical to brain states. So, in this view, it is not *just* that there is a correlation between a person's mental states and brain states. Rather, mental states just *are* brain states; beliefs, hopes, desires, sensations, and so on just *are* particular states of the brain. Scientists have shown, for example, that when particular areas of the brain are stimulated, say, by a small electric probe, that people have certain mental experiences. This is because, they say, those mental experiences simply are cases of being in particular brain states.

There are two main versions of identity theory: token identity theory and type identity theory. A token is a particular, individual thing—for example, a particular donkey named Guinness. A type is a *kind* of thing, such as the species donkey. So Guinness is a token of the type donkey: He is an individual that belongs to a certain kind of thing (the kind donkey). According to token identity theory, tokens of mental states are identical to tokens of brain states. In this view, for instance, a person's individual belief that donkeys are friendly is identical to a particular brain state. According to type identity theory, types of mental states are identical to types of brain states. For instance, the belief that donkeys are friendly is a kind of mental state, and it is identical with a kind of brain state.

One argument for identity theory is that it explains mind-body interaction. To illustrate this point, first consider an opposing view of mind, namely, dualism. According to dualism, mind is nonphysical. One problem for this view is that it is difficult to explain how a nonphysical mind can have an effect on a physical body, or vice versa. Yet a commonsense view is that what goes on in one's mind can have an effect on the body, and vice versa. For instance, a desire to eat chocolate can cause a person's hand to put a piece of chocolate in her mouth; stubbing one's toe seems to cause the mental experience of pain. If, as dualists claim, mind is nonphysical, how can it interact with the body in such ways? It has seemed to many philosophers that dualists cannot account for mind-body interaction. In contrast, identity theory addresses the issue by identifying mental states with brain states. Because brain states are physical, mental states (such as the desire for chocolate) would seem to have no difficulty in causing physical motion (such as putting chocolate in one's mouth). Physical causes have physical effects, as when raking a leaf-strewn yard causes leaves to move into a pile; on identity theory, mental states can be one kind of physical causes.

Another argument in favor of identity theory is that, as compared to nonmaterialist views of the mind such as dualism, identity theory is simpler. That is, it explains mind in a simpler way than dualism does, and in that respect identity theory is a better view. Analogously, consider two explanations for the fact that every time one turned the key in the ignition of a car, the car started. One explanation for this is that turning the key in the ignition awakens a tiny elf, who then sets into motion a physical process in the engine. Another explanation is that the key directly sets into motion a physical process in the engine. Both of these explanations explain why the car starts when the key turns in the ignition. However, the second explanation is simpler. The view that there is an elf involved raises questions that the second explanation does not (where does the elf live in the car? why do we never see the elf?).

Moreover, there seems to be no need to suppose there is an elf in the first place, because the second explanation gives an adequate account of why the car starts. Dualism is often regarded as rather like the explanation involving the elf: It raises a lot of questions that identity theory does not (how can a nonphysical mind interact with a physical body?), and it introduces a nonphysical mind when there is no need to do so. There is no need to do so, according to proponents of identity theory, because identity theory gives a sufficient account of mind. In addition, science has shown that there is a very close relation between the mind and brain, and identity theory explains this very close relation.

Often the identification of mental states with brain states is compared to well-known identifications in science. For example, lightning is identical to electrical discharge in the atmosphere. People did not always know, of course, that lightning is identical to electrical discharge in the atmosphere, but eventually scientists discovered that it was. In the same way, according to identity theorists, over time science will fully explain the identification of mental states with brain states. This point is important because it might be tempting to argue against identity theory this way: We know about our mental states just by looking inward; one knows that one is happy, for instance, just by looking inward. But a person does not know what physical and chemical properties her brain has just by looking inward. If mental states are identical to physical states, how can this be? In answer, consider that people could not tell just through everyday observation that lightning is electrical discharge. That discovery took scientific research. In the same way, the identity theorist might argue, scientific research is needed to learn all about our mental states (looking inward is not enough). Critics of materialism have argued that materialism is an assumption, and an unproven one at that, not a fact. Nonetheless, it is the most prevalent philosophical and scientific view today.

Thomas Hobbes

Thomas Hobbes (1588–1679) was an English philosopher who is best known today as an important thinker in political philosophy; however, he based his political philosophy on his metaphysical views. Hobbes was a materialist. He argued that thought, dreams, imagination, and indeed all mental activity can be explained in materialist terms, specifically in terms of mechanical matter in motion. That is, according to Hobbes, all mental activity is a matter of material stuff moving in a mechanical way. For instance, Hobbes claimed that sensations can be explained by external material objects somehow exerting pressure on the sensory organs—a person perceives a yellow banana, for example, when the banana exerts physical pressure on the eye (today we would say that photons reflected off the surface of the banana strike receptors in our eyes), and this pressure causes physical pressure in the brain. Hobbes was also an empiricist, believing that all knowledge depends on experience and on sensations in particular: Without sensations, we could not acquire knowledge, and indeed for Hobbes all knowledge is ultimately based on sensations. So, not only are our immediate mental experiences, such as seeing a tree, based on physical sensations, but also our memory of seeing a tree is a matter of images of those sensations that have been stored in our brain. Even our ability to imagine things that we have never directly experienced—for example, a purple cow—is the result of having experienced seeing cows and seeing the color purple and blending them in our minds.

Hobbes believed that not only human (and any nonhuman) thought and cognitive experience have physical causes but so, too, do human

Portrait of Thomas Hobbes, ca. 1670 (Painting by John Michael Wright)

desires. So, one has the desires one has because they are the result of a particular physical chain of events; in this way, one's desires are determined. No one chooses her desires because no one chooses the physical chain of events that cause them. Hobbes nonetheless believed it was possible for a person to be free. For Hobbes, freedom is not freedom to choose one's own desires but rather freedom from opposition; it is the ability to do what one wants. Suppose, for example, that a person wants to grow a garden. She does not freely choose to have that desire, which is just the result of a physical chain of events. However, she is free with respect to that desire as long as she is able to act on it. Hobbes thus offers a version of what is called compatibilism, that is, the view that it is possible for humans to be free even though their actions are materially caused; in other words, freedom and causation are compatible.

Universals and Particulars

Abstract Objects and Universals

Many sorts of things seem to exist, ranging from trees and paper clips to numbers, colors, and qualities. The distinction between abstract objects and concrete objects is between two supposedly very different kinds of things. Because the distinction describes the kind of things that exist, abstract objects are a significant issue in metaphysics (the study of reality) and ontology (the study of existence). Objects such as trees and paper clips are concrete in the sense that they have definite physical properties. They occupy space, exist in time, and they have certain perceivable qualities such as being shiny, smelling a certain way, and so on. Contrasted with such concrete objects are abstract objects, such as the number four. Abstract objects are typically thought to include the following:

- numbers
- types (such as kinds of things)
- propositions (such as the meaning of sentences)
- universals (such as redness)

However, although these objects seem fundamentally different than concrete objects such as trees and paper clips, there is considerable controversy not only about what objects are abstract but also about precisely what distinguishes abstract objects from concrete objects.

Because of these difficulties, some philosophers believe that there are no abstract objects.

A common criterion for distinguishing between abstract objects and concrete objects is whether an object has spatiotemporal properties; that is, whether it exists in space and time. According to this criterion, although concrete objects have such properties, abstract objects do not. A tree, for example, takes up a certain amount of space: It grows to a certain height and has certain dimensions. It is possible to bump into a tree in part because it occupies space. It has temporal properties in the sense that it exists in a certain time, say, in the year 2008, and began its existence at a certain time, say, in 2003. In contrast, it would not be possible to comply with a request to "Go look for the number two," because the number two does not seem to be anywhere in particular. It seems to be outside of space and time. Although it is true that we write the numeral two on chalkboards, computer screens, and other places, these written markings are not identical with the number two; if all written or typed twos ceased to exist, the number two itself would continue to exist (assuming that it does exist at all). As the number two does not seem to be anywhere in particular, and as its existence is independent of any particular time period, the number two lacks spatiotemporal properties.

Although this criterion seems to make sense for objects such as two, it is less clear when applied to abstract objects such as Stanford University. Stanford University, some claim, is an abstract object because it is not identical with its buildings, professors, or students. Although some buildings are destroyed and others built, and professors and students come and go (and even academic programs come and go), Stanford University itself seems to continue to exist regardless of these changes. For instance, it seems conceivable that Stanford University would continue to exist even if it temporarily lacked a physical campus (say, if an old campus shuts down while another is being built). These considerations suggest that Stanford University is an abstract object. Yet it seems mistaken, on the face of it, to suppose that Stanford University has no spatial properties at all. Although the university is not identical with a campus, it does have a campus, and insofar as that campus has certain dimensions and occupies space, Stanford University arguably has spatial properties. In addition, Stanford University seems to have temporal properties in the sense that the university was founded on a specific date. However, if it is possible for an abstract object to have spatiotemporal properties, then the possession of spatiotemporal properties cannot distinguish abstract objects from concrete objects.

Another criterion that has been proposed to distinguish abstract objects from concrete objects is the possession of causal powers. According to this view, concrete objects participate in causal relations and abstract objects do not. What this means is that concrete objects are involved both in causing events and being the effects of events. For example, when a tree falls in the woods, it flattens smaller plants beneath it. The falling of the tree causes the flattening of plants: The tree causally participates in the flattening of the plants, because if the tree had not fallen, the plants most likely would not have been flattened. The tree itself is the result of other causal relations involving concrete objects, for example, the planting of an acorn and a certain amount of rainfall. On the view now being considered, abstract objects do not similarly participate in causal relations. The number two does not cause any events, and nor is it the effect of any event. A person might write the numeral two, but in so doing, a person is not causing the number two. The number two cannot cause plants to flatten, people to do arithmetic, or anything else.

A significant objection to this view is that if abstract objects do not participate in causal relations it is difficult to see how humans can come to know about them. This is because we typically acquire knowledge of objects through causal interactions with them. We can acquire knowledge of a tree, for example, through observations of the tree (through sight, hearing, touch, and so on), and these observations depend on causal interactions. Light waves causally interacting with the human eye, for example, allow us to see the tree. If an object cannot causally affect even our brain activity, then it is mysterious how we could ever come to know about that object. Yet we do seem to have knowledge of abstract objects. We have mathematical knowledge, knowledge about redness, and other presumably abstract objects. Some philosophers have attempted to resolve this problem by offering fuller accounts of what it is to participate in causal relations.

Among the abstract objects that have especially been of concern to philosophers are universals. Universals, as opposed to particulars, are said to be those things that are general in nature. While there might be many instances of, say, white patches, white itself (or whiteness) is said to be a universal. Universal terms, then, are said to refer to those universal things, rather than to the particular instances of that universal. The word *white,* then, refers not simply to some particular patch(es) of white but to the universal abstract object that is whiteness. Philosophers have held different views about what they call the problem of universals. Some believe that universal terms really do refer to universal abstract objects, and this view is often called realism. Others deny that universals exist; they claim that only particular, concrete objects actually exist. For the sake of convenience, we use universal terms, but these are merely empty names that do not really refer to anything (other than, perhaps, the collection of all of those particular things that have that feature or characteristic that the universal term denotes; for example, *white* does not refer to some universal abstract object, but—if it refers at all—to all the white particulars in the world). This view is usually called nominalism. Finally, some philosophers say that universal terms do refer, but not to some abstract objects out there in the world; rather, they refer to concepts in our minds. This view is seen as a midway point between realism and nominalism; it is usually called conceptualism.

Plato: Realism

The ancient Greek philosopher Plato (ca. 428–348 B.C.E.) elaborated many extraordinarily influential doctrines, but perhaps the most enduring is what is usually called the Doctrine of Ideas (or Forms). The Greek word that Plato used was *eidos,* which is often translated as "idea." However, the word *idea* has the connotation for many people of some thought in someone's mind. This is not the sort of thing that Plato was writing about when he used the word *eidos.* When he spoke of, say, the Idea of Good or the Idea of Beauty or even the Idea of Tree, he meant not some thought in someone's mind but whatever it is that matches the correct definition of something that was being defined. The following example will make this clear.

In our everyday lives, we encounter many individual trees (the two in my front yard and the one in my neighbor's yard, for instance). We also can think of the many kinds of different trees that there are: pine trees, birch trees, elm trees, maple trees, willow trees, etc. In addition, there are other individual things and kinds of things that are not trees (my two

Bust of Plato in the Museo Pio-Clementino in Rome *(Roman copy after a Greek original from the last quarter of the fourth century)*

cats, my neighbor's truck, rocks, flowers, etc.). The word *tree,* then, must refer to certain things and not other things. For Plato, this meant that there must be some features or conditions that some things had in order for them to be trees. Also, for those things that are not trees, there must be some features that they do not have, which is why they are not trees. Whatever those features are that determine whether something is or is not a tree, those features are the essence of Tree. A correct definition of *tree* would include exactly those features. The Idea of Tree, then, for Plato, is whatever it is that matches those essential features. Of course, different trees, and even different kinds of trees, have different features. For example, some trees have leaves that fall off in the autumn, while other trees have leaves that do not; some trees have light-colored bark, while other trees do not; some grow in certain kinds of soil, while others do not, etc. Nonetheless, said Plato, for these things to all be trees, there must be some features that they all share in common—otherwise, they would not all be trees. The correct definition of tree provides just those essential, common, and unique features of trees. In effect, such a definition provides the ideal form of trees (which is why the term *Form* is sometimes used instead of Idea).

For Plato, there were levels of reality, with Ideas being the highest level. Some things that are real are particular and fleeting. For instance, a tree might cast a shadow if it is in the sunlight. The shadow is certainly real; it exists. However, if the Sun goes behind a cloud or sets, the shadow goes away; it no longer exists. The physical tree that cast that shadow is also real, in fact, it is more real, said Plato, than the shadow, since the physical tree continues to exist even when the Sun goes behind a cloud or sets. Just as the physical tree is more real than the shadow of a tree, the Idea of Tree is even more real than the physical tree, said Plato. This is because the Idea of Tree can exist even if that tree dies or is cut down. In fact, even if all trees somehow went away, the Idea of Tree would still exist, like the Idea of Dinosaur can exist even though there are no dinosaurs anymore. In addition, for Plato, there can be Ideas of things that are abstract. For example, there is the Idea of Circle, even if there are no true, perfect circles in the world. Also, there are Ideas of things such as white. If someone says that a piece of paper is white, the word *white* must refer to something. Just as with trees or anything else, there must be some correct definition of *white* and, for Plato, there must be some Idea of White that matches that definition. Beyond merely matching a definition, Plato claimed that Ideas cause the physical, everyday instances of them, much like those physical, everyday instances cause the shadows of themselves. That is, just as the shadow of a tree could not exist without that physical tree existing and causing the shadow (along with some light source), so, too, Plato claimed, the physical tree must be caused and the cause is the Idea of Tree. More broadly, his point is that lower levels of reality are caused by corresponding higher levels of reality. Also, Ideas can exist independently of the particular instances of them existing (that is, the Idea of Circle can exist even if no true circles exist in everyday experience, and the Idea of Tree could exist even if no trees existed). Plato's Doctrine of Ideas was a fundamental part of his view that while everyday experience seems to show that things are constantly changing, there is an underlying permanent reality (the reality of Ideas).

This Doctrine of Ideas has been immensely influential in philo-sophical thought ever since Plato, but it has also been critiqued. In fact, Plato himself raised some questions and doubts about this view in some of his own later writings. For example, he asked whether there is an Idea of Hair and an Idea of Dirt, etc. Plato had earlier identified Ideas with what is ideal and incorruptible and good, so Ideas of Hair and Dirt (and any other unpleasant notions) seemed questionable. In addition, Plato's student, Aristotle, said that there must be an infinite series of levels of Ideas. This is because if there is an Idea for any concept, that is, for any-thing that can be defined, then there would be, say, an Idea of Maple, as well as an Idea of Tree, as well as an Idea of Living Thing, as well as an Idea of Thing That Can Be Defined, etc. Furthermore, said Aristotle, just because we have words or terms that can be defined, it does not nec-essarily follow that there must exist something that matches those defi-nitions. For instance, we could define *unicorn*, but that does not mean that, therefore, there must be actual unicorns or an Idea of Unicorn. Some words or terms (and their definitions) are only about imaginary things. Other philosophers have rejected the view that things (must) have essences. Still other philosophers, however, have defended the underlying notion of Ideas and related conceptions of ideal, unchang-ing things that are real (a view often today called realism or Platonism).

Aristotle on Form and Matter

Form and matter are two fundamental concepts in metaphysics. In particular, they relate to what kinds of things there are in the world and the nature of those things. For example, in our everyday experi-ence we encounter many different kinds of things: cats, trees, water, clouds, oxygen, etc. Some things we think of as objects (such as cats and trees), but other things we think of as events (such as a party or a hur-ricane or a toothache). Those things we think of as objects have various features or characteristics. For instance, a cat has legs and fur, while a tree has leaves and bark, a cloud is puffy, and water flows. Philosophers sometimes call these features or characteristics properties. The things that have those attributes are sometimes referred to as substances. So, flowing or being puffy or having leaves are all properties of certain sub-stances (in this case, water, clouds, and trees, respectively).

A long-standing philosophical debate centers on how to understand substances and properties. This debate goes as far back as Plato and Aristotle (in fact, even further, but they focused attention on it). Plato argued that words referred to things. So, when we say, "Some dogs are black," the words are meaningful, and they refer to something or other. For instance, *dog* refers to a particular kind of object, and *black* also refers to a particular kind of object. For Plato, they do not refer simply to actual physical objects that we encounter every day. Instead, dog refers to an Idea (or Form). Ideas, for Plato, were whatever matches the ideal definition of some word. Since there are lots of different kinds of dogs that we encounter (for example, Chihuahuas and Great Danes), there must be something they all have in common for them all to be dogs (and there must be something that non-dogs lack for them not to be dogs). In other words, there must be some essence to being a dog. So, for Plato, *dog* really refers to whatever that essence is. The same was true, for Plato, for the word *black*. That is, he claimed that there must also be an Idea of Black, or something—some substance—that matches the essence of black.

Plato's student, Aristotle, disagreed. He claimed that *black* refers not to a substance, or thing, but to a property. For Aristotle, a substance is a thing, and he speaks of two sorts of substances: primary substance and secondary substance. A primary substance is a concrete, specific individual thing, while a secondary substance is a more general kind of thing. So, for him, *dog* does not refer to a primary substance, but "Lassie" or "Fido" (that is, the name of some specific dog) does. *Dog* refers to a secondary substance.

For Aristotle, everyday objects are made up of both matter and form. The matter is the physical makeup of objects. The form is the structure that the matter has such that the particular substance is what it is. As an example, one could have a pile of wood (matter) and with that wood one could make, say, a specific table. But, one could take that same pile of wood (matter) and make, say, a specific desk. Each of those two specific things is a different primary substance; that is, they are two distinct individual things. For Aristotle, a given table is certain matter (those pieces of wood) structured into a certain form (the form or structure of that specific table). If that same matter (those pieces of wood) are structured into a different form, then the substance we have would be a different (primary) substance; it would be that specific desk rather than that specific table. The general point, for Aristotle, is that every substance must have both form and matter. A specific table is not simply a pile of wood; rather it is wood in a particular structured form. For Aristotle, there can be no matter without form and no form without matter. That is to say, for Aristotle, all matter has some structure or other (so there is no formless matter), and all form has matter; that is, there cannot exist a substance that is merely a structure with no physical components (so there is no matterless form). Plato was wrong, then, he said, to think that there could exist some Idea of Dog or Idea of Black (or Idea of anything), if that meant some ideal, nonmaterial structure. Plato, he said, confused substances with properties. For Aristotle, Plato's Ideas really just refer to the (ideal) properties of substances. Aristotle's views were influential on later thinkers who—in opposition to the realism associated with Plato—advocated the views of nominalism and conceptualism.

William of Ockham: Nominalism

William of Ockham (ca. 1280–1349) was a medieval philosopher and theologian who today is mostly known for his rejection of metaphysical realism. William is believed to have been born in the town of Ockham, near London. He studied at Oxford University and was ordained in 1306. Because of his empiricist views, he met with disfavor from some of his teachers and other clerics, eventually being summoned before Pope John XXII to defend himself against charges of heresy. After several years of house arrest, he fled to Bavaria (now Germany), where he wrote a number of works that were critical of the hierarchy of the Catholic Church. He is believed to have died of the Black Death.

William is now best known for what is called Ockham's razor. Ockham's razor is a reference to the principle that explanations should be as simple as possible, but not too simple. In Ockham's writings, he frequently remarked that "plurality is not to be posited without necessity" and "what can be explained by the assumption of fewer things is vainly explained by the assumption of more things." So, there are two ways that this has been understood. One way is in terms of what is real. In this case, Ockham's razor is said to suggest that one should not assume the existence of things unless the assumption is necessary (or at least reasonable). We might be able to explain noises in the attic by

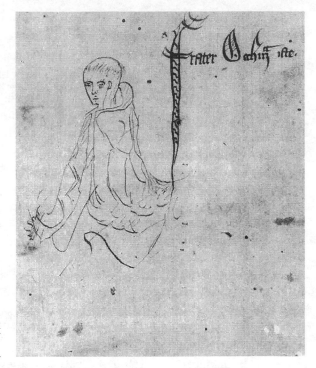

Sketch of William of Ockham from a manuscript of his *Summa Logicae*

claiming that there are goblins up there who are stomping around, but we could probably explain those noises without assuming the existence of goblins. The second, and related, way that Ockham's razor has been understood is more explicitly about explaining (and not about what things there are to be explained). So, even if the noises in the attic are made by, say, squirrels and not by goblins, we should explain this by, say, claiming that the squirrels are looking for food or shelter, not that they are having a dance party.

With respect to the issue of universals, William rejected them outright. His view is often referred to as nominalism (from the Latin word *nomina,* meaning "name"). For William, universal terms such as *white* or *dog* referred not to some independently existing real object but rather they were convenient names that we use to speak about particular objects, such as white patches or different individual dogs. We notice similarities and resemblances between various particular individual things, and because of this noticing as well as for our convenience, we label them under the same name. So, for William, if there are four dogs in a room, there are only four objects in that room, not five (four particular dogs plus the form or essence of Dog).

The reason we speak of universals, said William, is that we recognize, or perhaps formulate, similarities between objects that we encounter and then form concepts based on those similarities. If universal terms refer to anything at all, they could only refer to these concepts. (This is one reason that some philosophers have claimed that William actually held a view called conceptualism, not a hard-core view of nominalism.) Our knowledge comes from bumping into the world, so to speak, and forming concepts out of our perceptions of things. Not only is there no reason to think that universals actually exist and are real, but also, for William, there is reason to think that they do not exist and are not real. In a word, he thought that realism about universals was incoherent; it is a view that contradicts itself. This is because, he said, metaphysical realism must claim that a universal is both one thing and many things at the same time. For example, the universal term *humanity* must refer to one thing, what is common to all humans, but must also refer to many things because it is a property of each and every human. This, he claimed, was to say that humanity is both one thing and many things at the same time, which he found incoherent.

Peter Abelard: Conceptualism

Peter Abelard (1079–1142) was a medieval philosopher and theologian who rejected the view of metaphysical realism. Today, he is best known for his famous and troubled love affair with a woman named Héloïse, whose family, irate over the situation, ended up attacking and castrating Abelard. To philosophers, however, he was a rigorous and complex thinker. Abelard was born in the town of Pallet (in what is now France). He studied under a number of well-known thinkers, but his combative personality led to strained relationships with most of them. As he challenged the views of his teachers and some standard claims of the Catholic Church, he became ever more caught up in controversy. During his life, a number of his writings were officially condemned by the Church, and for a while he was excommunicated.

With respect to the issue of metaphysical universals, Abelard rejected them. He argued that the universality of a universal term, such as *white,* was simply that it could be truly spoken of with regard to many individual things. In other words, the term *white* could be applied to (or predicated of) many different individual things: this white piece of

Illustration of Peter Abelard and Héloïse at the Paraclete monastery *(H. Clerget)*

paper, that white cloud, that other white shirt, etc. So, *white* was universal not, for Abelard, because it refers to some additional thing that exists (namely, whiteness) but simply because it could be correctly applied to many things. Nonetheless, for Abelard, although universals themselves are not real, the common features of real things (that is, real particular individuals) account for and justify the application of universal terms to them. That is, the term *white* correctly, or truly, applies to some things (and not to others), but not because there is some thing—whiteness—that is real and, in some sense or other, causes the whiteness in particular white things. As Abelard put it, there is not common cause; there is common conception.

This notion of conception was important for Abelard. If universal terms refer to anything, it is a concept, not some independent abstract object. This view—that what a universal term refers to is a concept—is today called conceptualism. (Some scholars have claimed that Abelard was more of a nominalist than a conceptualist, meaning that he denied that universal terms referred to anything, even to concepts.) In laying out his view, Abelard spoke of the power of abstraction. Abstraction is our ability to focus on one aspect of something while ignoring other aspects of it. For example, we can look at a rug and just focus on its shape, while ignoring its color. (Perhaps we wonder if it will fit well in a particular room and do not care about its color.) Universals, he said, were, in effect, the products of our ability to think abstractly. Although what actually exists, for Abelard, is a particular piece of paper, we can ignore some of its features and just focus on its color. We can do this with other pieces of paper with the result that by mentally abstracting the color away from all of the other features of different pieces of paper, we have the concept of a given color, say, white. But, for Abelard, this is only an abstract concept, not a real thing independent of our abstraction. The concepts, or at least our conceptions, are real and might very well be the result of experiencing real features of things (that is, different pieces of paper really are white), but concepts can also reflect certain interests that we have as opposed to other interests. For example, there might be something common between a dog and a table (they have legs) or between a bird and a rocket and a balloon (they all fly, in some sense). We can even have concepts of imaginary things that do not exist (such as unicorns or elves). The point, again, is that, for Abelard, universal terms do not presuppose the existence of universal objects.

Causality and
Knowledge of the World

David Hume

David Hume (1711–76) was a Scottish philosopher whose influence in philosophy continues to be evident in such diverse areas as epistemology (the study of knowledge), metaphysics (the study of reality), ethics (the study of right action), and philosophy of religion. He was born in Edinburgh to a family that was relatively well-off, and he studied at the University of Edinburgh, intended by his mother to become a lawyer. However, Hume disliked law and found philosophy more interesting. When he was in his 20s, he published *A Treatise of Human Nature,* hoping to achieve literary fame and success. The book was not successful, and Hume later revised it and published it as *An Enquiry Concerning Human Understanding* and *An Enquiry Concerning the Principles of Morals.* He worked in various positions (such as a secretary to a general and a tutor to a mad nobleman) but was not able to attain a position as professor of philosophy. While working as a librarian, he wrote works on the history of Britain, finally establishing a literary reputation on the basis of these works rather than his strictly philosophical writings. Although many of his contemporaries disapproved of Hume's antireligious views, he was well liked for his witty and kindly personality.

Hume was an empiricist influenced by philosophers John Locke (1632–1704) and George Berkeley (1685–1753). He is famous for his skepticism. He believed that the mental content of the human mind consists of ideas and impressions. Impressions are more lively than ideas—that is, they are more vivid. Impressions include sensations, passions, and emotions. Ideas are copies of impressions. For instance, a person might see a brilliantly orange sunset, and while watching that sunset she has an impression. Later, when she remembers the sunset, she has an idea of that sunset; her memory of the sunset is a faded copy of the original impression (seeing the sunset is more vivid than remembering the sunset). Ideas can be combinations of impressions, and in this way it is possible to have an idea of something one never actually encounters. For instance, a person might see mountains and the color gold and can combine the idea of mountain with the idea of gold to form the idea of a golden mountain, despite having never seen a golden mountain. An idea that has no basis in an impression (or combination of impressions) has no sense, according to Hume—it is meaningless. For this reason, Hume rejected metaphysical concepts that could not be traced back to impressions (a view that later influenced a 20th-century school of thought called logical positivism).

Hume's version of empiricism shaped his view of personal identity, the issue of what makes a person *that* person. You are not the same person as your friends, your teacher, or your family members; something makes you *you*. But how is it that you are you? Put another way, what are the criteria for your identity or your self? Moreover, are you the same person over time? For example, is the you that attended kindergarten the same you that exists now? Philosophers have addressed these questions in various ways. It is, perhaps, natural to suppose that one has a single, permanent self—that all that one experiences happens to one's same self, a unified entity. Consider what seems to be yourself as a five-year-old and yourself as a 10-year-old, or even what seems to be yourself an hour ago and what seems to be yourself at this moment. Suppose an hour ago you were hungry and now you are not; an hour ago you were outside and now you are inside; an hour ago you were looking at a grassy field and now you are looking at text. One view is that it is the same self—the same you—that underwent or is undergoing all these experiences. Hume, however, denied that there is such a self, a single, unified entity that undergoes different experiences but itself is the same thing throughout those experiences. It is in this sense that Hume was a skeptic about the existence of the self.

To see why Hume thought this, recall that Hume claimed that an idea that has no basis in an impression is meaningless—it is literally *of* nothing. But, according to Hume, no one has an impression of the self (in the sense of a unified, permanent entity). Whenever he was conscious of himself, Hume noted, he was conscious only of an impression—for example, a sensation of heat or a feeling of love. But he was never conscious of a single, unified self. Similarly, if an hour ago you were walking outside, you were conscious of impressions such as the sight of green grass. Now, as you read this, you are conscious of the sight of the words you are reading. If an hour ago you were hungry, you were conscious of that feeling of hunger, but suppose now you are not. In such cases, by Hume's lights all that you are aware of is some impression or impressions, but you are never aware of some single, unified self. In general, if there is no impression of the self, the idea of self is empty; it has no meaning. In short, there seems to be no self at all. Rather, according to Hume, the self is just a bundle, or collection, of impressions, such as the feeling of fullness, the perception of text, and the memory of being outside an hour ago. There are, then, no essential features of what makes a person the *same* person. To talk about one's self is just a convenient way of talking about the bundle of impressions.

Perhaps most famously of all, Hume expressed skepticism about the notion of cause. Very often people believe that one event in the world causes another. For instance, kicking a soccer ball seems to cause it to move; boiling an egg seems to cause it to cook; viruses are thought to cause illnesses. There seems to be a necessary connection between such events, so that kicking a soccer ball will always cause it to move, and boiling an egg will always cause it to cook (under the appropriate conditions), and so on. So, nature seems to be uniform: Certain types of events that caused certain other types of events in the past will continue to cause those other certain types of events in the future. On the basis of this belief, scientists formulate general laws, stating, for instance, that the freezing point of water will remain in the future what it has been in the past. However, Hume denied that the belief that events necessarily cause another (and the belief in the uniformity of nature) is based on reason. Consider when one billiard ball hits another. It looks as if the first ball's striking the other causes the second ball to move. But it is not logically necessary that the second ball will move upon being struck by the first:

It is not a logical contradiction to suppose that it won't. In addition, our past experience of billiard balls also does not tell us that the ball will move in the future upon being struck. By Hume's lights, it is a mistake to argue that because the ball moved in the past when struck it will move again in the future when struck. It is a mistake because what is wanted is a justification for thinking that nature is uniform. To say that nature was uniform in the past and therefore will be uniform in the future is just to assume the very thing we want to prove (the uniformity of nature).

Hume's point was not that a billiard ball would not move when struck. Of course, he believed it would. His point was that the belief that there is a necessary connection between types of events (such as the

18th-century portrait of David Hume *(Painting by David Martin)*

event of one ball striking the other and the event of a ball moving) is not based on reason. Rather, according to Hume, our belief that one ball will move when struck by another is based on habit, or custom. We have seen one ball move when struck by another so often that we have seen a constant conjunction of events (that is, one event [the ball moving] constantly follows another [the ball being struck]). This constant conjunction gives rise to our belief that there is a necessary connection between the events. But the belief is a matter of custom, not of reason. Hume did not think there was anything wrong with this custom; in fact, he thought a belief in causes—and in general a belief in the uniformity of nature—was necessary. It was not a good idea, he noted, to throw oneself out a window (even if one's belief that doing so would cause pain is a matter of custom, not reason). Nonetheless, Hume's reasoning has far-reaching consequences, insofar as science is based on scientific laws and the view that nature is uniform. Hume's reasoning implies that science is based on custom rather than reason. The problem above concerning the uniformity of nature is known as the problem of induction, and Hume's writings have been very influential concerning it.

Causality

The concept of cause is fundamental not only to philosophy and to science but also to everyday life. We take it for granted that when something happens, there is a cause (or set of causes) for it happening, even if we do not know what the cause(s) might be. We even take it for granted that when something does *not* happen, there must be some cause for that. Aristotle provided the first sustained philosophical analysis of cause. He spoke of four causes, or four components of understanding the cause, of things. Included among these four causes, for Aristotle, was the notion of final cause, or purpose. That is, he argued that whatever exists or happens is purposive, there is some goal or end to be met that is part of the explanation for things. This view is called teleology (from the Greek word *telos,* meaning "purpose" or "end"). While many philosophers and scientists accepted Aristotle's views about cause, others rejected it, especially with the onset of the scientific revolution.

The basic concept of cause is still unclear. When we say that A causes B, one conception is that A is a necessary condition for B. In other words, in order for B to happen, A *must* happen; if A did not happen, then B could not happen. However, we commonly speak of one thing causing another, even if it is not a necessary condition. For example, we might say that smoking causes lung cancer. But some people contract lung cancer even though they do not smoke (or even inhale secondhand smoke). Another suggestion for cause is that if A causes B, then A is a sufficient condition for B. In other words, if A happens, that is all it takes for B to happen; perhaps some other things might bring about B, but it is enough that A does. However, once again, this notion of sufficient condition does not match common claims about cause. Again, we say that smoking causes lung cancer, but it does not always cause lung cancer. Some people who smoke do not get lung cancer, so, apparently, smoking is not a sufficient condition for lung cancer.

As we have seen, David Hume had quite a different conception of causality. According to Hume, the constant pairing of two events is all we can say that cause is. Of course, if that is all that cause is, then there is no difference between cause and very strong correlations between things. However, cause and strong correlations are not the same thing; in fact, we think that cause can explain why there are strong correlations, so cause cannot simply be strong correlations.

The German philosopher Immanuel Kant claimed that cause is not something out there in the world but is instead one of the categories of our minds. That is, he said it is one of the ways in which we necessarily are able to experience and make sense of things, but cause is not itself some thing or event in the world, like trees and cats. For Kant, we experience things and events as being caused, but that is, at least in part, a result of how our minds function.

Some additional philosophical issues that relate to cause are also relevant to the broader study of metaphyics. For example, there is the question of mental causation. We normally think of cause as being a physical interaction between things. Can there be such a thing as mental causation? If the mind is just the brain, then what we call mental causation is really just physical causation (because the brain is a physical organ). We speak of people acting from reasons (for example, I go to the store to buy chocolate because I like it), but what we call reasons seem to be explainable in terms of actions, which are physical.

There are also issues that relate cause more closely to the broader study of epistemology (or study of knowledge). These are issues about how we know cause or what would justify our claims and beliefs about cause. For example, one issue would be relating cause to explanation. Is explaining some thing or event just a matter of identifying the cause of it? Some philosophers claim that identifying a cause is all that there is to explaining something. In fact, the very word *because* is a shortened form of the phrase *by the cause of*. Other philosophers claim that cause is only a physical interaction (or, if Kant is correct, a mental category), and physical interactions are not themselves explanations but things that need to be explained.

Finally, there are also important issues that relate cause to the broad study of axiology (or study of values). For example, there is the issue of free will and determinism. If people's actions are (all) caused, then it seems that they are determined. That is, if something is caused, then it must happen and cannot not happen. It is puzzling to say that people's actions are not caused. We might not know the cause(s) of some choice that a person makes, but it is assumed that something caused whatever the choice was. On the other hand, how could someone be held to have any responsibility for one's actions if they are caused (and determined)? Yet, the practice of rewards and punishment only makes sense if we think that it causes future behavior. If punishment did not cause people to behave in certain way (or stop behaving in certain ways), then what would be the point of it? At very commonsense levels, then, we assume that people's actions are caused, although it is not clear exactly what that means.

Immanuel Kant

Immanuel Kant (1724–1804), one of a handful of towering figures in philosophy, developed the idea that rather than our knowledge conforming to objects, objects conform to our knowledge. This does not mean that objects do not exist unless we create them. To see what it does mean, consider that in an ordinary view, we experience what we do because objects in the world produce in us certain experiences. For example, one sees a red cup because the red cup produces in us the sensation of a red cup. But suppose, Kant thought, we see the red cup in part because the cup conforms to *how* we know: Rather than passively perceiving the cup, the mind actively structures how we experience the cup. It is in this sense that objects conform to our knowledge: What we know depends on how the mind structures experience. According to Kant, that the mind structures experience is what makes experience possible in the first place. For example, we experience what we experience in time and space. But, for Kant, space and time do not absolutely exist out there independent of the mind. Rather, the mind orders experience such that we always experience what we experience in space and time. Empiricists had argued that we acquire the idea of space through experience, by encountering objects outside of ourselves. In contrast, Kant argued, that we encounter objects outside of ourselves *presupposes* the notion of space: If we did not have the notion of space already, we would not experience objects as outside ourselves in the first place. So the idea of space is something the mind brings to experience, rather than something we encounter in experience. Similarly, the idea of time is something the mind brings to experience, rather than encounters in experience.

That the mind structures experience in terms of space and time explains how it is possible to experience sensible objects (that is, objects perceived through the senses). In addition, Kant thought, what explains understanding and knowledge of such objects is that the mind structures experience using certain a priori concepts (that is, concepts that are prior to or independent of experience). These concepts are concepts the mind actively brings to experience; it is only because the mind organizes experience by using these concepts that we can make sense of what we experience. So, without them, knowledge is not possible. Kant called these concepts categories. To show that we experience objects only through the categories, Kant again considered what is necessary for experience in the first place. It seems that we cannot experience objects as objects unless we have the concept of object. But, according to Kant, one cannot have the concept of object unless one also has the categories. In other words, the very concept of object involves certain a priori concepts. For example, the concept of object requires the concepts of substance and identity (or sameness), or the concept of something permanent (a cup, say, is a permanent object in the sense that it does not flicker in and out of existence even when it undergoes change; even painted blue, for instance, a once-red cup is the *same* cup, just colored differently). When we make judgments about the objects we experience, Kant argued, we do so according to certain logical forms of the mind, and we always use the categories to do so.

According to Kant, it is a mistake to suppose that all knowledge is based strictly on experience. This is because knowledge requires the application of categories, and the mind itself applies the categories. So the mind does not begin as a blank tablet (as Locke argued), passively receiving information via the five senses. Empiricists were wrong to think that it does. But, Kant thought, it is also a mistake to suppose that knowledge is based on reason alone. This is because knowledge requires that judgments (which involve categories) be applied to *something*: specifically, the objects of experience. In other words, the concepts themselves do not provide knowledge but merely a way of structuring experience. What we have knowledge of are the objects of experience (that is, of the things we experience). So, without sense experience—without perception—the concepts are empty, for they have nothing to apply to. But without categories, sense experience is blind, because we need the categories in order to experience.

An important component in Kant's thought, however, is that the categories apply *only* to the objects of experience. That is, they apply only to phenomena, the objects of perception—what we perceive through senses. Phenomena are contrasted with noumena, the objects of thought. Noumena are entities beyond the five senses: One can think about them, but one can never see, feel, hear, smell, or taste them. In Kant's work, noumena are things as they actually are (as he put it, things-in-themselves), independent of how they are perceived, while phenomena are the appearances of things (Kant uses *appearances* broadly, to include all perceptions, not just what one sees). For instance, a person might perceive an orange as round, orange-colored, and tart tasting. That is how the orange appears to one; the perceived shape, color, and taste of the orange are phenomena. Now consider the orange independently of how it is perceived, what the orange is in itself regardless of how it looks, feels, or tastes to anyone. That is the noumenon (singular of noumena) of the orange. Because the categories apply to phenomena, Kant believed that noumena are unknowable. Put another way, it is impossible for us to have knowledge of things in themselves, independent of how we perceive them. Knowledge, then, is confined to phenomena—the appearances of things.

Kant's views also had implications for the nature of the self. What we experience seems to be unified—it fits together as one. For instance, when a person lifts a rose to her nose and smells it, she experiences as one experience the scent of the rose, the feel of the rose, and the look of the rose. According to Kant, that experience is unified is possible only because the self is unified. So, the self is not just a collection of experiences (contrary to the view of David Hume). Of particular note here is Kant's concept of the transcendental ego. *Ego* is Latin for "self," so the transcendental ego is a kind of self. It is a transcendental self in the sense that it is a necessary condition for experience. So, it is not something that we encounter in experience. Rather, the transcendental ego is what makes experience possible in the first place; in that sense it transcends (goes beyond) experience. In addition, the transcendental ego also makes knowledge possible.

Consider that experience involves many different perceptions throughout time. For example, suppose on a trip in the desert, a person sees a cactus, a lizard, and a wild burro and feels happy at one time and tired at another. When a person experiences these various perceptions, those perceptions all belong to the same self—it is the *same* self that sees the cactus at one time and the wild burro at another, feels

Illustration of Immanuel Kant

happy at one time and tired at another. This self is the transcendental ego. We do not actually experience the transcendental ego, according to Kant; we do not even know anything about it except that it is necessary for experience and knowledge. To see why one knows nothing more of the transcendental ego, consider that one is never aware of a single permanent subject when mentally looking inward at one's self. Rather, all one is aware of is a particular perception at any given time, such as the sensation of being happy at one time and the sensation of feeling tired at another. The self that one is aware of at such times, the self one experiences upon looking inward, is the empirical self. But it is not the transcendental ego—the transcendental ego is the self that is the subject of *all* these perceptions throughout time. It is a unified self that experiences them all. Kant called the intellectual consciousness of one's unified self apperception, or the unity of apperception. It is intellectual consciousness in the sense that it is thought, not experienced empirically. (The transcendental ego is also known as the transcendental subject, because it is the unified subject of experience—that is, *it* is what has experience.)

The transcendental ego makes experience (and knowledge) possible by synthesizing one's various perceptions; it organizes perceptions using the categories. This is why it is possible for us to experience objects as objects, rather than as a hodgepodge of sensations. For instance, one typically perceives a cactus as a cactus, not as an unconnected stream of sensations such as the color of the cactus, its size, shape, and needles. In general, one's sensations are connected, or unified, so that we perceive single objects.

Among Kant's most important works is *Critique of Pure Reason*. In that book, Kant attempted to answer the question of whether synthetic a priori judgments are possible. A synthetic a priori judgment is a judgment that is knowable independent of experience (so, one can know it just by using one's reason) but whose content goes beyond the information contained in the subject of the judgment. To understand this, consider that an analytic judgment is a judgment whose content is contained in the subject of the judgment. One could just analyze the judgment to see that the content is contained in it. For instance, the statement "triangles have three sides" is analytic because what it says (that triangles have three sides) is contained in the subject of the sentence—*triangles* (triangles have three sides by definition). To say that a judgment is a priori simply means that we know it prior to experience; we do not need to investigate facts in the world to know certain things. This is contrasted with saying that we know something a posteriori (*post* meaning "after"), or only after investigating facts in the world. Kant claimed that everyday, common knowledge is synthetic a posteriori (that is, things that happen to be true or false and that we come to know by bumping into the world, so to speak). Another kind of knowledge is analytic a priori (that is, true or false by their very nature and knowable by our simply analyzing them). Metaphysical claims, however, Kant said, are synthetic a priori. A synthetic a priori judgment says something more than what is contained in the subject of the judgment. For instance, "rivers are cold" is synthetic, as it is not part of the definition of *rivers* that they are cold. If the judgment that rivers were cold were knowable a priori, "rivers are cold" would express a synthetic a priori judgment (in fact, however, it does not seem to be knowable a priori).

Whether synthetic a priori judgments are possible is controversial. Kant believed that they were (in particular, he thought that mathematical judgments and general statements in physics are synthetic a priori). The key to this view is Kant's claim that the mind organizes experience according to the categories. Consider, for example, the judgments in geometry. By its nature, geometry is about space. Now the possibility of experience presupposes the concept of space; so, we have the concept of space prior to experience. Geometrical judgments about space, then, are a priori. But they are also synthetic, Kant believed (roughly, they are not just a matter of definitions). So, geometrical judgments about space are synthetic a priori; given that we do make such judgments, synthetic a priori judgments are possible.

In general, Kant thought that synthetic a priori judgments are possible in mathematics and science. Another example regards the concept of cause. David Hume had famously argued that we experience no necessary connection between kinds of events (such as a connection between striking a match and the igniting of fire) and that we believe certain kinds of events follow other kinds of events because we have become accustomed to seeing those events occur at about the same time, not because we have reasoned that there is a necessary connection between those events. For instance, we commonly believe that fire produces heat, and that if fire has produced heat in the past, it will continue to produce heat in the future (that is, whenever there is fire, fire will produce heat). But such a belief, for Hume, is not based on reason but rather on our past experience that fire has been accompanied by heat. In general, Hume argued, the belief that certain kinds of events cause other kinds of events and that the future will be like the past is based simply on custom (what we have gotten used to experiencing). In contrast, Kant argued that laws of nature, including laws regarding causality, are valid; they are not simply based on custom. This is because, for Kant, the concept of causality (events causing other events) is one of the a priori categories by which the mind organizes experience. So, it is not possible *not* to understand what we experience without the concept of cause; our minds always structure experience using this concept (among others).

The Rejection of Metaphysics

Logical positivism, also called logical empiricism, was a philosophical movement that originated in the 1920s. It was born out of the Vienna Circle, a group of intellectuals (mathematicians, scientists, philosophers, and others) who met regularly in Vienna to share and discuss ideas. The philosophers Moritz Schlick (1882–1936), Rudolf Carnap (1891–1970), Friedrich Waismann (1896–1959), Otto Neurath (1882–1945), Carl Hempel (1905–97), and A. J. Ayer (1910–89) are all considered positivists. W. V. O. Quine (1908–2000) met with the Vienna Circle and is also associated with logical positivism; however, some of his ideas later helped undermine the movement.

The logical positivists were empiricists influenced by David Hume. They believed that knowledge is based on experience of the five senses. According to the classical logical positivist program, science is the only source of knowledge about the world, and most of the claims of religion, metaphysics, ethics, and aesthetics are neither true nor false, but simply meaningless. Logic and science, the positivists observed, had advanced even as philosophers continued to discuss the same metaphysical questions without ever arriving at answers. The problem was that these metaphysical questions were nonsense, and philosophy ought to dispense with them. Instead, positivists viewed the purpose of philosophy as using logic to analyze the concepts and the claims of science. Influenced by the logical work of Gottlob Frege (1848–1925), Alfred North Whitehead (1861–1947), and Bertrand Russell (1872–1970), positivists thought that they could clarify what concepts and claims

Moritz Schlick in 1930
(Photograph by Theodor Bauer)

mean. Science, in this view, tells us about the world, and philosophy makes it clear precisely what science tells us.

Fundamental to logical positivism was the principle of verifiability. Positivists formulated this principle in different ways, but in each case the idea was that according to the principle of verifiability, metaphysical claims were meaningless. In one version of the principle, sentences are meaningful only if they are either analytically true or if they are in principle verifiable through sensory experience. That is, meaningful sentences are true either because they are true in virtue of the meaning of the words (or the grammar of the sentence) or because it is, in principle, possible to verify the truth of the sentence through experience based on the five senses. For instance, the sentence "babies are young" is analytically true because part of the definition of *babies* is that babies are young. So, the sentence is meaningful. The sentence "the cat Happy Jack has black fur" is verifiable through sense experience because in principle it is possible to see Happy Jack and his black fur. So, that sentence is meaningful too. However, according to positivists, a metaphysical sentence such as "everything that exists is One" is neither analytic nor verifiable through sense experience. So, the sentence has no meaning: It is not false, it is just literally nonsense. On the basis of this reasoning, most ethical, aesthetic, and religious claims are also nonsense; it is not possible to verify, for example, the claim "The Mona Lisa is a good painting," since it is not true by definition and (at least for the logical positivists) there are no empirical facts that determine values such as good or bad. Also associated with positivism is emotivism, the view that ethical claims express a speaker's attitude but do not express anything true or false. For instance, to say that cruelty is bad is just to express one's own negative attitude about cruelty; it is not to say anything true (or false).

Influenced by the early work of Ludwig Wittgenstein (1889–1951), positivists thought the structure of language mirrored the structure of the world. As a very simple example, consider the sentence "Happy Jack is black." It is composed of a name (Happy Jack) for a cat and a predicate *(black)* that identifies the color black. Corresponding to the name *Happy Jack* is a cat (Happy Jack) and corresponding to *black* is the color black, which Happy Jack is. It is as if the sentence "Happy Jack is black" mirrors the actual state of affairs that Happy Jack is black. This is a very simple and rough example, but positivists thought that any true, meaningful, nonanalytic sentence similarly mirrors a state of affairs in the world. In addition, according to positivism, any meaningful, nonanalytic sentence can be reduced to a more basic statement about sensory experience. That is, any meaningful, nonanalytic sentence can ultimately be understood as saying something about sensory experience. For instance, "Happy Jack is happy" might be reducible to sentences that are about observing Happy Jack behaving in certain ways (such as purring). Exactly how to understand these kind of basic reports was controversial among logical positivists. Some positivists argued that basic statements should be about sense data—that is, information about individual sensory experiences, such as the sensation of seeing a patch of black color when looking at Happy Jack. Other positivists rejected this view on the grounds that it made scientific claims too subjective. The concern was that scientific claims are more objective than the sense data view suggests; scientific claims should not be understood as being about individual sensations.

A persistent challenge for logical positivists was how to understand the meaningfulness of the principle of verifiability itself. Of course, they believed the principle was meaningful. Yet by its own lights it was not obvious how. After all, the principle was not verifiable by sensory experience: No observation of the empirical world would seem to verify it or not verify it. Ayer claimed that it was analytically true, but this seemed unsatisfactory. First, it was not obvious that the definition of *meaningful* involved verifiability. Second, if the verifiability principle was analytic, it was not clear how the principle could be informative. An analytic sentence such as "babies are young" does not tell us anything new; it is just true by definition. Similarly, if the principle of verifiability were analytic, it would not seem to tell us anything new either. In part because of concerns over how to understand the principle of verifiability, logical positivism fell out of favor by the 1960s. Quine's rejection of the analytic/synthetic distinction was also influential, casting doubt on the notion that any sentences were analytic at all. Although logical positivism as a movement is now widely considered defunct, logical positivists were very influential in areas such as philosophy of science, philosophy of language, and analytic philosophy.

Emergentism

Emergentism

The idea of emergent properties is associated with the philosophers George Lewes (1817–78), John Stuart Mill (1806–73), and C. D. Broad (1887–1971). Very roughly, an emergent property is a property that emerges from its parts but is not the same as its parts and cannot be understood just by studying its parts. As an example, the harmony of a piece of music might be said to be an emergent property. It emerges from its various parts—the individual notes—and the relations between them. But it is not the same thing as those parts, and it cannot be understood just by studying its parts—just by studying each individual note, for instance, would not allow you to understand harmony itself. As another example, salt has properties that its individual components, sodium and chlorine, lack. For instance, sodium and chlorine have different chemical reactions than salt, even though salt is composed of sodium and chlorine. More precisely, an emergent property is a property that is not reducible to its parts and cannot be predicted beforehand. For example, perhaps no one could have predicted how salt would react chemically with other substances, even knowing how sodium and chlorine react with other substances.

Similarly, according to emergentism, mental properties such as consciousness are emergent properties. They emerge when matter is appropriately arranged and complex; in particular, mental properties emerge from the brain. No one could reasonably have predicted beforehand

Portrait of George Lewes from 1879 *(Painting by Ernst Hader)*

that they would do so. Of course, people can predict that a baby will be conscious when it is born or that it will become conscious; people can predict this on the basis of past experience (other infants were conscious or became conscious). However, prior to consciousness having ever arisen from matter in the first place (from humans, say), no one could have predicted that it would arise on the basis of the physical composition and structure of the brain. Knowing all the physical facts about the brain will not tell you that consciousness (or any other emergent property) will or will not emerge.

Emergent properties are also said to be nonreducible in an epistemological sense. That is, mental properties cannot be explained just by explaining everything about the physical stuff from which mental properties emerge. So, according to emergentism, the mind is not reducible to the body. (Sometimes, emergent properties are also taken to be nonreducible in an ontological sense, but they do not need to be taken in this way.) Some emergentists regard the emergence of mental properties as not calling for further explanation. The phrase is that such emergence is simply a brute fact. Consciousness, for instance, emerges from the brain just because that is the way it is. The stimulation of the body in certain ways leads to certain sensations (pain, ticklishness, the sensation of warmth, etc.) because that is just how things are. In this view, there is really nothing to be explained. Asking for an explanation of why consciousness emerges from the brain is like asking why the force of gravity is exactly what it is; arguably, that the force of gravity is what it is (rather than, say, being slightly stronger or slightly weaker) is not something to be explained. It just is, a brute fact that cannot itself be explained.

Some philosophers have not found this account of consciousness and other mental properties very satisfying. Typically, we look for explanations for natural phenomena, that is, phenomena that occur in the natural world. It is common to assume that there are such explanations, even if we do not always know what they are. Scientific theories account for many phenomena today that once seemed inexplicable— earthquakes, fire, magnetism, even the origin of life on Earth. Natural phenomena seem to happen for *some* reason or another, and these reasons have very often (eventually) fit comfortably into a scientific account. Some types of earthquakes occur because of the convergence of continental plates. At one level they can be explained in terms of laws of physics (laws that tell us what must happen when objects with certain physical properties collide in certain ways and with certain degrees of force). Scientists even offer explanations for fundamental laws such as the law of gravity; there is no consensus regarding such explanations, but some thinkers believe that there *is* some explanation, even if we do not yet know what it is. Arguably, perhaps consciousness should not be any different. To suppose that consciousness simply emerges from the brain with no explanation suggests that consciousness is somehow uniquely different from other natural phenomena. For critics of emergentism, why this should be is not obvious.

Another issue closely related to emergentism is that of downward causation. According to emergentism, mental properties can have causal effects on the physical realm, causing physical events. But this seems problematic. It is problematic because it implies that some physical events (such as one smiling, reaching out to pick up a brownie, running a marathon, etc.) cannot be explained in physical terms alone. They cannot be explained in physical terms alone because, according to emergentism, mental properties are not reducible to physical properties. So, any explanation of certain physical events must make reference to mental properties. The problem is that this conclusion is inconsistent with the claim that the physical world is causally closed—that is, that every physical event has a physical cause and can be explained in physical terms only. This principle, called the causal closure principle of the physical world, is a fundamental presupposition in contemporary science. So, according to critics, insofar as emergentism runs counter to this principle, emergentism is mistaken.

Images of the World

Wilfrid Sellars

Wilfrid Sellars (1912–89) was an American philosopher who wrestled with the issue of how to make sense of people's subjective experiences and encounters with science's objective descriptions and explanations, what he called two different images of the world: the manifest image and the scientific image. Sellars was the son of a well-known philosopher, Roy Wood Sellars (1880–1973). The younger Sellars received a master's degree in 1940 and taught at several universities before going to the University of Pittsburgh in 1963, where he stayed until his death.

Influenced by his father and also by the work of John Dewey (1859–1952) and other pragmatist philosophers, Sellars championed a view that is usually labeled as naturalism. This is vague, and different philosophers mean different things by it, but for Sellars it meant that only natural (as opposed to supernatural) objects, forces, and processes can meaningfully be taken to be real and to explain things and events. He rejected, then, abstract objects unless they could be shown to be consistent with a natural causal order of things. One way such things were talked about was to speak of theoretical entities. A theoretical entity is some entity that is unobserved and perhaps unobservable, but, for theoretical reasons, is postulated or assumed. For example, many scientists spoke of atoms long before they were said to be observed, and genes (as the unit of heredity) were spoken of long before biologists said they had observed them. For Sellars, theoretical entities were to be

Photograph of Wilfrid
Sellars

shunned unless there were good theoretical reasons for accepting, or at least assuming, them. This emphasis on the functional nature and importance of things was typical of the naturalist and pragmatist blend of Sellars's thought. This led to his general stance that to be is to be able to make a difference. That is, to take something as real and existing is to think that it makes a difference to other things if that thing is real and existing. For something to lack the ability to affect anything else would be, in essence, for it not to exist.

With respect to metaphysical concerns, Sellars is famous for remarking that the aim of philosophy is "to understand how things, in the broadest possible sense of the term, hang together, also in the broadest possible sense of the term." That is, the aim of philosophy is to give a coherent and complete as possible picture of all of reality. Particularly important for Sellars was that all of reality included what science tells us about the world and also our subjective experiences of the world. He referred to these as two different images of the world, a scientific image (that deals with things like molecules and physical forces) and a manifest image (that deals with subjective experiences and feelings). As an example of how these two images might be not only different but at odds with each other is how we understand the reality of colors.

The scientific, objective view about color has to do with wavelengths of electromagnetic radiation. So, red light is a particular wavelength (or spectrum of wavelengths) of electromagnetic radiation that can be measured precisely and described independently of any particular person. The manifest, subjective view about color has to do with what philosophers call qualia (singular quale, from Latin meaning "what kind"). Qualia are feels that we experience in our mental lives—for example, the sensation of seeing red, the taste of rhubarb, the emotion of joy, and the mood of restlessness. Philosophers debate the precise nature of qualia. On the surface, at least, it is not clear how qualia fit into scientific views about the world and about human minds. To illustrate this point, some philosophers have described particular thought experiments meant to show that there is more to mind than what is physical. For example, suppose a scientist comes to learn all the physical facts about color but never sees any color herself; she lives all her life in a room in which everything she sees is black, white, or a shade of gray. Now suppose she emerges from that room and sees the color red for the first time. According to this thought experiment, proposed by Australian philosopher Frank Jackson (1943–   ), the scientist would have learned something new about color: She would have learned what it was like to see red. If, however, she learned something truly new, then there is more to our mental lives than the physical facts. To put the point another way, there is something that it is *like* to see red, and all the physical facts about color do not capture this fact.

For Sellars, the important metaphysical issue is to show how these two images of the world—the manifest and the scientific—can be coherent. Neither image trumps the other, although when push comes to shove, for Sellars, the scientific image has greater weight because it goes beyond what is merely subjective. The scientific image is the result of a broader range of experiences than is the manifest image of any given person. Nonetheless, the scientific image, for Sellars, cannot negate the subjective experience of, say, seeing red; it must offer an account that is consistent with that subjective experience.

Personal Identity (the Self)

One of the aspects of the images of the world that Sellars talks about is the manifest, subjective image that pertains to persons. The important assumption of being a person underlies this image of the world and is an assumption that has generated great philosophical interest, in particular: What is a person, and what makes a given person that particular given person? Another way of expressing this is: What constitutes the self (or someone's personal identity)? The issue of personal identity is the issue of what, exactly, makes someone who he is. Another way of saying this is that personal identity is the issue of what is the essence or most basic features of someone such that, if those features were different, he would not be that person. Another term for personal identity is the *self*. That is, the issue of personal identity is: What is the self (or what constitutes a person's self)? This question of who am I? or: what makes me *me*? is one of the most fundamental philosophical questions of all.

There are two components to the issue of personal identity: the notion of person and the notion of identity. What, then, is a person? It is tempting simply to say that a person is a human. This is a way of defining what a person is in terms of being a certain kind of thing, namely a human. Philosophers say this is a way of defining persons in terms of some structural aspects, that is, in terms of having some basic structure (in this case, the biological structure of being a human). Under this conception of person, what it is to be a person is to be a human, so all persons are humans, and only humans are persons. If, under this conception, *human* is defined as having some basic structure (for example, having some appropriate genetic structure), then whatever has that genetic structure is human and therefore is a person. So, a human fetus is a person under this definition and even a dead human body is a person (since it has that appropriate genetic structure).

Some people claim that the notion of person is not exactly the same thing as the notion of human. For example, in legal and social contexts, a corporation might be treated as if it were a person. A corporation, for instance, might sue someone or be sued by someone; a corporation might be said to have acted in a certain way and, hence, be responsible for some outcome that resulted from its actions. Corporations are given tax identification numbers that function like social security numbers do for individuals. In various ways, then, corporations are treated as if they are persons, although corporations are not humans. In addition, many people treat the notion of person as not equivalent with the notion of human because the notion of person is not biological. After someone dies, people often remark that he was a wonderful person, but they do not think that the physical body that remains is itself that person or even a person at all. Even though the physical body is human (has a human genetic structure), in itself it is not seen as being a person.

Because of cases like corporations or bodies, many people define persons not in terms of having some structure but in terms of having some function or capacities. That is, they see persons as the sorts of things that can do certain kinds of things. The notion of person, then, is not so much biological as it is social. Persons, not human bodies, are the sorts of things, for example, that can have rights and responsibilities. One difficulty, however, is that there is no general agreement on what functions or capacities are the ones that make someone (or something) a person. Must someone have a certain level of awareness in order to be a person? Must someone be capable of communicating with others to be a person? Must someone be able to feel certain things (either in terms of sensations or in terms of emotions) to be a person? Just exactly what a person is, then, as opposed to what a human is, is not obvious.

The other basic component of personal identity (besides the component of person) is the component of identity, or being the same thing. There is a quantitative understanding of identity, which is that each individual thing is what it is and there are no two identical things. That is, identity is unique; something is the same as itself, but no two things are the same thing. We might think that there are two copies of the same book. However, each copy is unique, and one of them is, say, in a different room than the other one or is lying to the left of the other one. The two copies might be qualitatively the same, but they are not quantitatively the same. Qualitative sameness, then, is another understanding of identity, different than quantitative sameness. Along with the notion of qualitative sameness, there is a sense of identity that has to do with relevant similarity. That is, if two different things are similar enough in ways that are relevant to certain concerns, then we speak of them as identical. So, again, if there are two copies of some book, and we want to read a page from that book, it would not matter to us which copy we looked at. Both copies are similar enough with respect to our concerns, namely, to be able to read some particular page. As far as we are concerned, in such a case, the two copies are identical (even though they are not quantitatively identical).

The issue of personal identity, then, is about what makes a person who he is, or, again, what makes me *me*? What is *my* identity, such that it is my *self*? One way that philosophers often approach this question is by asking what kinds of change are needed for someone no longer to be who he is, or how much change is needed for someone no longer to be who he is. For example, would you be the same person if you had had different parents? Would you be the same person if you had been born the opposite sex than you in fact were born? What or how much would have to be different for you to be a different person than you are? Philosophers have tended to take four broad views with respect to the issue of personal identity: (1) mind continuity, (2) body continuity, (3) social continuity, and (4) no continuity (no personal identity).

The mind continuity view claims that what makes a person the same person over time—and, therefore, what constitutes the person's self—is that there is a continuity over time of one's memories and thoughts. The true essence of someone, according to this view, is memories and thoughts, not physical structure. If I am the same person today that I was yesterday or a year ago or 10 years ago, it is because I had certain experiences and I remember them. I remember what I did yesterday or I remember where I lived 10 years ago, etc. Of course, I do not remember *everything* that I did yesterday or 10 years ago, but there is a continuity of memories over time. It is this continuity of memories over time that makes me the same person over time. If I completely lost all memory (and, perhaps, could never regain it), according to this view, I would not be the same person as I was before I lost my memory. The same body might exist, but I would not be the same person. A famous philosopher, among many, who held this view was John Locke (1632–1704).

The body continuity view disagrees. This view claims that a person is who he is even if he entirely loses his memory (and, perhaps, could never regain it). The reason is because what makes some experience (or memory or thought) the experience of some person is that it is causally connected to a particular body. For example, I can remember what I did yesterday or a year ago or 10 years ago because I did certain things. The experiences (or memories or thoughts) are not just floating around in the world; they are *my* experiences because they are connected to *me*, a particular organism. What makes them *my* experiences and not yours is that they belong to me. The me is not the experiences themselves, but the experiences of someone. If I lose my memory, I do not cease to exist, says this view; rather, I have lost my memory. A famous philosopher, among many, who held this view was A. J. Ayer (1910–89).

One way of quickly seeing the difference between these two views is by using a science fiction example. Suppose there are two people, Al and Betty, and the minds of each were somehow placed inside the bodies of the other (so that Al's mind is placed inside of Betty's body and vice versa). Standing side by side, the person on the left is (or has) Al's mind in Betty's body, while the person on the right is (or has) Betty's mind in Al's body. The mind continuity view would say that Al is on the left, while the body continuity view would say that Betty is on the left.

The third broad philosophical view about personal identity is the social continuity view. This view claims that what makes someone who he is ultimately is a matter of social interaction. That is to say, our self is largely constructed by our interactions in the world. We are not merely bodies, says this view. On the other hand, our self-consciousness is not our self because our self arises out of our actions and interactions with others. If people treat us a certain way, that creates certain experiences, and those experiences generate future actions as desires and plans. Our understanding of our self and, in fact, the actual self, emerges out of these interactions. We are not born with a self, says this view, instead it develops as a result of the continuity of social interactions. How people treat us because of the way we look or speak or act, etc., shapes our development and how we see ourselves. Different interactions over time would result in a person being a different person. One's personal identity, then, is not a matter of having either some specific mental features (like the mind continuity view) or some specific physical features (like the body continuity view) but of having certain social interactions. If persons Al and Betty suddenly had their minds switched into the bodies of the other person, for the social continuity view, neither person would be Al or Betty, because the stream of social interactions would be new and different. A famous philosopher, among many, who held this view was George Herbert Mead (1863–1931).

The no continuity view is the view that there is no self, at least no self that underlies our actions or thoughts. In other words, much like the social continuity view, the no continuity (or no self) view claims that there are no core memories or bodily structure that makes someone who he is. Who someone is simply is a collection of interactions and experiences. To talk about a self is merely a convenient way to talk about these interactions and experiences. There is no self that has interactions and experiences; the self just is a way of speaking of such interactions and experiences. The illusion of the self is a notion that is included in much Buddhist thought. A famous philosopher, among others, who held this view is David Hume.

Although the issue of personal identity can seem abstract, it is a basic question of human life. It underlies issues of what kind of life one wants to live and of what choices one ultimately wants to make. Beyond that very fundamental question of who am I? (and, following that, who do I want to be?), there are very practical aspects of the issue of personal identity. For example, if someone committed a crime, normally it would be unfair and unreasonable to hold someone else responsible for that crime (and perhaps even punish that other person). That is, we should punish the same person who committed the crime. But, what makes someone the same person over time—and, so, responsible for some past action—is exactly the issue of personal identity. What about a person who commits a crime and is arrested but genuinely cannot remember having done it? Is the person who committed the crime the same person as the one who is arrested? Given the body continuity view of personal identity, yes, they are the same person. No one else committed the crime; it was this person, whether or not he remembers having done it. However, given the mind continuity view, they are not necessarily the same person. It would be improper to punish someone for something he cannot at all remember having done. From that person's perspective, it is as if he is punished for someone else's crime. However such a case is settled, the point is that important, practical social issues such as responsibility (and punishment or reward) rest in part on the underlying issue of personal identity.

Theseus's Ship

The story of Theseus's ship has its origin in Greek mythology. Over time, a ship belonging to Theseus has its parts replaced one by one. At one point, call it T_1, the ship is built and is made up of many parts. Eventually, every original part of the ship is replaced, so that at some point in time, call it T_2, there is no original part of the ship left. The question arises: Is the ship at T_2 the same ship as the ship at T_1? Another way of putting the question is this: Assuming that the newly built ship was given a name, call it *Explorer*, does *Explorer* refer to the same thing at time T_2 as it referred to at time T_1?

This issue points to an underlying concept of identity: What makes something what it is? It also relates to the issue of permanence: How much change or what sorts of change can something undergo and still remain the same thing (or what remains permanent in the midst of change)? Is Theseus's ship the same ship over time, even though the ship at time T_2 has no parts in common with the ship at time T_1? On one hand, we are inclined to say that it is the same ship, but it has undergone many changes. However, the question remains: What makes it the *same* ship? It cannot be the parts that make it up, since they are all different by the time of T_2. On the other hand, if it is not the same ship, when did it become a different ship? When the very first part was replaced? That is puzzling; it is as if when someone loses a fingernail, the person is no longer the same person, which, at the very least, runs counter to common sense. If at T_2, it is not the same ship, did it become a different ship when exactly one part more than 50 percent of the original parts was changed? That seems somewhat arbitrary.

This puzzle becomes even more complex in this case: Suppose, as each part of the original ship, which is docked in the water, is replaced, the original parts are stored in a warehouse. Eventually, all of the original parts have been replaced on the original ship, but all of the original parts are stored in the warehouse. Now, what if someone puts together again all those original parts, so that now there are two ships? Assuming that the name *Explorer* referred to the ship docked in the water, even on the day when the last original part was replaced, does the name *Explorer* now refer to the ship with all the newly replaced parts or does it refer to the ship in the warehouse, the one with all the original parts that have now been reassembled? This puzzle, as noted above, relates to the issues of identity and permanence, but also to the issue of personal identity (that is, what makes a person the same person over time).

Consciousness and Freedom

Consciousness

There are many things that distinguish creatures that have consciousness from things that do not. A normal, awake human, for example, thinks, feels, and plans; a rock does not. Yet exactly what consciousness is and what things have it, or even what things could have it, remain controversial. For instance, spiders seem to be aware at some level, mending their webs and capturing prey. But it is not clear that a spider has consciousness. Computers perform very complex calculations, but it is not obvious that any computer (no matter how sophisticated) could ever have consciousness. The questions of what consciousness is and what could have it are important topics in the philosophy of mind. Other topics related to consciousness are whether consciousness is physical or nonphysical, whether consciousness has a function, and what we can know about consciousness.

Philosophers use the word *consciousness* both to talk about creatures and to talk about mental states. That is, we say some creatures (such as normal, functioning humans) have consciousness and that some mental states are conscious states. A mental state is just a state of mental activity—for example, the state of believing that whales are mammals, the state of feeling pain, and the state of seeing a redwood forest. In addition, consciousness is not the same as just being awake. This is because one can be conscious while dreaming, for example, in the sense that one has feelings and desires during the dream. Inspired by the philosopher Thomas Nagel (1937–   ), one very common way of describing consciousness is to say that, if a creature is conscious, then there is something that it is like to be that creature. There does not seem to be anything that it is like to be a rock, for instance—a rock lacks consciousness. But, arguably, there is something that it is like to be a bat (something involving being nocturnal and finding food through echolocation). Similarly, there seems to be something that it is like to experience pain. So, states that exhibit consciousness are states that there is something it is like to be in those states.

On the surface, conscious mental states seem to be rather different than brain states. A brain has various features, such as having a certain shape and weight. However, a person's thoughts do not seem to have a shape or weigh anything. In addition, sensations such as joy are features of some conscious mental states but are not obviously features of the brain: It seems unlikely that a careful examination of the brain would uncover the sensation of joy. In part because the mind and the body do seem different, some philosophers have advocated dualism. According to dualism, consciousness is nonphysical. Most (but not all) contemporary philosophers reject dualism. They seek to explain consciousness in physical terms only. It is apparent that there is a close relation between the brain and consciousness. For example, a person who is brain-dead lacks consciousness, and some drugs that affect the brain also seem to cause conscious mental states, such as hallucinations. Such facts suggest that consciousness can be explained in physical terms alone; perhaps if we knew everything there is to know about the brain and how it works, we would understand consciousness. Perhaps consciousness just *is* a matter of processes in the brain. If this were so, it would explain the very close relation between consciousness and the brain. Some views in the philosophy of mind, such as identity theory and functionalism, attempt to explain consciousness just in physical terms.

However, *how* to account for consciousness just in physical terms has proven difficult. There is often said to be an explanatory gap when it comes to consciousness. The idea is that we are unable to explain the connection between physical states and consciousness. Just examining the physical properties of the human brain would not seem to tell us why a human would be conscious. We know *that* there is a close relation between the mind and the brain, but it is difficult to see *why* there is such a relation. Humans feel pain when certain physical fibers in the human body (C-fibers) are stimulated. But why should stimulating C-fibers cause pain and not some other sensation, such as heat? There seems to be no explanation for why certain physical states should be related to certain conscious states. Moreover, there is another important objection to views that regard consciousness in only physical terms. The objection is that knowing all the physical facts about a given conscious experience will not tell us what it is like to *have* that experience. For example, knowing all the physical facts about a bat (how its brain works, say) does not seem to tell us what it is like to be a bat. This is a problem for physicalist views of consciousness because it suggests that there is more to consciousness than physical processes.

Freedom and Determinism

If someone has an epileptic seizure and, in the throes of thrashing around, breaks a lamp, did that person act freely? If someone points a gun at you and demands your wallet, which you then hand over, did you act freely? If a six-year-old boy, immediately after watching a TV advertisement for a new toy, announces "I want that," did he act freely?

There are various senses of freedom. In philosophy, one broad sense has to do with political freedom, that is, freedom with respect to the government or other people. For example, this sense is concerned with people having the right to free speech or free expression. A second broad sense has to do with metaphysical freedom, that is, free will, or people's ability to act on their own. For example, this sense is concerned with people being free to make some choice (say, choosing chocolate ice cream over vanilla ice cream), as opposed to that choice being determined by something outside that individual's control.

Within these two broad philosophical concerns (political and metaphysical), there are different senses of freedom. One sense is sometimes called negative freedom, meaning the absence of some imposed constraint. For example, we speak of someone as being (negatively) free to ride a bicycle if that person is not prevented from doing so by, say, being in jail. Another sense is sometimes called positive freedom, meaning having the conditions or ability to do something. So, we speak of someone being (positively) free to ride a bicycle if that person has a bicycle and knows how to ride it. Negative freedom is often referred to as freedom from, meaning being free from constraints, while positive freedom is often referred to as freedom to, meaning being free to do something (not merely being free from constraints).

With respect to constraints on freedom, some are said to be external and some are said to be internal. For example, being locked in chains is an external constraint; the chains are external to the person himself. So, for example, being locked in chains is an external constraint to one's being free to ride a bicycle. On the other hand, being ignorant is an internal constraint; the ignorance is internal to the person himself. So, being ignorant of how to ride a bicycle is an internal constraint to one's being free to ride a bicycle. Generally speaking, things such as locked doors, barred windows, chains, etc., are external positive constraints, while obsessive thoughts, compulsive mental disorders, and even severe headaches are internal positive constraints. These are positive constraints because there is something that has a direct impact on one's freedom; there is something added, so to speak, to a person that constrains him. There are also negative constraints, which are cases in which the absence or lack of something is what constrains one's freedom. External negative constraints would be cases such as having a lack of money or lack of transportation. For instance, a person is not free to buy a book if that person does not have enough money to do so. In this case, it is the lack of something external to him that constrains him. Internal negative constraints would be cases such as having a lack of knowledge or strength or ability, etc. So, a person is not free to order food in a Swahili restaurant if that person does not speak Swahili (or cannot communicate effectively). The constraint is internal because what is lacking is not some object or thing but some ability or capability.

A fundamental metaphysical issue is that of trying to understand the notion of freedom, or free will, that is, our (apparent) ability to act freely. While the issue might seem fairly abstract, it has immediate practical implications. For example, would it be reasonable to hold someone responsible for her actions if those actions were not free? Notions and practices of reward and punishment, praise and blame, presume that people are responsible for their actions, which in turn, seems to presume that people act freely.

Given the various kinds of restraints on freedom that were noted above, it is clear that what it means to say that someone is free, or acts freely, is complicated. One intuitive sense of what freedom of action is is that a person has the ability to choose. Without such an ability how could one be said to act freely? However, the very notion of choosing presupposes that there are available alternatives of actions. That is, choosing implies choosing one thing rather than another. So, a person living in 1800 could not choose to watch television, since televisions did not exist then. Furthermore, that person could not have chosen to fly to, say, London rather than take a ship to London, since airplanes did not exist then. (There is a sense in which there is always an alternative; that sense is that one is always faced with doing action A or not doing action A.)

Many philosophers also claim that for an act to truly be free, not only must alternatives be available, but the actor must be aware of the alternatives. For example, suppose I want to drive from point A to point B, and the road I usually take is blocked. If I only knew it, I could take another route to get from point A to point B, but I do not know about another route. Some philosophers, at least, say that in such a situation, I am not truly free because I cannot choose an alternative if I am not aware of it. Furthermore, as noted above when speaking of constraints on freedom, to speak of someone truly acting freely, it might be that there is an assumption of authenticity or genuine autonomy by that person. What is meant here is that sometimes when people act in situations of extreme stress they do not make a genuine choice but simply respond or react without thinking or deliberating. For some people, at least, actions in such situations are not truly free but are mere automatic responses, similar to, say, a physical spasm or tic.

The major metaphysical question that is usually asked is: Are we indeed free? We certainly think we are. That is, we certainly think that we make choices and have the ability to do otherwise than what we actually do. That is, we assume that if we choose to buy chocolate ice cream instead of vanilla, we could have done otherwise; we could have chosen vanilla (again, assuming that vanilla was an available option and we knew that it was). Of course, everyone recognizes that some of our actions are not free. There are many kinds of human behaviors over which we normally have no control. The issue is whether or not there are any of our actions that are truly free.

Philosophers have tended to give two broad answers to this question. These two broad answers (or views) are usually called incompatibilism and compatibilism. Incompatibilism says that if an action is caused, then it is not free, and vice versa. That is, causation and freedom are incompatible; if something is caused, then it is determined, not free, while if something is free, then it must not be caused (or determined). Compatibilism says that causation and freedom are compatible; they are not mutually exclusive.

There are two broad versions of incompatibilism: metaphysical libertarianism and metaphysical determinism. Metaphysical libertarianism says that some of our actions are free, and therefore they are not caused. Metaphysical determinism says that all of our actions are caused (determined), and therefore none of them are free, even if we think they are. (One word about the term *libertarianism:* There is a political philosophy called libertarianism, which is not the same thing as metaphysical libertarianism. Metaphysical libertarianism, which is the kind discussed here, is simply about the issue of human free will, not about any political values or systems.) Libertarians claim that, while some of our actions are caused, some are not, because at any given moment, we have the ability to choose otherwise. Again, suppose that I am faced with the choice of selecting chocolate ice cream or vanilla ice cream. If I choose chocolate, say the libertarians, there are of course reasons, even causes, for why I made that choice. But the fact is, they say, that I could have chosen otherwise. We do this sort of thing all the time. More precisely, libertarians claim that some human actions are chosen and performed by agents (that is, humans) without there being any cause(s) of that action prior to the action itself such that the cause(s) prevented an alternative action being chosen.

Metaphysical determinism, on the other hand, rejects the libertarian view. It might seem to us, they say, that we act freely, but we do not. Every action, they say, is determined because every action is caused. For every action that occurs, there are previous events and circumstances that are the cause(s) of that action, so that, given those previous events and circumstances, it is not possible that the event in question does not occur (or that some other event could have occurred). Human actions, they say, are physical events in the world and, therefore, the results of previous physical events that led up to them. Of course, we might not know what those preceding events are or how they caused the event in question, but they did. Determinists often point to increased scientific knowledge of the world, including scientific knowledge about human biology and psychology, to support their claims. We know more and more, they say, about how the brain causes certain behaviors. Humans are, after all, biological organisms and are subject to physical and biological laws. Determinists do not necessarily deny that people make choices (after all, we do select chocolate ice cream over vanilla sometimes); rather, they say that the choices that we make are determined. We choose, but there are causes for those choices, and those causes are determined.

Although libertarians and determinists sharply disagree, they all agree that freedom and causation are incompatible. There are, however, many philosophers who reject this incompatibility. They represent the second broad answer to the question of human free will: compatibilism. Compatibilists say that actions can be caused and yet also be free at the same time. They claim that, of course, there are causes for people's actions and choices. The very notion of responsibility presupposes that actions are caused. For example, the reason that we praise or reward someone for good actions and blame or punish them for bad actions is because we believe that the praise/reward or blame/punishment will cause them to behave in certain ways in the future. By praising/rewarding people for certain actions, we assume that this will cause them to act in similar ways in the future, while blaming/punishing them for certain actions will cause them to behave differently in the future. So, say the compatibilists, responsibility requires the notion of actions being caused, otherwise, there would be no point to praise/reward or blame/punishment. To that extent, the determinists are right. However, it is also the case that we assume that people have the ability to choose otherwise (that is, that they are free), or else praise/reward and blame/punishment make no sense. We assume they will have a causal effect, but only in the sense that people in the future can and will have the ability to choose. Furthermore, they say, the only sense of freedom or free will that really matters is one in which we assume that people can do otherwise than what they actually do. Freedom does not mean uncaused for compatibilists, since, of course, people's actions are caused; rather, it means having the ability to select among alternatives. Once a choice is made, yes, of course, we could (at least, in theory) give a causal explanation for how and why that choice was made, but for the compatibilists, being caused is not the same thing as being determined (i.e., as necessary).

Both the libertarians and the determinists reject the compatibilist view. Libertarians say that compatibilism is simply determinism in disguise, a soft determinism, because it agrees that all actions are caused. Determinists say that compatibilists also are, in the final analysis, just weak determinists, who are uncomfortable with simply embracing full-fledged determinism because they believe that without some sense of freedom, morality and responsibility make no sense. The dispute between the compatibilists and incompatibilists continues!

Modality and Possible Worlds

Gottfried Leibniz

Gottfried Leibniz (1646–1716) developed a system of metaphysics in addition to writing on epistemology, ethics, the problem of evil, and free will and determinism. According to Leibniz, reality consists of simple substances called monads. There must be simple substances, he thought, because some things are composed of parts; these things must be composed of something, and what they are composed of are monads. A tree, for example, is composed of monads—at a fundamental level, it consists of simple substances that we cannot perceive through our senses. We cannot perceive monads through our senses because monads lack extension; they do not extend into space (so, they are not physical). Monads are simple in the sense that they cannot be divided. They are unique in the sense that no monad is just like any other monad. They are eternal in the sense that they neither can be created nor destroyed, except by God. Indeed, for Leibniz, nothing can causally affect a monad or be affected by a monad. That is, a monad does not cause anything and what happens to a monad is not caused by anything outside the monad itself. This idea stems in part from the traditional idea that substances are independent, which Leibniz took to imply causally independent. Each monad has a sort of active force, a kind of life principle. A person's soul is a monad. But there are also monads throughout a person's body—for example, in a person's hands and feet. As an analogy, a fishpond can be understood as a pool with fish in it. But the fish themselves can be understood as

Statue of Gottfried Leibniz in Göttingen, Germany *(Used under a Creative Commons license)*

composed of monads, each with its own life force. For Leibniz, even inorganic objects consist of monads, and because monads have a sort of life principle, all nature is full of life. However, some monads are more conscious and more rational than others.

Monads do undergo change, but they do so according to their own internal nature. A monad, Leibniz wrote, is pregnant with its future: It contains within it the potential for what will happen to it in the future. In addition, monads contain within themselves what has happened to them in the past. One might wonder, if reality consists of monads and these monads do not interact, then how is it that what happens in the world seems to fit together. Consider, for example, that when a person intends to dive into a pool of water, her body moves and dives into the water. How does the person's intention correspond with the body's motion, if the soul (a monad) does not interact with the body? For that matter, if the body is itself a collection of monads, how is it that each separate monad within the body somehow acts in concert such that the body dives into the water? Leibniz's answer is that there is a pre-established harmony between monads. The soul does not cause the body to move, nor does the body cause the soul to feel a certain way. Rather, God has arranged it such that the actions of the one correspond with the other. His view is sometimes referred to as a version of parallelism.

Parallelism is a philosophical position about how the mind and the body are related to each other. In a commonsense view, what goes on in one's mind has an effect on what goes on with one's body, and vice versa. The usual philosophical way of putting this is that mental events can cause bodily events and bodily events can cause mental events. For example, suppose the water in one's shower suddenly turns ice-cold. It is likely that a person would yelp in discomfort and quickly move to turn the water off. So the bodily event of the cold water striking one's skin seems to cause the mental event of the sensation of pain. Also, the mental event of a person desiring to stop the cold water seems to cause the bodily event of the person reaching for a valve in the shower.

However, according to parallelism, it is a mistake to think that mental events cause any bodily events, or that bodily events cause any mental events. Rather, mental and bodily events are parallel: They simply occur at the same time (or about the same time). But neither causes the other. Leibniz gave the following analogy. If two clocks are set to show the same time, then throughout the day, the clocks will show the same time: They are parallel to each other. But neither clock causes the other clock to show a certain time. In the same way, according to parallelism, mental events and bodily events are parallel, but neither causes the other. It is as if the mind and the body were both set at the same time. Why are mental events and bodily events parallel? As noted above, Leibniz's answer is that God has arranged it this way (so there is a pre-established harmony between mental events and bodily events).

Parallelism is often associated with substance dualism, the view that mind is a nonphysical substance and body is a physical substance (a substance is, roughly, a kind of stuff). A difficulty with substance dualism is that it seems mysterious how a nonphysical mind could have any effect on a physical body (or vice versa), that is, how mental events could cause bodily events (or vice versa). Because parallelism denies that mental events and bodily events can have any effect on each other, the view escapes this difficulty. However, parallelism faces difficulties of its own. First, few philosophers believe there is an adequate explanation for why mental and bodily events would be parallel. Second, if parallelism is true, then nothing that we think, believe, feel, or want has any effect on anything we physically do; moreover, nothing that happens to our bodies has any effect on what we think or feel. Many philosophers find this too far-fetched to accept parallelism.

Modality (Necessity and Possibility)

People often speak of things or events as being possible or as being necessary. For example, we might claim that it is possible that there is life on Jupiter; it might be the case that there is life on Jupiter, even if we do not know it. Similarly, we might claim that a father is necessarily older than his daughter; it must be the case that he is older than she is. These notions of necessity and possibility (what might be or must be) are what philosophers call modalities (modes, or ways, that something is). We often distinguish possibility and necessity not only from each other but also from two other concepts, actuality and contingency. That is, we sometimes distinguish something as being possible from something as being actual. For instance, it was possible that Babe Ruth could have run for governor of New York, but in actuality he did not. Likewise, while it in fact happened that Babe Ruth hit more than 700 home runs, he might not have; it did not have to happen, so it was contingent (not necessary) that it happened. Philosophers also speak of sentences as being contingent (for example, "bachelors are ugly"), which means that those sentences are true sometimes, but not always, as well as other sentences being necessary (for example, "bachelors are unmarried"). In the latter case (sentences being necessary), they can be either necessarily true, such as "bachelors are unmarried" (also called tautologies), or necessarily false, such as "bachelors are married" (also called contradictions).

These notions seem common and mundane. However, a closer look at them shows that they raise a number of conceptual and philosophical issues. One such issue is that there are different kinds of necessity and possibility. For example, philosophers speak of logical possibility as opposed to physical possibility. To say that something is logically possible simply means that it does not involve a contradiction. For instance, it is logically possible that a person could jump from the Earth to the Moon, but it is not physically possible. The law of gravity is relevant to physical possibility, but not to logical possibility. However, it is logically impossible for a square to be round, but not physically impossible (at least, if we take geometrical figures to be nonphysical, abstract things, so physical possibility or impossibility is irrelevant). People also speak of other kinds of possibility (or necessity), such as technological possibility (it might be logically and physically possible to fly faster than light, but it is not now technologically possible). In addition, we might speak of temporal possibility (or necessity), that is, possibility or necessity related to time and a sequence of events. Philosophers even speak of epistemic possibility (or necessity), meaning what might or must be known.

Another issue about modalities, besides the various kinds of possibility and necessity, that philosophers deal with is whether or not necessity and possibility are properly spoken of as of the world or only as in language. For example, if we say that something is possible—for example, it is possible that there is life on Jupiter—does that simply mean that the sentence "there is life on Jupiter" is not a contradiction or does it mean that there is actual possible life on Jupiter? The first case could be restated as "it is possible that there is life on Jupiter." In this case, the possibility is about the truth of the sentence, that is, that the sentence is possibly true (and not a contradiction). The second case could be restated as "it is the case that there is possibly life on Jupiter." In this case, the possibility is about life-forms, not about the sentence. Philosophers refer to the first case as *de dicto* (from Latin, meaning "of language"), and they refer to the second case as *de re* (from Latin, meaning "of things"). The reason this distinction is made is because there

Thomas Aquinas is shown reading in this 15th-century painting. *(Gentile da Fabriano)*

are conceptual questions about claiming that there are possible things, that is, that there are actually things that are possible. For instance, the 20th-century American philosopher W. V. O. Quine (1908–2000) asked: Are there more possible thin men in the doorway than possible fat men? His point was that the notion of *de re* possibility raises questions and concerns that lead philosophers astray, while *de dicto* possibility does not. Other philosophers disagree.

In the history of philosophy, a major topic related to necessity and possibility has been the topic of (the possibility of) a necessary being. Is there anything that *must* exist? Or, for that matter, is it even possible that anything must exist? The notion of a necessary being, that is, something that is necessary (or necessarily exists), is usually raised in the context of talking about God. Many philosophers have argued that while everyday things that we experience are contingent, there is one thing that is necessary (or, necessarily exists), and that is God. A famous argument for God's existence came from the medieval philosopher Thomas

Aquinas (1225–74). Aquinas offered various arguments to prove God's existence. One of those arguments was that not only did God exist but that necessarily God exists (or, that God is a necessary being). His argument ran like this: Our everyday experience shows us that in nature there are things that are contingent. In other words, it is possible for them to exist or not exist. Indeed, the things that we encounter every day are things that come into existence and go out of existence. If it is true that for everything in nature it is possible for it not to be (that is, it is the case that at some point in time it did not exist and then it came into existence), then at some point in time there would have been nothing at all. That is because, as contingent things, it is impossible for them always to exist (by their definition as being contingent). However, if that is true, namely, that at some point in time there was nothing at all, then there would still be nothing at all, because things can only come into existence by being caused by something else. Or, you cannot get something from nothing! (For example, a person can only come into existence by the actions of his parents, or a table can only come into existence by the actions of some tablemaker.) Obviously, there are things that exist now, so it could not be the case that at some point in time there was nothing. There must be something, then, that is not contingent but is necessary. That thing is God. Although Aquinas (and many others) found this argument to be persuasive, many others have not. For those who are not persuaded, some are not because this argument presumes, but does not prove, *de re* necessity, as opposed to *de dicto* necessity.

David Lewis

David Lewis (1941–2001) was an American philosopher who had tremendous influence among philosophers in developing the notions of modality (that is, possibility and necessity) and what came to be called possible worlds. Lewis was born in Oberlin, Ohio, and studied philosophy as an undergraduate student at Swarthmore College. He received his doctoral degree in philosophy at Harvard University. After teaching at UCLA during the late 1960s, he went to Princeton University in 1970, where he stayed until his death.

Lewis is probably best known for his view called modal realism. This is the view that possibilities (or, possible worlds) really exist. At a time when most philosophers said that possibility is *de dicto* (that is, about language), he claimed that possibility is *de re* (that is, about things). For example, if someone says it is possible that there could be a cat that is 15 feet tall, then what that really means is the sentence "There could be a cat that is 15 feet tall" is not a contradiction (or necessarily false). This would be to say that possibility is *de dicto,* or about the sentence; the sentence is not a contradiction; it could be true (even if it is not). Lewis, however, argued that possibility (and necessity) is actually *de re.* It is not merely about sentences and whether or not they are true, but it is about extralinguistic things. Lewis claimed that there is an indefinite number of possible worlds, where a possible world is one that differs from our actual world in some way or other. So, one possible world is one that is exactly like our actual world, except the tree in my yard is an elm tree, not a walnut tree; another possible world is one that is exactly like our actual world, except the shirt I am wearing is blue rather than white. Some possible worlds are much more radically different than our actual world; perhaps one such world is one in which dinosaurs still live or one in which basic laws of physics are different than in our world. (To say something is necessary means that it is true in all possible worlds.)

Lewis argued that these possible worlds do not exist in some different manner than our actual world; rather, they exist and simply are different. This, he said, was a better way of understanding modality than to treat it as being just about language. So, when someone says that it is possible that there could be a cat that is 15 feet tall, that means that in some possible world(s), there really is a cat that is 15 feet tall, not merely that the sentence is not a contradiction. In fact, said Lewis, the reason that it is not a contradiction is because there is some possible world(s) in which it is true. Lewis acknowledged that this view seems to many people to be strange, and he was often met with incredulous stares, but he claimed that it made much better sense of how we can understand modality and counterfactuals, statements that are contrary to fact.

Concluding Discussion Questions

1. What are the strongest arguments in favor of idealism? Against idealism?
2. What is the problem of universals? Why have philosophers considered it a problem?
3. What are realism, nominalism, and conceptualism? What are the problems associated with each of those views?
4. What are the philosophical problems associated with the nature of causation?
5. What does Wilfrid Sellars mean by the scientific image of man and the manifest image of man? How would these two images relate to the notion of emergent properties?
6. What is modality? How does it relate to the problem of free will versus determinism and to the issue of personal identity?

Further Reading

Aune, Bruce. *Metaphysics*. Minneapolis: University of Minnesota Press, 1985.

Carroll, John W., and Ned Markosian. *An Introduction to Metaphysics*. Cambridge: Cambridge University Press, 2010.

Conee, Earl, and Ted Sider. *Riddles of Existence: A Guided Tour of Metaphysics*. Oxford: Oxford University Press, 2007.

Divers, John. *Possible Worlds*. New York: Routledge, 2002.

Garrett, Brian. *What Is This Thing Called Metaphysics?* New York: Routledge, 2006.

Gracia, Jorge J. E. *Metaphysics and Its Task*. Albany: SUNY Press, 1999.

Hoy, Ronald C., and L. Nathan Oaklander, eds. *Metaphysics: Classic and Contemporary Readings*. Beverly, Mass.: Wadsworth, 1991.

Lowe, E. J. *A Survey of Metaphysics*. Oxford: Oxford University Press, 2002.

Moreland, J. P. *Universals (Central Problems of Philosophy)*. Montreal: McGill-Queen's University Press, 2001.

Taylor, Richard. *Metaphysics*. 4th ed. Englewood Cliffs, N.J.: Prentice Hall, 1992.

Van Inwagen, Peter. *Metaphysics*. Boulder, Colo.: Westview, 1993.

Van Inwagen, Peter, and Dean W. Zimmerman, eds. *Metaphysics: The Big Questions*. New York: Wiley-Blackwell, 1991.

Glossary

categories   basic kinds or classifications of metaphysical entities, for example, events are a different category of things than objects are.

cause   that which brings about or makes happen; it is difficult to define the notion of cause because it is so fundamental, and because of this difficulty, some philosophers have been skeptical about the concept.

conceptualism   the view that universals (that is, things nonparticular) have meaning because they refer to concepts (as opposed to actual objects); for example, the term *white* is said to refer to the concept of white, not to particular patches of white objects or to some real abstract object that exists.

emergentism   the view that certain features or properties of things come about, or emerge, from their parts but are not the same as their parts and cannot be understood just by studying their parts; for example, the property of being harmonious comes from the relationship between musical instruments being played and is not the result of the playing of any one of those instruments by itself.

idealism   in metaphysics, the view that ideas or mental content are what is (most) real; some philosophical idealists say that only ideas (and minds) are real, while other philosophical idealists say that being conceived by a mind is a necessary condition for something to be real; as opposed to materialism.

logical positivism   a 20th-century philosophical school of thought that rejected metaphysics as being meaningless because (they said) metaphysical claims could not be verified; this included the view that metaphysical claims are not merely false, they are literally nonsensical.

materialism   in metaphysics, the view that only what is material, or physical, exists; what counts as being material (matter) can include forces and interactions of material objects; as opposed to idealism.

modality   a mode, or way, of being; in metaphysics, this usually refers to the notions of contingency (or actuality), possibility, and necessity; for example, some particular tree might actually exist, but it might not have (so, it is not necessary), while that tree might (possibly) be in a different location than it actually is.

nominalism   the view that universals (nonparticulars) do not exist in the world and universal terms are merely names that refer to particular instances of things.

ontological commitment   a commitment to the existence of something; for example, modern physics assumes (and requires) the existence of atoms in order to explain the world, while religious believers are ontologically committed to the existence of God or gods.

ontology   literally, the study of being (from Greek *ontos,* meaning "being"); it is the philosophical discipline that focuses on the nature and existence of broad kinds of beings (such as objects, events, relations, etc.).

particulars   specific individuals, as opposed to kinds or categories or universals; most philosophers agree that particulars can be objects (such as a particular person), but not all philosophers agree on whether there can be other sorts of particulars (such as a particular relation or property).

possible worlds   a nonactual world that differs in some way from the actual world; some philosophers speak of these possible worlds as being real, while others speak of them only as ways of talking about modality.

realism   in metaphysics, the view that universals (nonparticulars) have meaning because they refer to real things; for example, the term *white* is said to refer to some real, abstract thing, namely, whiteness.

substance   literally meaning "standing below" (or "under"); in metaphysics, substances are taken as basic kinds of things that undergo change; for example, a person can undergo many physical and mental changes over time, so having, say, dark hair is not a substance, but hair itself might be.

universals   kinds of things, as opposed to particulars; for example, there are particular instances of white things, but whiteness itself is a universal.

verifiability/verificationism   the view that for a sentence to be meaningful there must be some way to test or verify its content; only those sentences that are verifiable are considered to be meaningful; usually associated with the view of logical positivism.

Key People

Abelard, Peter (1079–1142) *Medieval philosopher who wrote on the problem of universals, Abelard rejected both realism (that universal terms refer to real things in the world) and nominalism (that universal terms are merely names that refer to nothing), claiming, instead, that universals are conceptual abstractions (that is, universal terms refer to real, yet "only" conceptual objects). In the selection below, he says that universals name things, but not objective, independently existing things.*

Let us return to our universal conceptions, which must always be produced by way of abstraction. For when I hear "man" or "whiteness" or "white," I do not recall in virtue of the name all the natures or properties in those subjects to which the name refers. "Man" gives rise to the conception, indiscriminate, not discrete, of animal, rational, and moral only, but not of additional accidents as well . . . That is why a universal concept is correctly described as being *isolated, bare,* and *pure:* i.e., "isolated from sense," because it is not a perception of a thing as sensory; "bare," because it is abstracted from some or from all forms; "pure," because it is unadulterated by any reference to any single individual, since there is not just one thing, be it the matter or the form, to which it points, as we explained earlier when we described such a conception as indiscriminate.

. . . We do not want to speak of there being universal names when the things they name have perished and they can no longer be predicated of many and are not common names of anything, as would be the case when all the roses were gone. Nevertheless, "rose" would still have meaning for the mind even though it names nothing. Otherwise, "There is no rose" would not be a proposition.

[Abelard, Peter. "Glosses on Porphyry." In *Readings in Medieval Philosophy,* edited by Andrew B. Schroedinger. Oxford: Oxford University Press, 1996.]

Statue of Peter Abelard in the Louvre *(Sculpture by Jules Cavelier; photograph by Marie-Lan Nguyen)*

Berkeley, George (1685–1753)   *Irish empiricist philosopher who argued that all that exists are minds and ideas (or, at least, minds and what is dependent upon minds).*

In the passage below, Berkeley argued that ordinary objects (such as tables) exist but that they are dependent for their existence on a perceiving mind. We experience only ideas, according to Berkeley, but ideas are mind-dependent.

> The table I write on I say exists that is, I see and feel it; and if I were out of my study I should say it existed—meaning thereby that if I was in my study I might perceive it, or that some other spirit actually does perceive it. There was an odor, that is, it was smelled; there was a sound, that is to say, it was heard; a color or figure, and it was perceived by sight or touch. This is all that I can understand by these and the like expressions. For as to what is said of the absolute existence of unthinking things without any relation to their being perceived, that seems perfectly unintelligible. Their *esse* is *percipi,* nor is it possible they should have any existence out of the minds or thinking things which perceive them.
>
> . . . It is indeed an opinion strangely prevailing amongst men that houses, mountains, rivers, and, in a word, all sensible objects have an existence, natural or real, distinct from their being perceived by the understanding. But with how great an assurance and acquiescence soever this principle may be entertained in the world, yet whoever shall find in his heart to call it in question may, if I mistake not, perceive it to involve a manifest contradiction. For what are the forementioned objects but the things we perceive by sense? And what do we perceive besides our own ideas or sensations? And is it not plainly repugnant that any one of these, or any combination of should exist unperceived?

[Berkeley, George. *A Treatise Concerning the Principles of Human Knowledge*. In *Works*, vol. 2. Edinburgh: Thomas Nelson, 1710.]

Hume, David (1711–1776) *Scottish empiricist philosopher famous for expressing skepticism about cause/effect; he argued that we do not experience a necessary connection between cause and effect but expect one kind of event to follow another because we have seen those kinds of events occurring together in the past. In the following passage, Hume claims that we expect kinds of events to occur together (such as one billiard ball to move when struck by another, or the event of a fire's ignition to produce heat), not because we infer through our reason that there is a connection between such events, but rather because we are in the habit of experiencing those events together.*

. . . And it is certain we here advance a very intelligible proposition at least, if not a true one, when we assert that, after the constant conjunction of two objects—heat and flame, for instance, weight and solidity—we are determined by custom alone to expect the one from the appearance of the other. This hypothesis seems even the only one which explains the difficulty, why we draw, from a thousand instances, an inference which we are not able to draw from one instance, that is, in no respect, different from them. Reason is incapable of any such variation. The conclusions which it draws from considering one circle are the same which it would form upon surveying all the circles in the universe. But no man, having seen only one body move after being impelled by another, could infer that every other body will move after a like impulse. All inferences from experience, therefore, are effects of custom, not of reasoning.

Custom, then, is the great guide of human life. It is that principle alone which renders our experience useful to us, and makes us expect, for the future, a similar train of events with those which have appeared in the past. Without the influence of custom, we should be entirely ignorant of every matter of fact beyond what is immediately present to the memory and senses. We should never know how to adjust means to ends, or to employ our natural powers in the production of any effect. There would be an end at once of all action, as well as of the chief part of speculation.

[Hume, David. "Section V: Sceptical Solution of These Doubts." In *Enquiries Concerning Human Understanding and Concerning the Principles of Morals*. 2nd ed. Edited by L. A. Selby-Bigge, M.A. Oxford: Clarendon, 1902. Available online. Online Library of Liberty. URL: http://oll.libertyfund.org/title/341/61956. Accessed June 28, 2011.]

Kant, Immanuel (1724–1804)   *German philosopher who made what he called the Copernican revolution, arguing that objects conform to our knowledge, rather than knowledge conforming to objects; he believed that the mind structures experience according to certain categories, and therefore he advocated neither rationalism nor empiricism. Kant here relates the laws of nature to how the mind categorizes experience; he claims* *that experience is possible at all because the mind structures experience according to certain concepts (categories). So, for example, because the mind applies the concept of cause to experience, laws regarding causes are among the laws of nature (we cannot experience nature without such laws).*

> We shall here . . . be simply concerned with experience, and the universal and a priori given conditions of its possibility, and thence determine Nature as the complete object of all possible experience. I think it will be understood, that I do not refer to the rules for the observation of a nature already given, which presuppose experience, or how through experience we can arrive at the laws of Nature, for these would not then be laws a priori, and would give no pure science of Nature; but how the conditions a priori of the possibility of experience are at the same time the sources from which all the universal laws of Nature must be derived.

> We must first of all observe then, that, although all the judgments of experience are empirical, i.e., have their ground in the immediate perception of sense, yet on the other hand all empirical judgments are not judgments of experience, but that beyond the empirical, and beyond the given sensuous intuition generally, special conceptions must be superadded, having their origin entirely a priori in the pure understanding, under which every perception is primarily subsumed, and by means of which only it can be transformed into experience.

> [Kant, Immanuel. "The Second Part of the Main Transcendental Problem. How Is Pure Natural Science Possible?" In *Kant's Prolegomena and Metaphysical Foundations of Natural Science*. 2nd rev. ed. Translated and with a biography and introduction by Ernest Belfort Bax. London: George Bell and Sons, 1891. Available online. Online Library of Liberty. URL: http://oll.libertyfund.org/title/361/54872. Accessed June 25, 2011.]

Leibniz, Gottfried (1646–1716) *German rationalist philosopher who believed the world consists of monads, or simple substances; he also argued that mind and body are composed of different kinds of monads* *that have no causal interaction with the other. Instead, as he claims in the passage below, material and mental (or spiritual) monads have a pre-established harmony running along parallel tracks, which explains why physical events seem to cause mental events (such as stubbing one's toe seems to cause pain).*

1. The monad of which we shall here speak is merely a simple sub-stance, which enters into composites; *simple,* that is to say, without parts . . .
3. Now where there are no parts, neither extension, nor figure, nor divisibility is possible. And these monads are the true atoms of nature, and, in a word, the elements of all things . . .
10. I take it also for granted that every created being, and conse-quently the created monad also, is subject to change, and even this change is continuous in each.
11. It follows from what has just been said, that the natural changes of the monads proceed from an *internal principle,* since an external cause could not influence their internal being . . .
63. The body belonging to a monad, which is its entelechy or soul, constitutes together with the entelechy that may be called a *living being,* and together with the soul that may be called an *animal.* Now this body of a living being or an animal is always organic, for since every monad is in its way a mirror of the universe, and since the universe is regulated in a perfect order, there must also be an order in the representative, that is, in the perceptions of the soul, and hence in the body, through which the universe is represented in the soul . . .
78. These principles have given me the means of explaining naturally the union or rather the conformity of the soul and the organic body. The soul follows its own peculiar laws and the body also fol-lows its own laws, and they agree in virtue of the *pre-established harmony* between all substances, since they are all representa-tives of one and the same universe.

[Leibniz, Gottfried Wilhelm. *The Monadology and Other Philosophical Writings.* Translated with introduction and notes by Robert Latta. London: Oxford University Press, 1898.]

Lewis, David (1941–2001) *American metaphysician best known for his advocacy of modal realism, that is, that there exist possible worlds that* *are similar to, yet different from, the actual world in which we live. In the selection below, taken from his book* On the Plurality of Worlds, *he states that the belief in possible worlds is (theoretically) fruitful and that that is reason enough to proceed on the belief that they exist.*

> . . . I advocate a thesis of plurality of worlds, or *modal realism,* which holds that our world is but one world among many. There are countless other worlds, other very inclusive things . . . [These worlds] are isolated: there are no spatiotemporal relations at all between things that belong to different worlds . . .
>
> Nor does [our] world differ from the others in its manner of existing. I do not have the slightest idea what a difference in manner of existing is supposed to be. Some things exist here on earth, other things exist extraterrestrially, perhaps some exist no place in particular; but that is no difference in manner of existing, merely a difference in location or lack of it between things that exist . . .
>
> Why believe in a plurality of worlds?—Because the hypothesis is serviceable, and that is a reason to think that it is true . . . Modal realism is fruitful; that gives us good reason to believe that it is true.

[Lewis, David. *On the Plurality of Worlds.* Malden, England: Blackwell, 1986.]

Mill, John Stuart (1806–1873) *British philosopher best known for his work in ethics and political philosophy. However, he also wrote extensively on epistemology and metaphysics. In particular, he wrote on the nature of induction and of causation. The selection below, taken from his book* A System of Logic, *speaks to his rejection of the reduction of properties of living beings to the properties of the material parts that make up those living beings (and, so, is part of his endorsement of the notion of emerging properties).*

> . . . I shall give the name of the Composition of Causes to the principle which is exemplified in all cases in which the joint effect of several causes is identical with the sum of their separate effects.
>
> This principle, however, by no means prevails in all departments of the field of nature. The chemical combination of two

John Stuart Mill in 1884

substances produces, as is well known, a third substance with properties different from those of either of the two substances separately, or of both of them taken together. Not a trace of the properties of hydrogen or of oxygen is observable in those of their compound, water. The taste of sugar of lead is not the sum of the tastes of its component elements, acetic acid and lead or its oxide; nor is the color of blue vitriol a mixture of the colors of sulphuric acid and copper . . .

If this be true of chemical combinations, it is still more true of those far more complex combinations of elements which constitute organized bodies; and in which those extraordinary new uniformities arise, which are called the laws of life. All organized bodies are composed of parts similar to those composing inorganic nature, and which have even themselves existed in an inorganic state; but the phenomena of life, which result from the juxtaposition of those parts in a certain manner, bear no analogy to any of the effects which would be produced by the action of the component substances considered as mere physical agents. To whatever degree we might imagine our knowledge of the properties of the several ingredients of a living body to be extended and perfected, it is certain that no mere summing up of the separate actions of those elements will ever amount to the action of the living body itself.

[Mill, J. S. In "On the Composition of Causes." In *A System of Logic, Ratiocinative and Inductive.* 8th Ed., Book 3, Chapter 6. New York: Harper & Brothers, 1882.]

Ockham, William of (ca. 1280–1349) *Medieval philosopher who championed the view of nominalism (that is, the view that universal terms refer not to actual, real things in the world but rather are convenient terms that we use to talk about [collections of] individuals); for Ockham, only individuals exist, not universals. The selection below is from his book* Summa Logicae.

For it can be evidently proven that no universal is any substance existing outside the soul. First, as follows: No universal is a singular, numerically one substance. For if it were said that it is, it would follow that Socrates would be a universal. For there is no greater reason why a universal should be one singular substance rather than [any] other. Therefore, no singular substance is any universal . . .

This can be confirmed by reason too. For every universal, according to everyone, is predicable of many. But only an intention of the soul or a voluntary instituted sign, and not any substance, is apt to be predicated. Therefore only an intention of the soul or a voluntary instituted sign is a universal . . . Again, there is no proposition except in the mind, in speech, or in writing. Therefore, its parts are only in the mind, in speech, or in writing. But particular substances are not like this. Therefore, it is clear that no proposition can be put together out of substances. But a proposition is composed out of universals. Therefore, universals are not in any way substances.

[Ockham, William of. "Summa Logicae." In *Readings in Medieval Philosophy,* edited by Andrew B. Schroedinger, 605–607. Oxford: Oxford University Press, 1996.]

Parmenides (fl. 485 B.C.E.)   *Pre-Socratic philosopher who argued that reality is One, eternal, and unchanging; all change is mere appearance and cannot even be talked or thought about. The fragment below of Parmenides' writings is meant to show that any change or motion of what is real is impossible, because that would mean that there is some state of being that is not currently real.*

> One way only is left to be spoken of, that it *is*; and on this are full many signs that what *is* is uncreated and imperishable; for it is entire and without end. It *was* not in the past, nor *shall* it be, since it *is* now, all at once, one, continuous; for what creation will you seek for it? How and whence did it grow? . . . How could what *is* thereafter perish? And how could it come into being? For if it came into being, it is not, nor if it is going to be in the future. So coming into being is extinguished and perishing unimaginable.

> [Kirk, G. S., and J. E. Raven, eds. and trans. *The Presocratic Philosophers.*
> Cambridge: Cambridge University Press, 1957.]

Plato (ca. 428–348 B.C.E.)   *Extremely influential philosopher who shaped much of later Western thought and who argued that there are levels of reality, with the world of Ideas (or universals) as the most real. The selection below is taken from his work* Phaedo. *Here he claims that universal terms such as equality are not the same thing as particular equal objects or relations but exist independently of those particulars.*

> And shall we proceed a step further [said Socrates], and affirm that there is such as thing as equality, not of wood with wood, or of stone with stone, but that, over and above this, there is equality in the abstract? Shall we affirm this?

> Affirm, yes, and swear to it, replied Simmias, with all the confidence in life.

> And do we know the nature of this abstract essence?

> To be sure, he said.

> And whence did we obtain this knowledge? Did we not see equalities of material things, such as pieces of wood and stones, and gather from them the idea of an equality which is different

from them?—You will admit that?—Or look at the matter again in this way; Do not the same pieces of wood or stone appear at one time equal, and at another time unequal?

That is certain.

But are real equals ever unequal? Or is the idea of equality ever inequality?

That surely was never yet known, Socrates.

Then these (so-called) equals are not the same with the idea of equality?

I should say, clearly not, Socrates.

And yet from these equals, although differing from the idea of equality, you conceived and attained that idea?

Very true, he said . . .

And must we not allow, that when I or any one look at any object, and perceive that the object aims at being some other thing, but falls short of, and can not attain to it—he who makes this observation must have had previous knowledge of that to which, as he says, the other, although similar, was inferior?

Certainly.

And has this not been our own case in the matter of equals and of absolute equality?

Precisely . . .

Well, than I should like to know whether you agree with me in the next step; for I can not help thinking that if there be anything beautiful other than absolute beauty, that can only be beautiful in as far as it partakes of absolute beauty—and this I should say of everything . . . And that by Greatness only great things become great and greater greater, and by Smallness the less become less.

[Plato. *Phaedo.* In *The Works of Plato,* translated by Benjamin Jowett.]

Sellars, Wilfrid (1912–1989)   *American philosopher whose writings in metaphysics, epistemology, and philosophy of science were very influential. In particular, he was known for his efforts to show the interconnections of philosophical analysis of basic concepts with people's understanding of the world in their everyday experiences. The passage below speaks of his famous remarks about two images of humans (the manifest, or experiential, image and the scientific image).*

The aim of philosophy, abstractly formulated, is to understand how things in the broadest possible sense of the term hang together in the broadest possible sense of the term. Under "things in the broadest possible sense" I include such radically different items as not only "cabbages and kings," but numbers and duties, possibilities and finger snaps, aesthetic experience and death . . .

For the philosopher is confronted not by one complex many dimensional picture, the unity of which, such as it is, he must come to appreciate; but by *two* pictures of essentially the same order of complexity, each of which purports to be a complete picture of man-in-the-world, and which, after separate scrutiny, he must fuse into one vision. Let me refer to these two perspectives, respectively, as the *manifest* and the *scientific* images of man-in-the-world . . .

Thus, to complete the scientific image we need to enrich it *not* with more ways of saying what is the case, but with the language of community and individual intentions, so that by construing the actions we intend to do and the circumstances in which we intend to do them in scientific terms, we *directly* relate the world as conceived by scientific theory to our purposes, and make it *our* world and no longer an alien appendage to the world in which we do our living.

[Sellars, Wilfrid. "Philosophy and the Scientific Image of Man." In *Frontiers of Science and Philosophy*, edited by Robert Colodny. Pittsburgh: University of Pittsburgh Press, 1962.]

Vienna Circle   *Name for a group of philosophers and other academics who met and worked in Vienna at the beginning of the 20th century; they formed the core of the school of thought called Logical Positivism, advo-*

cating the view that philosophy needed to be more scientific and that the only meaningful claims are ones that can be verified. The passage below is from a manifesto authored by three members of the Vienna Circle (Hans Hahn, Rudolf Carnap, and Otto Neurath), in which they state their scientific world conception.

The scientific world conception is characterized not so much by theses of its own, but rather by its basic attitude, its points of view and direction of research . . . We have characterized the scientific world conception essentially by two features. First it is empiricist and positivist: there is knowledge only from experience, which rests on what is immediately given. This sets the limits for the content of legitimate science. Second, the scientific world conception is marked by application of a certain method, namely logical analysis. The aim of the scientific effort is to reach the goal, unified science, by applying logical analysis to the empirical material. Since the meaning of every statement of science must be statable by a reduction to a statement about the given, likewise the meaning of any concept, whatever branch of science it may belong to, must be statable by step-wise reduction to other concepts, down to the concepts of the lowest level which refer directly to the given.

[Neurath, Otto. *Empiricism and Sociology.* Dordrecht, Germany: Kluwer Academic Publishers, 1973.]

PART II

Philosophy of Religion

Introductory Discussion Questions

1. Can anyone know, rather than merely believe, that God does or does not exist? How?
2. Should there be a separation of church and state? What, if any, is the proper role of religion in politics and law?
3. Are reason and faith in opposition to each other? Could scientific findings refute any part of religion? Could religious belief refute any scientific finding? Why or why not?
4. Can God be described? If so, what are the characteristics of God? If not, why not, and how could one have any connection to God?
5. The Russian writer Dostoyevsky remarked that if there is no God, then everything is permitted (meaning that there would be no moral constraints on people's actions). Is that correct?
6. What aspects of religion, if any, are independent of God? For example, could humans have a soul even if there were no God?

What Is Philosophy of Religion?

The term *religion* is vague. Given the many different beliefs, values, attitudes, actions, and traditions that are called religion, it is practically impossible to have a precise definition, or even conception, of exactly what religion is. Everyone is aware of the fact that there are said to be many different religions: Christianity, Islam, Judaism, Buddhism, Hinduism, etc. What is it that makes all of these religions *religions,* as opposed to being something else? One approach to answering this question is to look for necessary and sufficient conditions for something to be a religion. That is, one approach is to look for features or characteristics that these different religions have in common and, at the same time, features or characteristics that nonreligions do not have in common with them. This turns out to be difficult, but there are various features that are more or less shared by different religions. Just about anything that is a religion involves some belief in supernatural or divine beings (God or gods). In addition, religions usually make a distinction between sacred and profane objects, that is, things that are special and related in some way or other to what is divine (those are the sacred things) or are not related (those are the profane things). There are usually rituals, or stylized actions, that focus on divine beings or sacred objects. There is also a pronounced sense of awe or mystery or some other feelings that people relate to what is divine or sacred. Beyond that, religions formulate and embrace particular moral codes, ways of behaving that are seen as related to what is divine or sacred. That is, religions speak of what types of human actions are forbidden or permitted or required by people.

Almost always, religions speak of humans not only individually but also collectively, that is, in terms of a religious community. For instance, Muslims speak of the *ummah,* or collective set of the world's Muslims. An aspect of this sense of human religious collective is the issue of theocracy, that is, the notion of a state or political unit that is religious in nature. Common to religions is the sense that particularly important aspects of people's lives, such as marriages or baptisms, have meaning because of their connection to what is divine and sacred. These important aspects are usually highlighted, and even legitimated, through rituals, such as marriage ceremonies. Of course, some of these features of religion(s) also apply to things that are secular (or, not considered religious). For example, there are rituals that are common, such as birthday parties, which are secular. There are moral codes that do not relate to anything divine or sacred. There are meaningful human collectives that are not religious. These various features, then, are not necessary and sufficient conditions of religion, but they certainly are typical and important for those things that are considered to be religions.

From the perspective of philosophy, what is important about religion has to do with metaphysics (the study of reality), epistemology (the study of knowledge), and axiology (the study of value). That is, there are metaphysical aspects of religion, as well as epistemological aspects and axiological aspects. Among the metaphysical aspects of religion are questions of what kinds of things exist. In particular, there is the question of divine beings: God (or gods), but also, say, angels or demons. The part of religion that is especially centered on God (or gods) is called theology, from the Greek words *theos,* meaning "god," and *logos,* meaning "study." Theology focuses not only on the existence of divine beings (for example, *that* God is) but also on the nature of divine beings (that is, *what* God is). It also focuses on the existence and nature of lesser divine beings (such as angels or demons) as well as on the relationship between divine beings and human beings (and the natural world in general).

Among the epistemological aspects of religion are questions about knowledge of what is divine and sacred. One standard issue is how we know that there are divine beings and also how we know how we are related to them. There are usually two claims made here. One—and this is often called natural theology—is that we know, or at least can know, about what is divine and sacred, as well as our relationship to them, by knowing the natural world around us. One phrase that is sometimes used is that we can come to know the creator by studying creation. In other words, there is evidence in the natural world that gives us knowledge of what is divine and sacred. A common example of this view is referred to as the design argument, namely, the orderliness of the world and things in the world show that it is the result of being designed (not random), and that implies a designer (God).

A second claim for religious epistemology—that is, how we can have knowledge of the divine and the sacred—is often called revelatory theology. This is the notion that things are revealed to us by divine beings, often in the form of direct scripture or sacred writings. Many people also speak of mystical revelation, that is, a personal, direct revelation from a divine being (as opposed to scripture or interpretations of events).

Yet another aspect of religious epistemology is the issue of *how* we can know of our relationship to the divine and sacred. In particular, one issue is that of prayer. Prayer as a means of relating to what is divine includes the notion of faith, itself also an epistemological aspect of religion.

Among the axiological aspects of religion are values as they relate to ethics and morality. One component of the ethical and moral issues has to do with what kinds of actions and behaviors are forbidden or permitted or required. A typical example of this is the Ten Commandments in Judaism and Christianity. Related to this is another component of ethical and moral issues, namely, the very nature and justification of moral codes. In other words, what makes some particular kind of action good or bad; is it because it has been divinely required or permitted or forbidden, or are there good/bad actions independent of divine sanction?

Another axiological aspect of religion is values that relate to collective human action, especially in the sense of social and political collectives. This is the issue of the relation of religion and politics. There is, of course, a variety of perspectives on this relation. For example, many people have claimed that religion is a personal, private matter, while politics is a social, public matter. This attitude has been expressed in a number of ways, for instance: "Render unto Caesar what is Caesar's and unto the Lord what is the Lord's," which has been understood by many to mean that worldly matters, such as politics, are not significant religious matters. On the other end of the spectrum, many people have argued explicitly for political institutions and structures to be very closely tied to religion, because, they say, religious truth applies to all aspects of people's lives.

Finally, a major axiological aspect of religion is the issue of meaning, especially the meaning of life. For many people, a secular and scientific understanding of the world, including of its things and events, is—and can only be—descriptive. That is, even if science could some day provide a complete account of the physical, natural world, it could not provide any account of meaning. Some people have claimed that science answers (and can only answer) the question of how something is, not why something is. The question of why, they say, is religious, because it speaks to something beyond a mere description of things or events. The question why speaks to the origin and identity and destiny—that is, to the meaning—of things and events.

While many people see religion and philosophy as very closely related, in some senses they are and in some senses they are not. Both are concerned with broad and fundamental questions of reality and knowledge and values, and certainly much of the history of religion and the history of philosophy overlap and intertwine. However, many of the goals and methods of religion and philosophy, as well as the content, are quite distinct. For example, where religion might focus on how to worship God, philosophy will focus on arguments for (and against) God's existence. Or, philosophy might focus on the nature of perception or what it means to give an explanation of something (as opposed to a description); these are not at all central to the concerns of religion.

Theism/Atheism/Agnosticism

Simply stated, theism is the view that God (or gods) exists, while atheism is the denial of such a view. However, this simple statement is actually somewhat misleading, or at least not complete. Philosophers distinguish theism from two other views that also claim that God exists. One such view is deism. Deism holds that God exists, that God created the world, but not that God interacts with humans or is the subject of personal revelation or experience. For deism, God is basically the creator and, perhaps, designer of the world, but that is all. The other view that theism is distinct from is pantheism. Pantheism is the view that God is all things (and all things are God). *Pantheism* comes from the Greek words *pan,* meaning "all," and *theos,* meaning "God." In effect, God the creator is identical with God the creation. Theism, as distinct from these two views, holds that God is indeed the creator of the world but is not the same thing as the natural world. For theism, God is a single, indivisible being with features that go beyond merely being the creator of the world and that go beyond the features of things in the natural world. So, for example, God is all-knowing and all-good and eternal. In addition, God sustains the world and is worthy of worship.

Just as theism is not simply the view that God exists, so atheism is not simply the denial of such a view. To begin with, atheism is not the same thing as agnosticism. Agnosticism is the view that one does not, and perhaps cannot, know about God. It does not directly deny the existence of God but also does not accept the existence of God. Agnosticism is neutral because, it says, the issue is not, and perhaps cannot be, settled. Atheism is not neutral; it does deny the view that God exists, but it does so in various ways. One way is to reject specific claims and arguments that are given for God's existence. Another way is that it claims that the very name, or concept, *God* is meaningless. Under this view, to say that God exists is no more meaningful than to say that Glub exists; it is literally nonsense and gibberish. So, too, it would be meaningless to deny that Glub exists or that God exists. That is, since the word *glub* does not refer to anything at all, to say that Glub does not exist makes no more sense than to say that Glub exists; both are simply nonsense. Likewise, under this version of atheism, to say that God does not exist makes no more sense than to say that God exists. Again, both are nonsense.

Philosophers do not take claims about God (either for or against) on faith. That is, they do not simply say that these issues are merely a matter of what someone wants to believe. Instead, they claim, there is a truth of the matter. In other words, they claim that if God does in fact exist, then atheism is wrong, and if God does in fact not exist, then theism is wrong. In either case, there must be evidence and arguments, not merely faith or belief, to settle the matter. (Not all philosophers hold this view, but most do. The Danish philosopher Søren Kierkegaard [1813–55] was one who regarded this issue of God's existence as a matter of personal, subjective belief.)

Both theists and atheists put forth their views in two ways. One way is to argue in favor of their own views, and the other way is to argue against the opposing views. For example, theists claim that there are proofs for God's existence and for God's nature (that is, not only *that* God is, but also *what* God is). They also claim that the arguments in favor of atheism are faulty. Likewise, atheists offer both rejections of the proofs of the theists as well as arguments to show that God does not exist.

For philosophers, the debate between theism and atheism has aspects that are related to metaphysics, epistemology, and axiology. With respect to metaphysics, the very issue of God's existence is metaphysical. That is, if we seek a full description of what is real, would God be included? Such metaphysical issues would also focus on God's nature. A common example of this is the age-old question: If God is all-powerful and can do anything, can God create a stone too heavy for God to lift? That is, this is a question about reality, specifically, if there is, or could be, a real thing that is indeed all-powerful. There are other metaphysical issues about God. For instance, there is the question of whether or not God exists in time or outside of time.

Besides metaphysical aspects of the theism/atheism debate, there are epistemological aspects, or aspects about what we can know and how we can know it. For example, related to the metaphysical issue just mentioned, namely, whether God exists in time or outside of time, how could we know? How can humans make any claims about God with any kind of certainty or for that matter with any verifiable evidence? Again, philosophers do not take faith as the basis for addressing these sorts of questions but instead look for arguments based on something else.

Finally, for philosophers there are axiological aspects of the theism/atheism debate. One major axiological question is what difference does it make? That is, how and why would it matter if theism turned out to be correct or incorrect? Another value-oriented issue is how theism (or atheism) relates to ethics and morality. In terms of people's actual behavior, it is certainly not the case that theists always behave in virtuous ways or that atheists do not. Both behave in good and bad ways. What, then, is the relation between theism (or atheism) and ethics and morality? In addition, how does theism or atheism relate to social and political values, and how should they relate?

Deism

According to deism (from the Latin word *deus*, meaning "god"), God exists and it is through our reason alone that we know God exists. So, deists reject revelation, the giving of knowledge to people directly by God or other supernatural means. Deism is often called a natural religion, meaning that deists base their belief in God on evidence in the natural world. For example, some deists are (or were) convinced by the design argument that God exists, believing that, because the world seems organized and functional, the world must have a designer, namely, God. Historically, deism was most prominent in the 17th and 18th centuries during the Enlightenment, particularly in England, France, and the United States. Beyond the emphasis on reason and the rejection of revelation, there has been considerable disagreement among deists about specific religious doctrine, such as whether there is an afterlife and whether God intervenes in the course of the world. However, deists tended to reject religious authority and often opposed significant components of orthodox Christianity.

In the 17th century, Lord Herbert of Cherbury (1583–1648) founded English deism (although he himself did not use the term *deism*) when he made the following claims: that there is one supreme God, who should be worshipped, that worshipping God means living virtuously, that people should repent their sins, and that in this life, as well as in the afterlife, God would reward good and punish evil. Prominent French

Early-17th-century portrait of Lord Herbert of Cherbury *(Painting by William Larkin)*

deists include Voltaire (1694–1778) and Jean-Jacques Rousseau (1712–78). Voltaire rejected the idea of providence, the view that all the events of the world unfold according to God's divine plan, satirizing that view in his novel *Candide*. He also advocated religious tolerance and attacked Christianity—and the Catholic Church in particular—for what he saw as its superstitions and its rigid insistence on Church doctrine. Important figures in the colonial and revolutionary United States were deists as well, including Benjamin Franklin (1706–90), Thomas Jefferson (1743–1826), and Thomas Paine (1737–1809). Franklin and Jefferson tended to regard Christianity less as a means for personal, religious salvation than as a useful system of morality, and American deists often saw God mainly as the designer and creator of the universe. The writer and political theorist Thomas Paine, who in his book *The Age of Reason* advocated a religion based on reason and denied both that Jesus was the son of God and that the Bible is God's revealed word, was one of the most public deists. Deism was in decline by the 19th century, and it has never regained the prominence it once held (however, it is credited with influencing religious movements such as Unitarianism).

Faith and Philosophy

Philosophy of religion is the analysis and evaluation of basic concepts and practices within religion and about religion. Although philosophy and religion often overlap in terms of the topics and issues they are concerned with—for example, both investigate the nature of the world and of people—philosophy of religion is a philosophical look at religion, so it is not the same thing as religion.

Historically, the particular topic of the existence and nature of God has been of primary interest to philosophers. Philosophers do not take God's existence as an issue of faith; instead, over the course of centuries, they have offered numerous arguments for God's existence (and other philosophers have offered numerous objections to those arguments). The arguments for God's existence have included the cosmological argument, the design argument, the ontological argument, the moral argument, and the experiential argument. The cosmological argument basically says that the universe (the cosmos) must have been created by something, namely, God. That is, everything that exists either comes from something else or is self-created, but the universe itself was not self-created, so it came from something else (God). The design argument says that the complexity and order that is found in the universe could not simply have happened (or is extremely unlikely to have simply happened). The fact that the universe and things in it seem to be so complex and yet so ordered shows that they were designed. Being designed, there must be a designer, and the designer of the universe and things in it is God.

While the cosmological argument and the design argument both point to features about the natural world, the ontological argument does not. The word *ontological* comes from the Greek word *ontos,* meaning "being." This argument says that the very being of God proves God's existence. The starting point is that God, by definition, is said to be the most perfect thing. For instance, God is all-knowing (perfect in the sense of knowing everything) and all-powerful (perfect in the sense of having the power to do anything) and all-good (perfect in the sense of being purely good). If God lacked something, then God would not be perfect. So, if God lacked some knowledge or some ability, for example, God would not be perfect. In addition, if God lacked existence, then God would not be perfect (because there would be something lacking in God, namely, existence). Therefore, because God is perfect by definition, and being perfect means that God does not lack existence, then God must exist. This is the ontological argument, that is, the argument for God's existence that is based strictly on God's nature (or being), not on aspects of the universe.

The final two arguments make the case for God's existence on the basis of relating God to human life (rather than on the basis of the universe or God's being). The moral argument for God's existence is that God is the ultimate source for all values. That is, standards and criteria for good and bad, for right and wrong, must come from somewhere. Things are better or worse relative to some standard or criterion. So, there must be some top standard (that is, something that is the best) that determines whether or not other things are better or worse. That top standard is God. Finally, the experiential argument says that people have actual experiences with God. They feel or hear God directly. For them to have such experiences, God must exist.

For each of these types of arguments for God's existence, many philosophers have offered counterarguments, attempting to show that these arguments simply do not work. The point here is that this issue of arguments for (and against) God's existence has been a major focus within the philosophy of religion.

Another major focus, one that is related to God's existence, is the nature of God. For centuries, philosophers have wrestled with understanding the nature of God. Some have claimed that this is a pointless task and that God is infinite and beyond the understanding of humans, who are finite. Others have claimed that humans can know God (or, at least, have some level of knowledge or justified belief) by saying what God is not. For instance, they say we can know that God is not limited in terms of knowledge or power or evil. Within many religions, although not all, God is said to be a perfect being.

Still others have argued that the notion of a perfect God makes no sense or at least contradicts other beliefs that we hold. There are two common arguments given along this line. The first is called the problem of evil. The problem of evil is this: If God is all-knowing, then God knows if evil happens; if God is all-powerful, then God could prevent evil from happening; if God is all-good, then God would not allow evil to happen. Some philosophers have said that if God is all-good, and if everything comes from God, then evil could not exist or else it would have had to come from an all-good God. So, if God is perfect, then God knows there is evil, has the power to prevent evil, and, being all-good, should prevent evil. So, if there is any evil in the world, then either God did not know about it (and, so, is not all-knowing) or could not prevent it (and, so, is not all-powerful) or did not prevent it (and, so, is not all-good). Those philosophers who have argued along this line, then, have said that either there is no God or else that God's nature is not that of a perfect being. Of course, many people have offered counterarguments to this.

The second argument that has often been made to question the nature of a perfect God is called the problem of divine foreknowledge. The problem is this: If God is all-knowing, then God knows everything that has happened and everything that is now happening and, in addition, everything that will happen. (If God does not know everything that will happen in the future, then God does not know everything, and, so, is not all-knowing and not perfect.) But, if God already knows what will happen in the future, then it seems that the future is already determined. For instance, if God knows what events will happen tomorrow, then those events must happen; otherwise, God would be wrong. So, if God already knows what a person will do tomorrow, then that person must do those things; that person's actions are already determined. If this is the case, then it seems that people do not have free will. The conclusion is one that many people find troubling or even unacceptable: If God is perfect, then people have no free will. There is even more to the argument, however. If God is perfect and people have no free will, then how can the notion of sin make any sense? After all, sinning seems to imply that people have a choice: They make a bad choice, they choose to sin. But if God is perfect, how can that be possible? Even more, if people's actions are determined (because God already knows what they will do), how could an all-good God reward or punish people for their actions? Once again, there are many people who have offered counterarguments to this problem. The point here is that these particular problems are ones that philosophers have dealt with in terms of trying to understand the nature of God.

Besides the issues of God's existence and God's nature, philosophers have focused on the relation between religion and morality and religion and society, as well as religious knowledge, human life and the relationship between religion and science.

Religious Epistemology and the Ontological Argument

Ontological Argument

The word *ontological* comes from the Greek word *ontos,* meaning "being." Ontology is the study of being and beings (that is, those things that are, or have being). Basically, ontology is about what kinds of things there are. For example, in everyday experience, we think of there being objects, such as cats and trees and electrons. But we also speak of there being events, such as an election or a storm or the occasion of someone buttering a piece of toast. We also speak of there being relations between things; for example, "being older than" is a relation between a father and a son (that is, there are two objects that are related to each other in a certain way). Ontology, then, is the study of what kinds of things there are and of the nature of being.

The ontological argument has to do with the question of God's existence. Philosophers do not take it as a matter of faith that God exists; rather, over the years they have offered arguments for and against the view that God exists. Among the arguments for God's existence are arguments that the universe must have come from something, and that something is God; that is, God created the universe. This is often called the cosmological argument. Another argument for God's existence is that the universe shows so much complexity and order that this must be the result of design, not of random physical forces. The apparent design of the universe and of things in the universe means there must be a designer, and this is God. This is often called the design argument or the teleological argument (teleological means "purposive" or "goal-directed").

While the cosmological and design arguments are ones that many people have considered (even if they have not used those terms), there is another argument that has been unique among philosophers: the ontological argument. The ontological argument claims to prove that God exists strictly on the basis of God's nature or being (so it has nothing to do with the physical universe). Philosophers usually attribute this argument to the early medieval philosopher Saint Anselm (1033–1109). The argument goes like this: By definition, God is said to be the greatest thing, something perfect. Anselm's phrase was "that than which nothing greater can be conceived." For example, we can think of someone who is strong (say, the boxer Muhammad Ali), but God is the strongest thing that can be thought of (conceived). That is, God is all-powerful, and nothing can be conceived that is more powerful. Or we can think of someone who is very knowledgeable (say, Albert Einstein), but God is the most knowledgeable (God is all-knowing), and nothing can be conceived that is more knowledgeable. Or we can think of someone who is very good (say, Mother Theresa), but God is the most good (indeed, all-good), and nothing can be conceived as more good than God. So, even if someone did not believe in God, said Anselm, he could at least understand and conceive what is meant by the phrase "that than which nothing greater can be conceived."

Now, said Anselm, something is greater if it exists than if it does not exist. That is, imagine two identical things (or gods). If both are all-powerful and all-knowing and all-good, but one of them actually exists while the other one is only part of someone's imagination, then the first one—the one that actually exists—is greater than the second one. So, if by definition God is "that than which nothing greater can be conceived," then God must exist. That is because if God did not exist—even if God were all-powerful, etc.—then there would be something greater that could be conceived, namely, a God that was all-powerful and did exist. So, again, that which is the greatest conceivable thing must be something that exists; that greatest conceivable thing is God; therefore, God exists. This is called an ontological argument because it involves nothing more than the very nature of being or, in this case, of

God's being. It does not involve anything else, such as the creation or design of the universe.

This argument was immediately criticized by other philosophers and then, in turn, defended and criticized by even more philosophers over the centuries. One criticism is that it seems to make God's existence dependent upon what people can conceive. That is, what if people cannot conceive of the greatest thing? It is one thing to say that we can conceive of the most powerful or most knowledgeable or most good thing, but can we really? For instance, can we conceive of the hottest thing (or hottest temperature)? Furthermore, what would it mean to conceive of the most powerful thing? Does it mean that there is nothing that this most powerful thing cannot do? But this leads to other puzzles, such as can God create a stone so heavy that even God cannot lift it? The point is that phrases such as *all-powerful* or *all-knowing* or *all-good* are not really concepts that people can conceive. But even if they could, the ontological argument still seems to suggest that God's existence is somehow connected to conceivability, which seems puzzling at best.

Philosophers also quickly said that conceivability cannot guarantee the existence of something. For example, we can conceive of numbers, but does that mean that they actually exist? Or what if we could conceive of the perfect island, that is, that island no greater than which can be conceived. Would that mean that such an island must exist somewhere? Conceivability certainly does not cause something to exist, so, again, there is a question about how this is relevant to God's existence. What seems to matter is not conceivability but God's perfection, or perfect nature. However, many philosophers claim that God's perfect nature cannot be assumed but must be proven (as well as God's existence). These debates, along with other very technical and difficult aspects of them, have continued from Anselm's time in the 11th century up to today.

Necessary Being

A necessary being is something that *must* exist. Things that we experience in everyday life exist, but it is not always necessary that they exist; on another day, they might not exist. Furthermore, those things have a lifetime; that is to say, they come into existence at some point in time and they go out of existence at some point in time. Philosophers speak of these everyday things as contingent (and not necessary). To say that something is necessary, then, is to say that it is not contingent. In addition, we sometimes speak of things as being possible. That is, there could be a mouse under one's bed right now, but in fact, there is not one. It is possible that there is life on another planet, say, Jupiter, but perhaps not. The point is that it is certainly not necessary that there is a mouse under one's bed right now or life on Jupiter. So, sometimes to say that something is necessary is to say that it is not merely possible; it is much more than *merely* possible. However, philosophers debate over the best understanding of something as possible and whether or not being possible has to do with things or has to do with how we talk about things.

The notion of a necessary being, that is, some *thing* that is necessary (or necessarily exists) is usually raised in the context of talking about God. Many philosophers have argued that while everyday things that we experience are contingent, there is one thing that is necessary (or necessarily exists), and that is God. A famous argument for God's existence came from the medieval philosopher Thomas Aquinas (1225–74). Aquinas gave various arguments to prove God's existence. One of those arguments was that not only did God exist, but that necessarily God exists (or that God is a necessary being). His argument ran like this: Our everyday experience shows us that in nature there are things that are contingent. In other words, it is possible for them to exist or not exist. Indeed, the things that we encounter every day are things that come into existence and go out of existence. If it is true that for everything in nature that it is possible for it not to be (that is, it is the case that at some point in time it did not exist and then it came into existence), then at some point in time there would have been nothing at all. That is because, as contingent things, it is impossible for them always to exist (by their definition as being contingent). However, if that is true, namely, that at some point in time there was nothing at all, then there would still be nothing at all, because things can only come into existence by being caused by something else. For example, a person can only come into existence by the actions of his parents, or a table can only come into existence by the actions of some table-maker. Obviously, there are things that exist now, so it could not be the case that at some point in time there was nothing. There must be something, then, that is not contingent, but is necessary. That thing is God.

While many philosophers have been convinced by this argument for God's existence, many others have not. They claim that there is nothing to rule out the possibility of an infinite series of contingent things. It might be difficult to conceive of such an infinite series, but there is nothing about Aquinas's argument that rules out such a possibility. In addition, as mentioned above, many philosophers claim that it is not things that are necessary (or necessarily exist) but our ways of speaking about them. For example, it might be that some sentence is necessarily true (for example, "Object X is either a cat or not a cat"), but that only means that the sentence is necessary, not what the sentence talks about.

Plantinga's Modal Argument

The notions of necessity and possibility (what might be or must be) are what philosophers call modalities (modes, or ways, that something is). We often distinguish possibility and necessity not only from each other but also from two other concepts, actuality and contingency. That is, we sometimes distinguish something as being possible from something as being actual. For instance, it was possible that Babe Ruth could have run for governor of New York, but in actuality he did not. Likewise, while it in fact happened that Babe Ruth hit more than 700 home runs, he might not have. It did not have to happen, so it was contingent (not necessary) that it happened. Philosophers also speak of sentences as being contingent (for example, "Bachelors are ugly"), which means that those sentences are true sometimes, but not always, as well as other sentences being necessary (for example, "Bachelors are unmarried"). In the latter case (sentences being necessary), they can be either necessarily true, such as "Bachelors are unmarried" (also called tautologies), or necessarily false, such as "Bachelors are married" (also called contradictions).

These notions seem common and mundane. However, a closer look at them shows that they raise a number of conceptual and philosophical issues. One such issue is that there are different kinds of necessity and possibility. For example, philosophers speak of logical possibility as opposed to physical possibility. To say that something is logically possible simply means that it does not involve a contradiction. For instance, it is logically possible that a person could jump from the Earth to the Moon, but it is not physically possible. The law of gravity is relevant to

Photograph of Alvin Plantinga telling a joke at a lecture at the Mayo Clinic in Rochester, Minnesota *(Used under a Creative Commons license)*

physical possibility, but not to logical possibility. However, it is logically impossible for a square to be round, but not physically impossible (at least, if we take geometrical figures to be nonphysical, abstract things, so physical possibility or impossibility is irrelevant). People also speak of other kinds of possibility (or necessity), such as technological possibility (it might be logically and physically possible to fly faster than light, but it is not now technologically possible). In addition, we might speak of temporal possibility (or necessity), that is, possibility or necessity related to time and a sequence of events. Philosophers even speak of epistemic possibility (or necessity), meaning what might or must be known.

Another issue about modalities, besides the various kinds of possibility and necessity, that philosophers deal with is whether or not necessity and possibility are properly spoken of as in the world or as only as in language. For example, if we say that something is possible—for example, it is possible that there is life on Jupiter—does that simply mean that the sentence "There is life on Jupiter" is not a contradiction or does it mean that there is actual possible life on Jupiter? The first case could be restated as "It is possible that there is life on Jupiter." In this case, the possibility is about the truth of the sentence, that is, that the sentence is possibly true (and not a contradiction). The second case could be restated as "It is the case that there is possibly life on Jupiter." In this case, the possibility is about life-forms, not about the sentence. Philosophers refer to the first case as *de dicto* (from Latin, meaning "of language"), and they refer to the second case as *de re* (from Latin, meaning "of things"). The reason this distinction is made is because there are conceptual questions about claiming that there are possible things, that is, that there are actually things that are possible. For instance, the 20th-century American philosopher W. V. O. Quine (1908–2000) asked: Are there more possible thin men in the doorway than possible fat men? His point was that the notion of *de re* possibility raises questions and concerns that lead philosophers astray, while *de dicto* possibility does not.

With respect to the ontological argument for God's existence (and nature), the American philosopher Alvin Plantinga (1932–   ) has argued that there is a modal argument for God's existence, meaning that there is a logical argument to prove, or at least support, the claim that God, as a necessary being, exists. His argument runs like this: To say that something is possible simply means that it might be the case. Philosophers sometimes speak of this as saying that there is a possible world in which that thing is the case. For example, although Babe Ruth did not run for governor of New York in the actual world, he might have (or there is some possible world in which it is true that he ran for governor of New York). To say that something is necessary means that in all situations something is the case (or, in all possible worlds that thing happened, or it is true to say it was the case). For example, if it is necessary that a father is older than his daughter, then it is true in all situations that a father is older than his daughter; there is no situation in which that is false or even might have been false. Philosophers would say that if something is necessary (or necessarily true), then that means that it is true in all possible worlds. In other words, there is no world (or situation) in which that turns out to be false.

Plantinga claimed that a theorem of modal logic is that if it is possible that something is necessary, then it is necessary. This seems puzzling! However, here is his reason: To say that it is possible that God is a necessary being (and therefore exists) means that there is at least one possible world (or situation) in which God necessarily exists. That is, he says it is not impossible, or a contradiction, to say that God necessarily exists. So, if it is possible that God necessarily exists, then, again, that means that there is at least one possible world (or situation) in which God necessarily exists. However, to say that God necessarily exists, even just in that one world, means, by the definition of necessary, that God exists in all possible worlds, including the real, actual world. So, if it is even possible that God necessarily exists, then God exists! Of course, not all philosophers are persuaded by this argument. For those who are not persuaded, some are not because this argument presumes, but does not prove, *de re* necessity, as opposed to *de dicto* necessity. That is, they claim that at most what the argument shows as necessity is about language, not about things in the world, and that language cannot determine existence, necessary or otherwise; language cannot create even possible things, much less actual or necessary things.

The Cosmological Argument

Cosmological Argument

The cosmological argument is an argument offered to prove that God exists. In its simplest form, it is probably the argument that most people would give if they wanted to prove that God exists. Quite simply, it is an answer to the question: Where did everything (that is, the cosmos) come from? The answer that is often given is: God. In a nutshell, God is the creator of the cosmos.

In more sophisticated versions, the argument runs like this: Everything that exists either always existed or was created. If it was created, it either created itself or was created by something else. This holds not only for things within the universe (or cosmos), such as people and trees and planets, but also for the universe itself, as a whole. It is not conceivable that the universe has always existed or that it created itself, therefore something else created the universe, namely, God.

Some version or other of this argument has been given by philosophers (and everyday people) over the centuries. A common version sometimes refers to God as the First Cause or the Prime Mover. This version simply says that everything that exists has some cause; that is, for anything that exists, something or other caused it to exist. So, if A (whatever A is) exists, then there must be something, call it B, that caused A to exist. Of course, this means that B exists, so there must be something else, call it C, that caused B to exist. As we trace these causes back in time, either the series of causes goes back infinitely or else there must have been a

First Cause. (This is also sometimes called the prime mover because *cause* and *motion* were taken by Greek philosophers basically to mean the same thing. So, the Prime Mover is the First Cause.)

Many other philosophers (and nonphilosophers) have rejected this argument for God's existence. One reason is because they claim that there is nothing that rules out the possibility of the cosmos having existed infinitely back in time. While an infinite past might be difficult to conceive, such a difficulty does not rule out the possibility. Although modern science now favors the view of the big bang, that the universe came into existence at some point in time (now believed to be around 13–14 billion years ago), this view is not generally seen as settling this concern. This is because critics still say that it is not unreasonable to say that it is this current universe that is the subject of the big bang, but the notion of the cosmos could include more than that. In addition, those who have favored the cosmological argument have not meant it to depend upon scientific evidence. They would favor it even if there were no evidence of a big bang.

A second reason that people have criticized the cosmological argument is that they claim that even if the universe came into existence at some point (and is not infinitely old), this in itself does not prove that God exists but only that the universe is not infinitely old.

A third concern raised by critics is that those who favor the cosmological argument do not explain how the universe was created (if it is not infinitely old) but merely put a label on its creation. This concern is much like a child's question: Who (or what) created God? That is, if the existence of the universe needs to be explained, then why not ask for an explanation of the cause of God. Is it not simply arbitrary to say that God caused the universe but nothing caused God (or that God was self-caused)?

Supporters of the cosmological argument have, of course, claimed that there simply is nothing that could explain the existence of the universe other than God. For them, it is arbitrary to claim that the universe might be infinitely old (and, indeed, modern science says it is not) or that it could somehow cause itself.

Aquinas's Five Ways

The Greek philosopher Aristotle (384–322 B.C.E.) wrote that God was the Unmoved Mover. For him, the concept of motion was similar to the concept of change. Things, for him, are moved in the sense that they change in some way or other; that is, they move from one state of being to another state of being. For instance, a person might move in the sense of walking across a room and, so, change position in that room. Another sense of motion, or change, for Aristotle, would be a piece of fruit ripening. Over the course of time, it changes from one state of being to another, as it ripens. Aristotle would have spoken of this as the fruit being in motion, even though the motion was in terms of maturing, not in terms of its location in space.

For Aristotle, all things in the natural world move (or change). However, there must be some cause(s) for any change. As we trace back a series of causes to account for any motion, Aristotle claimed that eventually we must get back to some first starting point, something that is itself not moved. This unmoved mover, he said, is God.

Depiction of Thomas Aquinas in a stained glass window *(Used under a Creative Commons license)*

The medieval philosopher and theologian Saint Thomas Aquinas (1225–74) was highly influenced by Aristotle, as well as by Christian doctrine. Among his vast writings, he offered five proofs (or Five Ways of proving) God's existence. One way is often called the proof from motion. It is simply Aristotle's argument of the Unmoved Mover. A second way, for Aquinas, was a closely related argument that he called the proof from efficient cause. It is essentially, the same point, that for any effect, there must be some efficient cause—call it C—that is, some thing that brought about that effect. But, then, there must have been an efficient cause—call it D—for C, and another efficient cause—call it E—for D, and so on. Aquinas said that this cannot go on back infinitely; there must be a first cause (or uncaused cause), namely, God.

Aquinas's third way of proving God's existence is from the notions of possibility and necessity. In nature, he said, we find things that exist, but they might not have existed. It is possible that George Washington might never have been born, say, if his parents had never met. George Washington's existence, then, was not necessary; that is, he did not necessarily exist. Aquinas claimed that this is true of all things in the natural world; if they exist, they might not have. To say that they exist, but do not necessarily exist, is to say that they exist contingently (which, again, simply means that they happen to exist, but not necessarily). Since all things in the natural world exist contingently, for Aquinas, there must have been some point back in time when nothing existed (because nothing *must* exist necessarily). However, if there was ever a moment in time when nothing existed, then there would still be nothing existing, since you can't get something from nothing! But, said Aquinas, this is false; things do exist! That means that there must be something that exists necessarily, namely God.

His fourth way of proving God's existence is called the proof of gradation. This refers to the notion that things can have comparable qualities, or grades. For example, one person might be tall, but another person is taller, or one rock is heavy, and another rock is heavier. Things can have more or less of some quality or feature (such as more or less height or weight). However, said Aquinas, to speak of gradations presupposes some standard by which to determine whether or not something has more or less of that quality or feature. Since people can be more or less good, he claimed that there must be a standard of goodness, or perfection. That is, there must be the thing that is the most good, or most perfect, namely, God.

Finally, Aquinas's fifth way was what he called the governance of the world. This is his notion that the universe is orderly, not chaotic. There must be some cause for this orderliness, and that cause is God. This is often spoken of as the design argument, because it says that the universe shows such orderliness and complexity that it must be designed, not random, and the designer is God.

Argument from Design

Design Argument

Over the centuries, philosophers have offered a variety of arguments to prove that God exists. One such argument is called the design argument (and sometimes the teleological argument). In a nutshell, this argument says that things in nature and the universe as a whole display such order that the most reasonable explanation is that this orderliness, or design, is the result of a designer, not of random chance events. The designer of the universe is God. So the orderliness of things shows that God exists.

The first question to ask here is: What are the sorts of features that we associate with something having been designed? They are orderly or at least organized; they are often quite complex or complicated; they seem purposive, that is, intended to fulfill some purpose or other; they are frequently quite precise or fine-tuned. The design argument says that when we look at nature, this is just what we find, an orderliness and harmony of things such that it makes the most sense to infer that these things were designed. And, of course, if there is design, then there is a designer. Again, the designer of nature is God.

A famous version of this argument came from the 18th-century British clergyman William Paley (1743–1805). He argued that nature is "more wonderfully organized than the most subtle human contrivance." Paley's famous analogy was that the world is like a watch and God is a watchmaker. Imagine, he said, that we were out in nature and we came upon a watch (or perhaps something that we did not know what it is or how it worked). The watch seems to be complex, that is, made up of many different parts; they seem to work together, that is, if any of the parts were missing, the watch would not function; they seem to be purposive, that is, they seem to work together to accomplish some goal. Is it not much more likely and reasonable to assume that the watch had a watchmaker than that it just happened to come about?

Since Paley's time, we have come to understand the world and things in it even more. The human eye far exceeds any camera in sensitivity and accuracy of reproduction; the human brain still cannot be duplicated by the most sophisticated computer; the merest one-celled microscopic organism exhibits a biochemical complexity and adaptation that taxes the analytic powers of our best science. Surely, it is more reasonable to believe that such organization and complexity is the result of intelligent design and not mere random physical forces and interactions.

Of course, plenty of people have not found this argument convincing. For one thing, they say, even though we can find lots of examples in nature of orderliness and complexity, we also find lots of examples in nature of the lack of orderliness! There are a lot of aspects of the natural world that seem disorderly. Beyond this, they say, while we can find lots of examples in nature of orderliness and complexity, it does not follow that there was necessarily an intelligent designer. The orderliness and complexity might well be the effect of nonintelligent causes. For example, we see orderliness and complexity in the structure of our solar system, with its eight planets and many moons (and other celestial objects). Each of these things has gravitational influence on all the others, yet somehow the solar system runs on and on in harmony, without planets and moons crashing into each other and in orbits that are highly structured. Intelligent design of this system is, of course, one explanation for the order that we see. However, these critics claim, the order might well be the result of nonintelligent forces. We can easily explain, say, the Moon's orbit around the Earth, as a balance of two forces, gravity and inertia. Gravity, which pulls the Moon toward the Earth is exactly balanced by the Moon's inertia to move off in a straight line away from the Earth. It is the balance of these forces that produces the Moon's orderly orbit. At least this is how a physicist would explain the order. If the forces had not been balanced, the Moon would not have its orbit. If gravity had been stronger, the Moon would have crashed into the Earth, or if the Moon's inertia had been stronger, it would have flown off away from the Earth. So, the fact that things are orderly or complex does not by itself demonstrate intelligent design.

Or with respect to living things and the complexity about them, a common example used to talk about organisms adapting to their environments is the peppered moth in England. There are two varieties, the darker-winged variety and the lighter-winged variety. Prior to industrialization, there was a certain survival rate of these two varieties. With the oncoming of industrial pollution from coal-burning factories and the resulting soot-darkened trees and buildings, the darker-winged variety could more easily blend into its environment and escape predators than the lighter-winged variety. As a result, the survival rates of darker-winged moths increased relative to lighter-winged moths. This was not evidence of any intelligent design; it was simply the result of environmental changes. The point, of course, is again that orderliness and complexity by itself does not demonstrate intelligent design. In direct response to Paley, the British biologist Richard Dawkins (1941–   ) refers to the blind watchmaker.

For philosophers, there are two major issues with respect to the design argument. The first issue is whether the apparent design that we see in the world is explained—or best explained—by appealing to something outside of nature. As seen above, supporters of the design argument have claimed that the best, and possibly the only reasonable, explanation is of a cosmic designer (that is, God). Perhaps some orderly aspects of the world can be explained without appealing to a cosmic designer, but certainly not all orderly aspects and certainly not with respect to the design of the universe as a whole. On the other hand, critics of the design argument have claimed either that there are no orderly aspects of the world that have not been explained by natural forces and interactions or that appealing to a cosmic designer does not actually explain anything; it merely puts a label or name in place of an actual explanation.

The second issue for philosophers is the nature of the argument. For many philosophers, this argument is an analogy. That is, they say that people are trying to get to a conclusion—namely, that God exists—on the basis of showing some similarity to another argument. For instance, as noted above, Paley said that upon investigating a watch, we would most reasonably conclude there was a watchmaker. Likewise, upon investigating the natural world, we would most reasonably conclude there was a world-maker (that is, a world-designer, or God). However, for many philosophers, analogies are suspect and can often lead to questionable conclusions. This is because analogies are not direct evidence for something but are means of persuasion. Two things might be analogous in various ways, but those same two things might also not be analogous in various ways (for example, there are lots of ways in which a watch and the universe are quite different). So, some analogies are good, and some are bad; some lead to good inferences, and some do not. The point for philosophers is that simply offering an analogy in itself is not much basis for a reliable conclusion. If there is a cosmic designer, some other argument is needed.

Evolution

Many things change over time, not only individuals and groups of organisms, but even abstract things such as organizations or institutions or attitudes. With respect to groups of biological organisms, the most commonly known account for their change is the theory of evolution. The theory of evolution does not merely say that groups of organisms, specifically species, change over time, but it puts forward an account of how and why they change over time. The theory actually is made up of a number of hypotheses and explanations. The 20th-century biologist Ernst Mayr (1904–2005) claimed that there are five broad theses within evolutionary theory: (1) evolution as such (meaning that things change and transform over time); (2) common descent (meaning that different species existing today can be traced back to some common ancestor species); (3) gradualism (meaning that the change and transformation of species usually takes place gradually over a relative long period of time); (4) multiplication of species (meaning that the change and transformation over time produces more and more different species); and (5) natural selection (meaning that the cause[s] of the change and transformation of species over time is the result of everyday physical forces and factors in the environment, not of design or divine intervention).

The theory of evolution is related to philosophy in a number of ways. One way is in terms of basic questions about human nature. This is sometimes addressed in the context of human origins. Were humans divinely created or at least divinely created separately from other species? Or did humans come about as a result of natural selection processes? Related, but separate, is the issue of human dignity and identity. If humans came about as a result of natural selection processes, what does this say about the value and importance of humans (that is, their dignity), and what does it say about what humans are (that is, their identity) with respect to other forms of life on Earth? Different people, of course, have given different answers to these questions. Another focus along the lines of basic questions about human nature—but also about the nature of the world at large—is the issue of what is often called the design argument. The design argument is an argument that the universe is, or at least appears to be, orderly and designed; but this implies that there is a cause of its orderliness, a designer. The designer of the universe is God. So, related to basic questions about human nature is the issue of design, including how (if at all) humans fit into such a design.

A second broad way in which the theory of evolution is related to philosophy is in terms of philosophical analysis of fundamental and important concepts within evolutionary theory. For example, evolutionary theory (and other aspects of biology) speaks of species. In fact, the focus of evolutionary theory is on species, not on individual organisms. Biologists remark that genes mutate, organisms adapt, but species evolve. However, there are conceptual questions about what exactly a species is. There is also a question about the unit of selection. That is, if natural selection is the (or an) explanation for how and why species evolve, what exactly gets selected naturally? Suppose one bird survives in a given environment better than another bird, say, because it is faster or because its plumage protects it better from predators. Then is it the speed or plumage that gets selected or is it the individual bird that gets selected or, because that bird's speed and plumage are caused in large part by its genes, is it the bird's genes that get selected? This is the question of what unit—the gene or certain traits or the individual organism or possibly even a larger group, such as a herd or whole species—is the unit of selection. Both philosophers and biologists wrestle with this issue, among other conceptual issues connected to evolutionary theory.

A third broad way in which the theory of evolution is related to philosophy is in terms of how evolutionary theory has influenced the content and practices of philosophers. One way it has done this is that, because of evolutionary theory, philosophers have reconsidered issues within axiology (the study of values), epistemology (the study of knowledge), and metaphysics (the study of reality). With respect to axiology, philosophers today commonly speak of evolutionary ethics. This means that philosophers investigate and analyze basic ethical values and beliefs in terms of how or why they would have evolved for humans. They look to the interaction of humans in their environments, rather than looking at abstract principles, to make sense of ethical behavior at all as well as specific moral values (for example, why incest is condemned or why people feel duties to others). With respect to epistemology, philosophers today often speak of evolutionary epistemology. That is, they investigate and analyze how beliefs form in people or how and why certain standards and patterns of reasoning are accepted and justified or what role the development of the brain has on mental states. In all of these sorts of concerns, philosophers today often look to the kinds of explanations that come from evolutionary theory in order to address these issues. With respect to metaphysics, many philosophers today speak of naturalism. By naturalism, they mean the basic assumption that things in the world arose as a result of natural forces and processes, so when philosophers raise questions about what is real, they need to address those questions with the assumption that the answers will involve only natural forces and processes. In particular, many philosophers today reject abstract, nonnatural philosophical concepts such as Plato's Ideas. Instead, they embrace the emphasis and assumption of change and transformation that is basic to the theory of evolution.

Creationism

The term *creationism* refers to a collection of related, although different, views about the nature of the universe and the nature of humans, in particular. Broadly speaking, creationism holds that the universe was created by God and humans were created by God as a particular, unique species. One point that is supported by most creationists is the rejection of the theory of biological evolution, especially evolution's claim about the origin of humans. A rejection of this evolutionary view, along with the claim of special creation of humans are basic to, perhaps even defining of, creationism.

Some aspects of creationism have a long history. For many centuries, people have engaged in what is called natural religion. Natural religion is the area of interest that sees the study of the natural world as a means to being closer to God. The notion is that the study of God's creation is a way of coming to know (either intellectually or spiritually) the creator, God. Related to natural theology is the view that God's existence and nature are revealed in God's creation. As part of this view, many people have put forth what is called the design argument. The design argument says that the study of the natural world shows that it is complex and orderly, which is to say that it is designed and not the result of random or chance events or processes. The best explanation is that there exists a designer, which is to say, God.

From a philosophical perspective, there are three broad areas of concern related to creationism: metaphysical, epistemological, and axiological. Metaphysics is the study of reality, focusing on basic questions of what kinds of things there are; epistemology is the study of knowledge, focusing on what knowledge is (as opposed, say, to belief or opinion) and how claims about knowledge can be justified; axiology is the study of value and values, focusing on what value is and types of value (such as ethical value or aesthetic value). With respect to each of these broad philosophical concerns, there are issues that relate to creationism.

In terms of metaphysical issues, one issue concerns the origin and age of the universe. While for a long time philosophers argued back and forth on the issue of whether or not the universe came into existence at some point in time or always existed (that is, whether or not the universe had a beginning), today few people, including philosophers, think this is a significant issue. Even fewer think it is a philosophical issue; to the extent that it is an important question, it is seen as a scientific question, and most scientists today support the view of the big bang, that the universe (as we know it) came into existence 13–14 billion years ago. For some creationists, this is the main point: The universe came into existence at some point in time, and the best explanation is that it was created by God. Some creationists, however, claim that the universe is only a few thousand years old; their evidence is taken from religious scripture, not from scientific investigations. In part, they claim, any scientific evidence that suggests a much older universe can be explained as God making things seem to appear that old.

In terms of epistemological issues, a major one is how we (can) know when the universe was created or when and how humans came into being. Opponents of creationism claim that the overwhelming evidence that comes from science rejects creationism. In addition, they say, the methods of science are objective and follow where the data take them, not to a predetermined desired result. Science, they claim, makes predictions on the basis of current information, and those predictions can be observed and tested. If the hypothesis or theory leads to false predictions, then they will reject the hypothesis or theory. Creationism, they claim, neither makes predictions nor is open to rejecting their view if evidence runs against it. Creationists deny that they fail to make predictions or that they fail to reject unsupported predictions. In addition, they claim, scientific evidence is not the only kind of evidence; scientific tests, they say, can only evaluate what they are designed to test and evaluate.

In terms of axiological issues, the main ones are related to a broad conception of what it is to be human and also are related to social and political policies. With respect to the conception of human nature, the issue of creationism is connected to what people see as the best (perhaps only) way to understand human nature and human identity. The issue of what something is—that is, its nature—is related to its origin and its destiny. In other words, some people argue that a thing's origin, where it comes from, is crucial to what that thing is. If humans are seen as coming from other species, then they are not unique or especially important, at least for creationists. Also, if they are seen as coming from other species, then they do not have a unique or especially important destiny. Besides this issue of the conception of human nature, there are social and political questions related to creationism. In particular, especially in the United States, there have been social and political conflicts over teaching creationism in public schools. Beginning with the notorious Scopes trial in the 1920s, there have been a number of court cases concerning the teaching of creationism (or the banning of the teaching of evolution) in public education. This has usually taken the form of whether or not to permit the teaching of creationism as an alternative theory to evolution with respect to the origin and nature of the universe and of humans. Creationists have argued that evolution is just a theory and alternative theories, such as creationism, should also be part of the school curriculum. Opponents have argued that creationism is not science and to include it, especially to mandate it, would both violate the separation of religion and the state as well as teach religion in the guise of science.

Creationism has been used less and less since the late 20th century and has been replaced by *creation science.* Even more, it has been replaced by what is called *intelligent design,* a view that claims that the best scientific evidence for many features of the natural world is that they are designed, not the result of mere physical, evolutionary processes. Critics have said that intelligent design theory is only the design argument updated and creationism packaged under a new label.

Anthropic Principle

As more evidence is gathered by scientists about the nature of the universe, some have claimed that this evidence supports the design argument for God's existence. This is sometimes called the *anthropic principle.* What this claim amounts to is that there are some very fundamental features of the universe that, if they were even very slightly different than they actually are, would result in the universe being radically different than it is (and perhaps not even existing). For example, if the gravitational constant were just slightly different, the universe would have evolved very differently. Or if the balance of matter and antimatter at the beginning of the universe were even slightly different, the universe would have evolved very differently. Some theists see the delicate balance of many fundamental features of the universe as evidence for design. Critics do not and see such information as only the latest version of the design argument, suffering the same problems as earlier versions.

Natural versus Revealed Religion

Natural Religion

Theology, in a literal sense, is the study of God (from the Greek words *theos,* meaning "God," and *logos,* meaning "study"), but it often includes the broader sense of the study of religion. Some forms or aspects of theology are called revelatory theology, or revealed religion, meaning they are concerned with revelations, or something being revealed. Usually this means some form of direct word of God being revealed to humans. For example, scripture—such as some Christian biblical passages, or the content of Muslim scripture, the Qur'an—are said to be the revealed word of God. Also, some people have claimed to have had direct communication with God (or some deity), that is, to have received divine revelations.

Natural theology (or natural religion) is the form or aspect of theology that is not concerned with direct revelation. Rather, the focus is on understanding signs in nature of what is divine, for example, signs in nature of God's existence or of God's nature or even human moral nature as it relates to God.

With respect to God's existence, natural theology focuses on the view that there is evidence in the natural world to demonstrate by reason—not by faith—that God exists. There are two very common sorts of natural theological arguments for God's existence. The first is the very existence of the world, or universe. This is often called the cosmological argument. In a nutshell, this argument says that anything that exists had to have come from somewhere or something. Things cannot create themselves. So, the world as a whole (the cosmos) must have been created by something, namely, God.

The second common sort of natural theological argument for God's existence is often called the design argument. This argument says that there is a lot of evidence for order and structure in the world. That is, there appears to be a lot of evidence that things in the natural world are designed, not random or haphazard. If they are designed, then there must be a designer, someone or something that does the designing. With respect to the design of the natural world, that designer is God. Probably the best-known version of this argument comes from the writings of William Paley, who in the 1700s proposed what is called the watchmaker argument. Paley said that if we found a watch in the middle of a forest, we would assume that it was made by a watchmaker. The fact that it is complex and yet orderly is much more likely to be explained by it having been made by a watchmaker than it having just been assembled by nature. The complexity, yet obvious useful function of the human eye (and many other things in nature), is much more easily explained, he said, by the assumption of a designer than by natural causes.

Besides God's existence, natural theology is also concerned with God's nature and humans' relationship with God. For example, many people have argued that events in the world are a sign of God's happiness or unhappiness with human actions. Also, many people have argued that there are lessons in nature for humans to learn about how they should act, lessons that are placed in nature by God for us to learn. For instance, some people have claimed that the industriousness of ants in their purposeful activities and in their collective work to build their colonies is a natural sign of how humans should behave. In addition, some people have argued that the competition for survival among nature's organisms and species is a sign that humans, too, are correct to be competitive, because such competition ensures the survival of the fittest (that is, the best).

One concern about natural theology has been to investigate if it ever conflicts with revelatory theology and, if it does, how to resolve that conflict. For example, do natural signs and evidence that the Earth is billions of years old conflict with any scriptural, revelatory information about the age of the Earth? This points to the even broader issue of the relationship between faith and reason as well as the relationship between religion and science.

Problem of Divine Foreknowledge

The problem of foreknowledge is the problem of making sense of humans having free will and at the same time God being all-knowing. For this reason, this problem is often called the problem of divine foreknowledge. One assumption of this problem is that if humans have free will, then their actions and choices are not determined or predestined ahead of time. That is, free will seems to imply that people have options at a given point in time and they might do one thing or another; they are free to choose. Another assumption of this problem is that God is all-knowing. This is taken as part of the nature of God; there is nothing that God does not know. Being all-knowing, however, does not simply mean that God knows everything that is happening right now, but also that God knows everything that has already happened and—most important for this problem—that God knows everything that will happen in the future. (If God does not know what will happen in the future, then God is not all-knowing.) The problem arises in the sense that if God already knows what will happen in the future, then it seems that humans do not have free will. That is, if God knows today that tomorrow some person will do X, then it seems that tomorrow she *must* do X; she is not free to do Y, because God already knows that she will do X. (If she ends up not doing X, then God would have been mistaken and not all-knowing.) Therefore, God being all-knowing seems to imply that humans do not have free will. It is important to note that this problem of divine foreknowledge does not say that God causes people to act in certain ways, but that *if God knows* what they will do, then they must do it (otherwise, God would not know). That is, the problem is one about knowledge, not about cause.

This conclusion leads to even more problems. If this conclusion is correct and people do not have free will, then how can they be held responsible for their actions? If their actions are already determined or predestined, then they have no choice about doing them. This would seem to mean that the concept of sin makes no sense, if sin is a matter of people intentionally choosing bad actions.

There have been a number of responses to this problem. One response, in fact, has been to embrace divine predestination, for example, as did the American theologian Jonathan Edwards (1703–58). Another response has been to deny that God sees into the future. In other words, some people have claimed that God is outside of time, so that the past, present, and future are all present to God. Time (including notions of past, present, and future) is an aspect of human experience, not divine experience. So, what some person does tomorrow is just as much present to God as what she did yesterday or what she does today. If this is true, then there is no problem about human free will, because knowing what she did yesterday or today does not mean that she had no choice; it simply means that her choice was known to God, and the same is true for her future actions. Many, but not all, philosophers accept this response to this problem. Those who do not accept it claim that we have no evidence for saying that God is outside of time and, in addition, that much religious tradition points to God acting in time, that is, directly engaging in human affairs. Others claim that such actions only show that God can act in time, but this does not mean God exists in time as humans understand it.

The Nature of God's Perfection

God

It is difficult to say what is meant or referred to or understood by the term *God*. One reason for this is that many people, both as individuals and as cultures, have had different conceptions of God (or gods). Another reason is that the term is difficult to define or even to characterize. Philosophers have tended to focus on four broad issues connected to the concept.

One broad issue is the nature of God. That is, what is God? In addressing this question, philosophers have usually spoken of what they call the attributes or features of God. For example, many philosophers (and nonphilosophers) have said that God is eternal, meaning that God did not come into existence and will not (cannot) go out of existence. Also, they claim that God is all-knowing (or omniscient), as well as all-good (or omnibenevolent) and all-powerful (or omnipotent). Some have said that God is infinite, meaning there are no limits at all on what God is or can do. In addition, some have said that God is Perfect Being. Sometimes people mean by this that God is infinite, but sometimes they say that perfection cannot be explained. Indeed, some people have claimed that there is no way that God can be (adequately) characterized; what God is cannot be put into words or even into human thought.

An issue that has been raised by some is that the very concept of God's nature as being all-powerful makes no sense. This is sometimes cast as the paradox of the stone. A paradox is a kind of argument in

Painting of Thomas Aquinas, panel from the altar of San Domenico in Ascoli Piceno
(1476) *(Painting by Carlo Crivelli)*

which the conclusion of that argument is unacceptable even though it follows from reasonable and acceptable assumptions. The word *paradox* comes from two Greek words, *para,* meaning "beyond" or "contrary to," and *doxa,* meaning "belief" or "opinion." The paradox of the stone is usually presented in the form of a question: Can God create a stone that is too heavy for Him to lift? The concern is that if God *can* create such a stone—that is, one that He is not powerful enough to lift—then, God is not all-powerful. On the other hand, if God *cannot* create such a stone, then it is also the case that God is not all-powerful, since there is something God cannot do. Some theists, including Thomas Aquinas, have responded by saying that being all-powerful does not mean that God can do what is logically impossible (such as creating a square circle or a stone too heavy for Him to lift). Critics, then, have asked what, exactly, omnipotence does mean?

Related to the broad issue of the nature of God is a second philosophical focus, namely, the existence of God. This is a separate issue because, even if we can speak of what something is, it does not follow that the thing in question exists. For example, we can speak of the attributes or features of a unicorn or of a hobbit, but that does not mean that unicorns or hobbits exist. In addition, philosophers do not take the issue of God's existence as given or a matter of faith; rather, they have offered various arguments intended to show that God exists. (Other philosophers have offered various arguments intended to show that God does not exist.) The most common philosophical arguments related to God's existence are the cosmological argument, the design argument, and the ontological argument.

Although the issues of God's nature and God's existence are in one sense separate, they are very closely related. For example, some philosophers have argued, in what is called the ontological argument, that part of God's very nature is that God exists. This close relationship has led to questions about both God's nature and God's existence. For instance, some people have argued that the existence of evil in the world is not consistent with the existence of a perfect God. In addition, some people have argued that God being all-knowing is not consistent with humans having free will.

A third broad issue related to God that philosophers have dealt with is the relation of God to the natural world and to humans. One notion is that God is transcendent. This means that God is not in the world or part of the world but beyond it. That is, God transcends the world; God is supernatural (simply meaning, above or beyond nature). On the other hand, there is the notion that God is immanent. This means that God is in the world, not outside of the world. One conception of God as immanent is that God has and does interact in history. For example, Christians claim that God became flesh in the person of Jesus Christ, and Muslims claim that God spoke (through the angel Jibril) to Muhammad, and Jews claim that God intervened to part the waters for the exodus of Moses from Egypt. Another conception of God as immanent is the concept of pantheism. The word *pantheism* comes from two Greek words, *pan,* meaning "all," and *theos,* meaning "god." Pantheism is the view that God is everything and that God is not separate from the natural world. (This is not exactly the same thing as panentheism, which is the view that everything is *in* God and God is *in* everything.) While many people who believe in God have embraced the view of pantheism (and also panentheism), because God is limitless—so God is everything—others have rejected pantheism (and panentheism) for the same reason, namely that God is limitless—claiming that the world is not limitless and, so, is not identical with God. Another way of saying this is that God is the creator, while the world is the creation.

Another way in which people speak of the relation of God to the world and to humans is as lawgiver and judge. That is, many people claim that standards of good and bad, right and wrong, come from God. In addition, God does and will judge human behavior. Related to this notion of God as related to the world and to humans is God as personal, meaning God as not an abstract concept but as having a direct, personal connection to people (for example, as hearing one's prayers or as the savior of one's soul).

A fourth broad philosophical issue related to God is the knowledge of God. This is the issue of what and how humans can know with respect to God. One aspect of this issue is the question of faith as a means of knowing. For instance, what exactly is faith? What is the relation between faith and reason? Closely connected to this is the aspect of religious experience. Again, what exactly is religious experience? How can one know if some given experience is religious, or how can one know if one's experience is truly an experience of God? Knowledge of

God is usually said to be of two forms: revealed knowledge and signs of nature. Revealed knowledge is knowledge of God that is revealed to people, such as sacred scripture or direct communication with God. In a word, revealed knowledge is revelation. Signs of nature function as knowledge of God by way of things in the world that point to God. For instance, many people claim that both the orderliness and complexity of things in the world are a sign that they are not random but designed, and that God is the designer.

Theodicy and the Problem of Evil

Problem of Evil

The problem of evil is the problem of how to make sense of the existence of evil if God is all-powerful, all-knowing, and all-good. So, the problem of evil is a challenge for forms of theism that view God as having these qualities. If God is omnipotent (all-powerful), omniscient (all-knowing), and omnibenevolent (all-good), then it seems as if there should be no evil in the world. This is because if God is all-good, then he would want to prevent evil, and if God is all-powerful and all-knowing, then he would have the ability to prevent evil and know how to do so. Yet evil exists. People murder, rape, and torture, and in various other ways needlessly inflict great harm on other people and animals. In addition, disease and natural disasters such as earthquakes cause enormous suffering on people and animals that do not seem to deserve it. If God is all-powerful, all-knowing, and all-good, then how can this be?

A common way of answering this question is by arguing that God allows evil to exist for the sake of a greater good. For example, one view is that God allows evil to exist because God wants humans to have free will; specifically, God wants people to be able to choose freely between good and evil. If people can choose freely between good and evil, it is likely there will be evil in the world, just because sometimes people will choose evil. But, in this view, free will is so important that it is worth the existence of evil: It is better to have a world with evil where people can freely choose good or evil than a world where there is no evil but people cannot freely choose. Often this view is based on the idea that the goodness of people who are good only because they have to be (they are not capable of being evil) is much less valuable than the goodness of people who can freely choose evil but do not. Consider, for instance, a sophisticated android who acts only in good ways just because its programming does not allow it to do anything else; plausibly such a creature's goodness is not as meaningful as the goodness of someone who freely chooses to be good. However, one difficulty with this answer to the problem of evil is that it does not address all forms of evil. That God wanted people to have free will might explain why humans suffer at the hands of other humans, but it does not explain the suffering caused by natural disasters and diseases such as cancer. In other words, not all evil comes as a result of humans exercising free will, and it is not clear why an all-powerful, all-knowing, all-good God would allow those forms of evil to exist too.

Another response to the problem of evil is the argument that evil makes people morally better than they would be if they never had to face evil. Evil gives us the opportunity to develop important virtues such as courage and compassion, for example. Sometimes in the face of evil humans are brave, kind, and compassionate, even heroic; they put themselves in harm's way to help others, such as by rescuing people from attackers or collapsing buildings. According to this argument, we could not develop these important virtues without facing evil. Perhaps someone whose life was risk-free, for instance, would never have the opportunity to develop courage. Similarly, perhaps a person would never develop the virtue of compassion unless there were people who needed compassion, that is, unless there were people suffering. So, God allows evil so that people can develop these important virtues. To put the point in a way popularized by John Hicks (1904–89), evil is soul-making. We have morally better, more complete souls for having developed virtues in response to evil. On this view, it is better to have a world with evil, where humans can develop these virtues, than a world without evil, where people cannot.

One objection to this argument regards the suffering of animals. Animals suffer too: They experience disease, hardship, starvation, and predation by other animals. Yet many animals that suffer do not seem capable of developing virtues such as compassion or courage. A chicken, for example, might suffer great hardship by being confined to a tiny cage throughout its life, but it seems unlikely that the chicken would develop virtues such as perseverance or bravery as a result. It seems that God could have made the world in such a way that evil is confined only to the humans who might benefit from it in soul-making ways, but it seems that God did not. Many philosophers have also questioned whether the sheer amount and intensity of suffering that exists is really necessary to develop such virtues. For example, was the Holocaust necessary for people to develop certain virtues or could they have developed those virtues in response to a lesser evil?

A third answer to the problem of evil also takes the view that God has a good reason for allowing evil in the world and that the world is better off with evil than it would be without, but adds that it is impossible for humans to understand why. Famously, the German philosopher Gottfried Leibniz (1646–1716) argued that this is the best of all possible worlds and that everything that occurs (including apparent evil) is for the best. But, according to this view, because humans are very limited compared to God (for example, God knows everything, and humans do not), human beings cannot understand just why everything that happens is for the best, including evil.

Best of All Possible Worlds

With the claim that we live in the best of all possible worlds, Leibniz believed he had provided an answer to the problem of evil, the problem of how to make sense of the existence of evil in the world if God is all-powerful, all-good, and all-knowing. If God is all these things, why would he allow evil to exist? Leibniz's answer was it was not possible for God to have created a better world.

An important element in Leibniz's reasoning is the principle of sufficient reason. According to this principle, if something is the case, then there must be a sufficient reason for why it is the case. Now it seems that God, being all-powerful, could have created a world different than ours: There were various possible worlds, and out of these possibilities, God chose to create this one. So, Leibniz reasoned, there must have been a sufficient reason for why God chose to create this world rather than

Eighteenth-century engraving of Gottfried Leibniz *(Portrait by Johann Gottfried Auerbach)*

another one. That reason, according to Leibniz, is that this is the best of all possible worlds. This is because God, being morally perfect, would have chosen to create the best world possible, with the least amount of evil possible. For Leibniz, then, the best of all possible worlds does not mean a world that has no evil; rather, it means the world with the least possible amount of evil.

The evil that does occur in the world, Leibniz argued, is ultimately for a greater good. To illustrate, Leibniz remarks that a general would rather receive a wound and win a victory than go unharmed and forfeit a victory. The idea is that it was necessary to be wounded in order to win a great victory. Somewhat in the same way, the evil that exists in the world is necessary for a greater good. This does not mean that humans are capable of understanding exactly how this is so. Indeed, with our finite minds—our inability to see and understand all the events of the world for all time, or the connections between them—we are not capable of understanding how each and every instance of evil contributes to the greater good. For example, it is not obvious how the

Voltaire in 1718 *(Painting by Nicolas de Largillière)*

September 11 attacks in the United States are ultimately for the best. But, for Leibniz, they must be, and if humans fail to understand how, God does not.

Leibniz's answer to the problem of evil has found both supporters and detractors. One famous detractor was the French writer Voltaire (1694–1778), who satirized the view that this is the best of all possible worlds in his 1759 book *Candide*. In that story, although evil and unjust things happen and people suffer, the main character unfailingly says that this is the best of all possible worlds and that it is all for the best.

Modern Science and Ethics

What is the nature of the relationship between science and religion? One view of the relation between them is that they conflict. That is, both religion and science make claims about the world or things in it, and those claims clash. For example, if a modern cosmologist says that the universe is 13–14 billion years old, and Bishop Usser (a theologian in the 1600s who claimed that the universe was created in the year 4004 B.C.E.) says it is only 6,000 years old and they are both making factual claims about the real age of the universe, then obviously they cannot both be true. They are making contrary claims, and they are rival views. Very often this is how religion and science are portrayed.

A second view of the relationship between science and religion is that they are really quite independent of each other. Each has its appropriate, relevant sphere of concern. They do not contradict each other because they are talking about different things. (There is an old expression that there is a big difference between the Rock of Ages and the ages of rocks.) So, when a theist says that God parted the waters or separated the land and the sea, this is not necessarily meant to contradict a scientific account of how the world works. The point is that religious claims are not necessarily meant as actual physical descriptions of the world, even if they sound like it. Instead, they are metaphorical or allegorical and are meant to speak about the meaning or significance of things and events in the world rather than descriptions of them.

A third view of the relationship between science and religion is that there is and can be important dialogue and integration across both their concerns. There might well be boundary questions that both speak to, so that they are not completely independent of or isolated from each other. For example, both religion and science wrestle with the question of the origin of humanity and the nature of who we are as people. Much of the history of science is testimony to religious believers trying to understand the physical world. This is often called natural religion (or natural theology), in which one studies God's creation in order to understand better or connect with God the creator. So, there might be areas of mutual concern between religion and science, and yet they have separate concerns as well. The question becomes when, if ever, religious claims are meant to be empirical (that is, about the world) and, hence, rival claims to science. Just as well, it would be appropriate to ask when, if ever, what is said in the name of science is meant to function like religion, that is, tell us about the meaning and significance of things and events. In terms of claims about the world, many—probably most—scientific claims are consistent with religious claims. There is nothing, say, about electrons having a negative charge and protons having a positive charge that runs against religious concerns. Even claims that might seem more controversial are not necessarily so. For example, a theist could easily agree that the Moon's orbit is the result of a balance of gravitational and inertial forces yet still hold to the belief that there is a creator of the universe or even intelligent design to the universe.

Certainly many people have taken the conflict view. Among those people, some hold to what is called fideism. Fideism is the view that faith is independent of, superior to, and perhaps even in conflict with reason as a means of knowing. For some fideists, reason (science) is fine as long as it does not contradict faith; faith is superior to reason, but in itself reason is not bad and might even be of service to faith. For other fideists, reason is seen as being in opposition to faith. (An early Christian theologian, Tertullian [ca. 110–220] is said to have asked: "What is Athens to Jerusalem?" meaning what is the relevance of reason [identified with Athens, as the home of Greek philosophy] to faith [identified with Jerusalem, as the home of Christian belief].) One particularly influential fideist was the Danish thinker Søren Kierkegaard.

Søren Kierkegaard

Søren Kierkegaard (1813–55) was a Danish philosopher and writer who wrote on a wide variety of topics, ranging from psychology and literary criticism to the Protestant Church, in addition to his more strictly philosophical work. He is often considered the father of existentialism. Kierkegaard's father raised him with a deep sense of melancholy and religious guilt, themes that often surface in Kierkegaard's work. During college, Kierkegaard lived a life focused on food, drink, and clothes, but after his father's death, he settled down, became engaged to be married, and planned to become a Lutheran pastor. However, Kierkegaard soon broke off his engagement and dropped his studies to become a pastor, believing God had called him to a less conventional life as a writer. This belief strengthened Kierkegaard's lifelong view of himself as an outsider.

A central concern of Kierkegaard's was the human individual, and he was very critical of philosophical work that emphasized abstract, systematic thought over the individual. Kierkegaard especially faulted the work of Georg W. F. Hegel, because he thought that Hegel overlooked the fact that particular, individual people exist in the real world and instead focused on abstract generalities. Kierkegaard famously wrote in his published journals that he sought an idea that was "true for him," an idea for which he himself could live and die. Kierkegaard saw the question of Christian faith—whether to believe in Christianity or not to believe—as the vital question of his life. For Kierkegaard, belief in Christianity was not a matter of reasoned argument; for example, an attempt to prove through logic that God exists is simply the wrong way to approach Christianity. There are two reasons for this. The first is that, according to Kierkegaard, there are logical reasons for thinking that Christianity is actually false: It seems absurd, for instance, that God could both be an eternal God and a mortal human (Jesus). For Kierkegaard, the second reason is that what is crucial is not simply *that* one believes in Christianity but *how* one believes; in particular, true Christian faith involves passionate feeling. To use Kierkegaard's term, faith involves inwardness. Because aspects of Christianity seem absurd, Kierkegaard saw faith as nonrational. Rather, it requires a leap of faith; the person who makes such a leap passionately commits herself to Christianity, even though she is not certain that Christianity is objectively true. Because she is not sure that Christianity is objectively true, faith involves risk—she does not know whether making the leap of faith is the right choice. Yet the fact that the truth of Christianity is always uncertain is, for Kierkegaard, the very thing that makes a faithful person's commitment to Christianity passionate. This is because if one is convinced of Christianity's truth by reasoned argument, no passion is necessary; one simply believes according to the rules of logic. What this means is that the person who believes in Christianity in the right way—passionately—must always keep in mind that whether Christianity is true is uncertain, even while she continues to believe. So, for Kierkegaard, a leap of faith must be repeated throughout one's life, and in that sense Christian faith involves continuous, passionate commitment. Kierkegaard describes the decision about whether to make such a leap as filled with anxiety or angst. At the same time, however, Kierkegaard saw the realization that one is free to make such a decision as a source of exhilaration; one can feel dizzy from freedom.

Kierkegaard's account of Christian faith points to two dominant themes in his work: first, an emphasis on the individual's personal experience, and second, the belief that ideas should matter emotionally to one's life (they are not just a matter of intellectual belief). Along these lines, Kierkegaard wrote in his *Concluding Unscientific Postscript* that "truth is subjectivity." Truth is subjectivity in the sense that it involves an individual subject's experience. Consider the belief, for example, that Jesus was God. Truth is not just a matter of whether this belief matches up to actual, historical events such as the birth of a divine Jesus. For Kierkegaard, truth has to do with *how* a person has this belief—in such a way that it matters emotionally to that person, for instance, or only in a distant, uninvolved way. So, the Christianity of someone merely going through the motions of Christianity, without feeling deeply about Christianity, is less true (for Kierkegaard) than the Christianity of someone who is passionate about it. Kierkegaard's claim that truth is subjectivity is focused overwhelmingly on Christianity, as is his account of faith; he does not consider whether his view of faith would apply also, for instance, to Islam.

In two important works, Kierkegaard examined making other fundamental choices. In *Either/Or*, Kierkegaard presents a dialogue between people who represent very different ways of living: the aesthetic life, focused on personal pleasure, and the ethical life, focused on duty and ethical rules. Kierkegaard did not intend for the book to suggest that one way of life is objectively better than the other; given Kierkegaard's emphasis on individuality and subjective experience, perhaps it would seem strange if he had. However, it seems equally clear that Kierkegaard favored the ethical life in the choice between the ethical and aesthetic.

Illustration of Abraham and Isaac, published in *The Children's Bible Picture Book* in 1875

For Kierkegaard, a third and yet better option regarding a way of living was the religious life, in which God is the focus. In *Fear and Trembling*, Kierkegaard wrote about the biblical story of Abraham, in which God asks Abraham to kill his son Isaac. Kierkegaard asks, "Is there such a thing as the teleological suspension of the ethical?" What he meant by this was whether a person could appropriately temporarily give up ethical rules (such as the rule that one should not murder) for some higher purpose. Kierkegaard's answer is yes and, specifically, that Abraham does so. Abraham suspends the rule that murder is wrong for the sake of the higher purpose of obeying God. Abraham's decision, by

Kierkegaard's lights, is an illustration of the religious life. However, one does not immediately live such a life; one reaches the religious by first going through an aesthetic stage and an ethical stage.

Mysticism

Philosophical discussions of mysticism tend to focus on the nature of mysticism and whether mysticism can be a source of knowledge (and, if so, how). There is no universally accepted definition of what mysticism is. Nor is there a single description of mystical experiences. Mystical experiences have been described in various ways from diverse religious traditions and even outside religious traditions. Some mystics describe experiencing union with God; others do not involve divinity at all. Some describe the feeling that everything that exists is one; others report coming to certain realizations about the nature of ultimate reality (sometimes divine and sometimes not). Another theme in mystical experience is that it is a state of consciousness that has no object, meaning that one is conscious, yet one's consciousness is not directed toward anything (so, a person is not conscious even of herself or her thoughts, though she is conscious). In addition to these themes, mystic experiences are often thought to occur beyond ordinary, sensory experience: That is, they are not *solely* the experiences of what a person ordinarily experiences with one's five senses. For instance, some mystics describe directly perceiving God or ultimate reality, but doing so in a way independently of the five senses. In addition, mystical experiences are often described as ineffable, incapable of being given an adequate description. Given the diversity of descriptions of mystical experiences, one philosophical question is whether mystical experiences share certain core features; the issue is controversial. Some philosophers also question whether it is even possible to have certain mystical experiences, such as the experience of consciousness that has no object.

The American philosopher William James (1842–1910) wrote that mystical experiences are "authoritative" for the people who have them. For instance, a person who believes she experienced union with God is inclined to believe that she did really experience union with God; a person who in a mystical experience seemed to realize that she is identical with some ultimate reality is inclined to believe that, in fact, she really is identical with that ultimate reality. Whether mystical experiences should

William James in the 1890s *(Photograph by Sarah Choate Sears)*

be authoritative or whether they are authoritative for those who have not experienced them are separate questions. Put another way, the question is whether claims based on mystical experiences (such as claims about the nature of oneself, God, or reality) are adequate grounds for accepting those claims. In one view, such claims are importantly different than claims based on nonmystical grounds. For instance, if someone claims that the Pacific Ocean is salty, this claim can be publicly tested. Anyone can go into the Pacific Ocean and take a sample and test it—or even simply taste it—so the claim can be based on repeated experience that is public in this sense. It is not obvious that a claim based on a person's private mystical experiences can be tested and verified in the same way. But whether such a claim cannot be tested in *any* important way—and whether it matters for its justification—is controversial.

Pascal's Wager

A person might believe in God because she is convinced by a logical argument that God exists or because she has had particular religious experiences. But another reason for believing in God is that it is beneficial, or likely to be beneficial, to do so. This is the approach to belief in God in Pascal's wager, an argument by French mathematician Blaise Pascal (1623–62). Pascal argued that it is rational to believe in God because a person stands to gain more from believing in God than she stands to lose. He gave three different versions of this argument. The most famous of these is the following.

Pascal approached the issue of belief in God as though it were a wager, from the standpoint of a person betting. Now when a person wagers, she typically calculates what she has to win or lose. Suppose, for instance, a person is considering buying a lottery ticket. If the lottery ticket costs just a few dollars, and the buyer could potentially win millions of dollars, she might buy the ticket on the grounds that she has little to lose (if she loses, she will have lost just a few dollars) and a lot to gain (if she wins, she will be rich). Pascal applied similar reasoning to belief in God. Now either God exists or he does not. If God does exist, and a person believes in God, then she stands to win everything: eternal happiness after death. But supposing that God does not exist,

Seventeenth-century
portrait of Blaise Pascal

and a person believes in God, she would have lost nothing: Her belief in God would not have harmed her. So, a person has everything to gain by believing in God but nothing to lose. In addition, suppose that she does not believe in God and God does not exist. Then she has neither won nor lost anything. However, if she does not believe in God, and God does exist, she has lost everything; she is damned for eternity. Therefore, for Pascal, it is rational to believe in God in the sense that believing in God promotes one's own best interests. Moreover, according to Pascal, a person *must* wager regarding belief in God, that is, must choose whether or not to believe in God. This is because to try to avoid making the choice is in effect to choose, because in avoiding choosing, a person refrains from believing in God.

Pascal's wager raises many issues, especially in the philosophy of religion and decision theory. One issue is whether it is true, as Pascal claimed, that reason alone cannot decide for a person whether or not to believe in God, in the sense that reason alone cannot establish whether or not God exists. Another is the role of choice in belief: That is, can a person choose to believe something just because she wants to do so, and in particular, just because doing so is in her own best interests? Suppose, for instance, that a person knew she would be better off if she believed she was the smartest person in the world. It is not obvious that this would be sufficient for her to be able to make herself believe this—especially if she thought she had evidence that she was *not* the smartest person in the world. Another issue is whether Pascal's wager establishes that it is rational to believe in the God of Christianity in particular (as Pascal evidently desired) or whether it could establish just as well that it is rational to believe in other gods.

Divine Command Ethics

Divine command ethics is the view that moral behavior consists of obeying God's commands. One ought, then, to obey God's commands, for that is just what it means to behave morally. Divine command ethics does not attempt to say exactly what God commands; the answer to that question varies according to religious doctrine. Divine command ethics does provide one answer to a very old philosophical question: What is the relation between morality and religion? According to divine command ethics, morality depends on God (if there were no God, there would be no morality). One apparent advantage of divine command ethics is that it provides an objective ground for ethics. If right actions are just those actions commanded by God, then it seems that right actions are objectively right—it is not just a matter of personal preference or opinion that some actions are morally right and some actions are morally wrong. Morality is also universal: God's laws would seem to apply to everybody. So, if divine command ethics is true, moral relativism is false, and insofar as moral relativism seems unlikely to be true, that is a good thing.

Philosophers as diverse as William of Ockham and Søren Kierkegaard advocated divine command ethics. However, divine command ethics have also long been a matter of controversy. Perhaps the most important criticism of divine command ethics comes in the form of a question posed in Plato's dialogue *Euthyphro*. In that work, Socrates asked, "Is what is holy holy because the gods approve it, or do they approve it because it is holy?" The question can be rephrased like this: Is right action right because God commands it or does God command right action because it is right? The problem for divine command ethics is that the two most obvious ways of answering this question are not very attractive answers by the lights of divine command theory. If right action is right because God commands it, then it looks as if God's commands are arbitrary. This is because if what makes actions right is just that God commands them, then God could just as well have commanded other actions, and *those* would have been right, because God commanded them. God could well have commanded us to murder our first-born children, for example. However, something seems clearly wrong with the view that murdering all first-born children would be good just because God commanded it. If *that* could count as right action, then it does not seem to make much sense to say that God is good; rather, it seems that God simply commands. Because of these apparent consequences, many philosophers deny that actions are right just because God commands them. Suppose instead, then, that God commands right actions *because* they are right. This eliminates the problem that God's commands are arbitrary. Moreover, the notion that God commands us to do certain things because those things are morally right fits with the traditional belief that God is morally good. However, answering Socrates' question this way is also problematic. If God commands certain actions *because* they are right, then it looks as if God is really irrelevant to the morality of that action. This is because those actions would have been right whether or not God commanded them—in this view God commanded them, after all, *because* they were independently right. Moral behavior, then, is less a matter of obeying God's commands than it is a matter of doing what is right in any case. But this view is contrary to divine command ethics.

Many philosophers, noting that both answers to Socrates' question seem unacceptable for divine command ethics, believe that divine command ethics is not a good theory: Although religion might be related to morality in various ways (for example, religious doctrines often include moral teaching), morality is not *dependent* on religion. However, other philosophers have attempted to respond to Socrates' question in a way that is still consistent with divine command ethics, without claiming either that God's commands are arbitrary or that morality is independent of God. For example, some have argued that divine commandments are unlike any other kind of commandment. If God is truly the source of these commandments, then that matters; their divine source *is* all that is needed to justify them. Bad commandments simply cannot come from an all-good source.

In addition to the question posed by Socrates, there are other important issues related to divine command ethics. One issue is the view that morality is a matter of obedience. Some philosophers believe that it is a mistake to view morality as consisting of obeying commands (divine or not), arguing instead that moral maturity requires more than just obedience for the sake of obedience. A child obeys commands. But one might expect an adult to acquire autonomy and the ability to reason thoughtfully about ethical issues and freely make moral decisions on the basis of that reasoning. Along these lines, one criticism of divine command theory is that it is contrary to human flourishing, which requires skills and abilities beyond simple obedience to commands. One defense of divine command ethics is that one can freely and autonomously choose to obey God's commands, and that doing so actually demonstrates moral maturity in the sense that one acts on the basis of recognizing certain facts (for instance, that one needs God's help to be moral) and takes responsibility for one's actions.

There are also issues related to the content of what God demands. First, how does one know what God commands and, hence, how to behave? Second, do God's commands tell us everything we need to know how to behave morally? Suppose, for instance, God's commands are just the Ten Commandments of the Old Testament. These commands do not seem to provide answers for every moral question one might face—for example, whether one should go to war to fight for a just cause or stay at home to care for one's ailing mother; whether to vote for one political candidate or another; or whether to disobey a racist law.

Theocracy

The term *theocracy* comes from two Greek words, *theos,* meaning "God" and *kratia,* meaning "rule." Theocracy is a form of government and usually is taken to mean that there is no official separation between the government and religion. More technically, however, a theocracy is a form of government in the sense that the structure of government is one in which religious officials are also governmental officials and religious doctrine forms at least part of the government. So, at the beginning of the 21st century, Iran is technically a theocracy, but Israel is not, even though Israel declares itself as a Jewish state. Most of Israel's laws and governmental structures are secular, as opposed to Iran, in which Islamic law, sharia, is also state law.

While the United States is a democracy (or, more technically, a republic), not a theocracy, the issue of the formal relationship between religion and government has been a part of American history from its beginning. The early colonies settled by European immigrants during the 1600s were involved in direct debate about the role of religion in their government. Some of the early colonies were, in fact, designed much along the lines of theocracies. For example, the Mayflower Compact that was adopted in 1620 by early English settlers spoke directly about forming a community ("a civil Body Politic") based on Christian scripture. Likewise, the Fundamental Orders of Connecticut from 1639 spoke of "an orderly and decent Government established according to God," with civil affairs to be "guided and governed" according to Christian laws.

On the other hand, Thomas Jefferson wrote explicitly of "building a wall of separation between Church and State," because, he wrote, religion is a private matter. In addition and for this reason, the U.S. Constitution included in the First Amendment the phrase that "Congress shall make no law respecting the establishment of religion, or prohibiting the free exercise thereof." Although there are religious symbols connected to government (for example, coins in the United States include the phrase "In God We Trust"), most aspects of religion are not part of the structure of government nor are they state law (even if some civil laws are motivated by and consistent with certain religious doctrine).

While most people see the issue of the formal separation of religion and government as a difference between democracy and theocracy, not everyone agrees or sees such a distinction. For example, many Muslim officials (including philosophers, theologians, and government officials) claim that no human has legitimate authority over any other human. All authority comes from and belongs to God. The only legitimate civil laws and, indeed, the only legitimate governments are those that rule in accordance with God's laws. Along these lines, the Muslim philosopher Abu'l A'la Mawdudi (1903–79) claimed that the only real democracy is a theocracy because no person, class, or group, not even the entire population of the state as a whole, can lay claim to sovereignty. God alone is the real sovereign; all others are merely His subjects. If God truly is the sovereign and lawgiver, then civil laws, those created and enforced by the state, need to be in accordance with the laws of God. Appropriate political power derives only from obedience to the laws of God, and people have an inherent right to overthrow inappropriate political systems just as much as they have an inherent duty to obey appropriate political systems. Nevertheless, most people (including many in Islamic countries) distinguish democracy and theocracy and advocate some separation between religion and government.

Nineteenth-Century Responses to Religion

During the 1800s, especially, there arose a new approach to religion. This approach was to look at religion from the outside, that is, from a sociological or psychological perspective. Religion was seen as a phenomenon to be studied and critiqued, just as governments or other social institutions might be studied and critiqued. Among the most influential critiques of religion were those offered by Karl Marx, Sigmund Freud, and Friedrich Nietzsche.

Karl Marx

Karl Marx (1818–83) was one of the most influential thinkers of modern times. His writings were not only important during his lifetime but also they shaped much of Western culture throughout the 20th century. His impact was vast in the areas of philosophy, economics, sociology, and politics. Marx was born in Trier, Prussia (now western Germany). His family background was Jewish, but his father converted to Christianity shortly before Marx was born. As a student, Marx studied philosophy and law at the University of Berlin and then at the University of Jena. For years, he worked as a journalist and newspaper editor, frequently criticizing his own government and other governments. In 1848, he published *The Manifesto of the Communist Party,* one of the most influential books of the modern era. After being banished from several European countries, he moved to Britain, where he lived in poverty but wrote hundreds of political and social articles and editorials. In 1867, he published *Das Kapital,* an analysis of economic systems and a critique of capitalism. He continued to live in Britain until his death in 1883.

Photograph of Karl Marx, published in *Reminiscences of Carl Schurz* in 1907

Marx famously described religion as the "opium of the people." Using opium can dull a person's suffering; however, it can also make a person sluggish and dull, and opium smokers are famous for spending their time dreaming opium-induced dreams. Similarly, according to Marx, religion is used by the people as a solace for their unhappy lives. Religion turns people's attention away from the alienation and unhappiness they suffer in a capitalist society and focuses their attention on illusions of an otherworldly realm. So, religion has the effect that people are more inclined to passively accept the conditions in which they live, rather than seek to change them, even when those conditions are oppressive (as Marx believed they were in a capitalist society).

Sigmund Freud

Sigmund Freud (1856–1939) is considered one of the most influential psychologists of the 20th century. Although he did not publish philosophy directly, his works on the nature of persons, the self, the mind, and human action had an important role in the writings of many philosophers since. Freud was born in Moravia (now part of the Czech Republic) and lived much of his life in Vienna, Austria. He attended medical school in Vienna and focused his studies on physiology and physics, both of which shaped his later ideas about human psychology. He later worked in France and Germany, practicing his new "science of psychoanalysis" and writing both the underlying theory as well as case studies. After the Nazis took power in Germany, Freud moved to Britain, where he stayed until his death.

Freud was openly an atheist and was very critical of religion, calling it "patently infantile." In various different writings, he spoke of religion as an illusion, that is, that the content of religion (at least, of many religious claims) simply does not match up with reality. Religion is, he said, an attempt to get control over the sensory world, not by means of science and technology, but by means of "wish-fulfillment." We might wish—and believe—that we could live forever, but for Freud, that is merely a wish. Further, Freud compared religion to a "childhood neurosis." Man is not made from the image of God, he said, but the reverse: God (or the concept of God) is made in the image of man. In particular, God is a father figure writ large. As young children, our fathers loom in our lives as almost larger than life. They are powerful, knowledgeable,

Photograph of Sigmund Freud, 1926 *(Photograph by Ferdinand Schmutzer)*

and dramatically shape what happens to us; they can be the source of bounty (they seem to be the source of food and shelter and love), but they can also be the source of punishment and retribution (they can punish us and make us behave to match their will). God is merely the "super" extension of a father figure.

Friedrich Nietzsche

Few philosophers have been as influential or as widely read as the German philosopher Friedrich Nietzsche (1844–1900). Although he is associated with existentialism, Nietzsche's work ranges beyond any one area of thought. He was appointed professor of philology (that is, language and classical texts) at the University of Basel in Sweden when he was just 24. Poor health forced him to resign in 1879, and for about the next 10 years Nietzsche lived a nomadic life in Europe, moving from place to place while he struggled with his health and continued to write. In January 1889, he collapsed on the street as he hugged a cab horse that had been beaten by its driver. He died 11 years later, without ever having recovered.

In one of his most important books, *Thus Spoke Zarathustra*, Nietzsche's character Zarathustra famously proclaimed that God is dead, a claim Nietzsche repeated in *The Gay Science*. By this Nietzsche did not mean that God had literally died; he did not believe God literally existed in the first place. Rather, Nietzsche's point was that God had ceased to play a significant role in people's lives. In other words, although people might talk as if they believed in God and lived by God's commands, as a matter of fact belief in God made very little difference to them. Yet the death of God (in this sense) raised serious questions. Many people had once regarded God not only as the source for meaning in life but also as the basis for morality as well. But if God does not make our lives meaningful, and if God does not tell us what is morally right and wrong, then what does? Regarding meaning, Nietzsche's answer was that meaning was to be found in *this* life and on this Earth—not in an afterlife or some other otherworldly realm. Rather than pinning one's hopes and goals on something outside our concrete lives, we can create meaning by making something of our lives in the world we actually live in. Nietzsche emphasized creativity as one aspect of an excellent, meaningful life, and in *Thus Spoke Zarathustra*, Nietzsche described the *overman* (sometimes translated as the *superman*). Man, Nietzsche wrote, is something to be overcome, and the overman is the meaning of the Earth. Humanity is something to be overcome in the sense that humans can become something much better than what we are now—freer, stronger, more creative, more affirming of life. The overman is the meaning of the Earth in the sense that what can give meaning to our lives is a striving to overcome—or, in Nietzsche's phrase, a striving to

Friedrich Nietzche, 1882 *(Photograph by Gustav Schultze)*

become what we *are* in the sense of striving to realize one's potential. In addition, with the diminished role of God in people's lives, we are free to create our own values. To put the point another way, because God does not provide the basis for morality, we must decide for ourselves what is good and what is not, what is worth valuing and what is not.

Although Nietzsche believed we are free to create our own values and decide for ourselves what is good and what is not, he clearly thought that some views about what is good (and what is not) are better than others. In *On the Genealogy of Morals* and other works, Nietzsche distinguished two different kinds of morality: master morality and slave morality. Master morality is positive in the sense that it is concerned mainly with the good, rather than being preoccupied with what it considers bad. For the master moralist, what is good has to do with creativity and excellence. Slave morality is a reaction against master morality and in that sense it is mainly negative. In particular, what motivates slave morality is resentment against the strong. Because the slave moralist fears and resents strength and excellence that he or she cannot (or, perhaps, does not) achieve, the slave moralist values weakness instead. Consider, for example, someone who would like to act as an individual rather than merely going along with the crowd but who does not have the inner strength to do so; she might come to resent the person who does. Similarly, someone who cannot achieve the greatness of a first-class artist or scientist, for example, might resent people who can. Reacting against them, she prefers to keep everyone at her level. So, whereas master morality strives for excellence, slave morality prefers that everyone remain mediocre. Whereas master morality is a morality of independence and achievement, slave morality is a morality of the "crowd" in a negative sense, or to use Nietzsche's term, *the herd.*

Nietzsche clearly preferred master morality to slave morality. However, he believed that in a historic struggle against master morality and slave morality, slave morality had won, and he associated slave morality with Christianity in particular. For example, he viewed traditional Christian virtues such as meekness and humility as being motivated by fear rather than by a genuine sense of harmony with others. In general, Nietzsche's critique of Christian morality is based largely on the view that it is life denying rather than life affirming. To put the point another way, Nietzsche regarded Christianity as being in opposition to a life of flourishing and achievement and in favor of a meek, passive existence instead. One reason for this is simply Christianity's focus on otherworldly entities such as God and soul; Nietzsche believed these were illusions and that Christianity irrationally focused on them at the expense of our real lives on Earth. In addition, Nietzsche charged Christianity with being life denying by rejecting human instincts (such as sexuality) and passions. In his assessment of Christianity, Nietzsche distinguished between Jesus and Christianity as a body of thought and was much more critical of the latter.

Twentieth-Century Philosophy

Today the primary metaphysical view of philosophers is a material-ist view, that is, that the world along with the things and events in the world are to be understood and explained in terms of them being material—not spiritual—things. For example, while earlier thinkers spoke of people as having both material features of the body, they also spoke of people as having mental features of the mind or as having spiritual features of the soul. However, more and more, philosophers have dismissed mental features of people as coming from some non-material source. Our mental features, such as memory or ability to think and comprehend, are seen as being purely material. As more is known about the brain, philosophers (and others) say that people's mental features can be understood and explained simply in terms of neurological (that is, material) causes and effects. As we come to know more about material causes of behaviors, we understand and explain people's actions in those terms. For instance, we understand that ill-ness is the result of physical causes, not the result of people's immoral actions or beliefs. At the same time as we rely on science and its basis in this materialist metaphysics, people around the world remain committed to religion and religious views about things and events in the world, highlighting perhaps more than ever questions about the nature of religion and its relationship with our scientific views.

Concluding Discussion Questions

1. Is the ontological argument for God's existence valid? Why or why not?
2. Is the cosmological argument for God's existence valid? Why or why not?
3. Is the design argument for God's existence valid? Why or why not?
4. How, if at all, is natural religion related to revealed religion? Can they be in conflict? If so, which is more important and why?
5. Is the problem of evil a genuine problem for theists? Why or why not? How does this problem relate to the problem of divine foreknowledge?
6. What, if anything, is wrong with theocracy? Does a theocracy follow from belief in divine command ethics? How, if at all, can someone accept either divine command ethics or theocracy and not accept the other?

Further Reading

Centore, F. F. *Theism or Atheism: The Eternal Debate.* Burlington, Vt.: Ashgate, 2004.

Dixon, Thomas. *Science and Religion: A Very Short Introduction.* Oxford: Oxford University Press, 2008.

Ford, David F. *Theology: A Very Short Introduction.* Oxford: Oxford University Press, 2000.

Haught, John F. *What Is Religion: An Introduction.* Mahwah, N.J.: Paulist Press, 1990.

Helm, Paul, ed. *Faith and Reason.* Oxford: Oxford University Press, 1999.

Hick, John. *Philosophy of Religion.* 4th ed. Englewood Cliffs, N.J.: Prentice Hall, 1989.

McGrath, Aliser E. *Science and Religion: An Introduction.* Oxford: Blackwell, 1998.

Noss, David S., and Blake R. Grangaard. *History of the World's Religions.* 12th ed. New York: Prentice Hall, 2007.

Peterson, Michael, William Hasker, Bruce Reichenbach, and David Basinger, eds. *Philosophy of Religion: Selected Readings.* 3rd ed. Oxford: Oxford University Press, 2006.

Pojman, Louis P., ed. *Philosophy of Religion: An Anthology.* 5th ed. Belmont, Calif.: Wadsworth, 2007.

Rowe, William L. *Philosophy of Religion: An Introduction.* 4th ed. Belmont, Calif.: Wadsworth, 2006.

Smart, J. J. C., and J. J. Haldane. *Atheism and Theism.* New York: Wiley-Blackwell, 2002.

Glossary

cosmological argument   an argument intended to prove God's existence by showing that the universe (or cosmos) exists because it was created by God.

deism   the view that God was the cause of the universe, but without any commitment to other religious claims (such as the divinity of Jesus or the existence of angels).

design (teleological) argument   an argument intended to prove God's existence by showing that things and events in the world, as well as the world itself, are so orderly and complex that they must be the result of design; God is the designer.

divine command ethics   the view that standards, criteria, and sources for moral and ethical claims are whatever is commanded by God.

evil, problem of   an argument intended to challenge or disprove God's existence by showing that the presence of evil in the world is inconsistent with a perfect God.

fideism   the view that faith is independent of, superior to, and perhaps even in conflict with reason as a means of knowing.

Five Ways   five arguments proposed by the medieval philosopher and theologian Thomas Aquinas to prove God's existence.

foreknowledge, problem of divine   an argument intended to challenge or disprove God's existence by showing that God's omniscience (or God being all-knowing) is inconsistent with human free will and also with other religious claims (such as human responsibility for sin).

materialism/dualism   views about the fundamental nature of persons, whether they are constituted only by their material, physical nature (materialism) or whether they are constituted by both material and nonmaterial, or spiritual, nature (dualism).

natural religion   the approach to religion that focuses on evidence from nature of the truth of religious claims; independent of, and sometimes seen in opposition to, revealed religion.

necessary being   a being that exists necessarily (in the terminology of some philosophers: a being that exists in all possible worlds).

omnibenevolence   a term that means all-good; commonly held to be a feature of God.

omnipotence   a term that means all-powerful; commonly held to be a feature of God.

omniscience   a term that means all-knowing; commonly held to be a feature of God.

ontological argument   an argument intended to prove God's existence by showing that the very nature of God as a perfect being (or as "that than which nothing greater can be conceived") implies God's existence; by definition, God must exist.

paradox of the stone   an argument intended to challenge or disprove God's existence, or at least God's omnipotence, by asking whether God could create a stone too heavy for God to lift; either answer (yes or no) implies that God is not all-powerful.

Pascal's wager   an argument intended to show that believing in God is more rational than not believing in God.

revealed religion   the approach to religion that focuses on some form of direct contact with divine being(s), either through direct personal experience or through sacred scripture based on direct contact; independent of, and sometimes seen in opposition to, natural religion.

theocracy   a form of government in the sense that the structure of government is one in which religious officials are also governmental officials and religious doctrine forms at least part of the government.

theodicy   religious concerns that focus on resolving the problem of evil and justifying religious belief.

Key People

Anselm (1033–1109) *Italian-born medieval theologian who became archbishop of Canterbury in England. He is most famous for formulating the ontological argument for God's existence, claiming that God, conceived of as the greatest thing possible, must exist. The selection below is from his work* Proslogium.

And so, Lord, do thou, who dost give understanding to faith, give me, and so far as thou knowest it to be profitable, to understand that thou art as we believe; and that thou art that which we believe. And, indeed, we believe that thou art a being than which nothing greater can be conceived. Or is there no such nature, since the fool hath said in his heart, there is no God? (Psalms XIV.1). But, at any rate, this very fool, when he hears of this being of which I speak—a being than which nothing greater can be conceived—understands what he hears, and what he understands is in his understanding; although he does not understand it to exist.

For it is one thing for an object to be in the understanding, and another to understand that the object exists. When a painter first conceives of what he will afterwards perform, he has it in his understanding, but he does not yet understand it to be, because he has not yet performed it. But after he has made the painting, he both has it in his understanding, and he understands that it exists, because he has made it.

Hence, even the fool is convinced that something exists in the understanding, at least, than which nothing greater can be conceived. For, when he hears of this, he understands it. And whatever is understood, exists in the understanding. And, assuredly that, than which nothing greater can be conceived, cannot exist in the understanding alone. For, suppose it exists in the understanding alone: then it can be conceived to exist in reality; which is greater.

Therefore, if that, than which nothing greater can be conceived, exists in the understanding alone, the very being, than which nothing greater can be conceived, is one, than which a greater can be conceived. But obviously this is impossible. Hence, there is no doubt that there exists a being, than which nothing greater can be conceived, and it exists both in the understanding and in reality.

And it assuredly exists so truly, that it cannot be conceived not to exist. For, it is possible to conceive of a being which cannot be conceived not to exist; and this is greater than one which can be conceived not to exist. Hence, if that, than which nothing greater can be conceived, can be conceived not to exist, it is not that, than which nothing greater can be conceived. But this is an irreconcilable contradiction. There is, then, so truly a being than which nothing greater can be conceived to exist, that it cannot even be conceived not to exist; and this being thou art, O Lord, our God.

[St. Anselm. *Proslogium; Monologium: An Appendix in Behalf of the Fool by Gaunilo; and Cur Deus Homo.* Translated from the Latin by Sidney Norton Deane, B.A., with an Introduction, Bibliography, and Reprints of the Opinions of Leading Philosophers and Writers on the Ontological Argument. 1903. Reprint, Chicago: Open Court, 1926.]

Aristotle (384–322 B.C.E.)   *Greek philosopher who today is considered probably one of the two most influential Western philosophers of all time, along with his teacher, Plato. With respect to religion, he is known for having given a version of the cosmological argument, claiming that God is the Unmoved Mover (or the ultimate cause of changes in the world).*

Since there must always be motion without intermission, there must necessarily be something . . . that first imparts motion, and this first mover must be unmoved . . . It is clear, then, that though there may be countless instances of the perishing of some principles that are unmoved but impart motion, and though many things that move themselves perish and are succeeded by others that come into being, and though one thing that is unmoved moves one thing while another moves another, nevertheless there is something that comprehends them all, and that as something apart from each of them, and this it is that is the cause of the fact that some things are and others are not and of the continuous process of change: and this causes the motion of the other movers, while they are the causes of the motion of other things. Motion, then, being eternal, the first mover . . . will be eternal also.

[Aristotle. *Physics. Book 8.* In *The Basic Works of Aristotle*, edited by Richard McKeon. New York: Random House, 1941.]

Augustine (354–430)   *Medieval philosopher and theologian, born in what is now Algeria. Among his writings, he is famous for having addressed the problem of evil and for having responded that evil is merely the lack or absence (what he calls a privation) of good and that greater good comes about as a result of the existence of some evil.*

What, after all, is anything we call evil except the privation of good? In animal bodies, for instance, sickness and wounds are nothing but the privation of health. When a cure is effected, the evils which were present (i.e., the sickness and the wounds) do not retreat and go elsewhere. Rather, they simply do not exist anymore. For such evil is not a substance; the wound or the disease is a defect of the bodily substance which, as a substance, is good. Evil, then, is an accident, i.e., a privation of that good which is called health . . .

All of nature is good, since the Creator of all nature is supremely good. But nature is not supremely and immutably good as is the Creator of it. Thus the good in created things can be diminished and augmented. For good to be diminished is evil . . . When, however, a thing is corrupted, its corruption is an evil because it is, by just so much, a privation of the good.

[Augustine. *Confessions and Enchiridion.* Translated and edited by Albert C. Outler. Philadelphia: Westminster, 1955.]

Freud, Sigmund (1856–1939)   *Austrian psychologist renowned for developing psychoanalysis and for arguing that people's actions often are shaped by nonconscious forces. He was critical of religion, saying that it was an "infantile obsession." The following passage is from his work* Civilization and Its Discontents.

In my *Future of an Illusion* I was concerned much less with the deepest sources of the religious feeling than with what the common man understands by his religion—with the system of doctrines and promises which on the one hand explains to him the riddles of this world with enviable completeness, and, on the other, assures him that a careful Providence will watch over his life and will compensate him in a future existence for any frustrations he suffers here. The common man cannot imagine this Providence otherwise than in the figure of an enormously exalted father. Only such a being can understand the needs of the children of men and be softened by their prayers and placated by the signs of their remorse. The whole thing is so patently infantile, so foreign to reality, that to anyone with a friendly attitude to humanity it is painful to think that the great majority of mortals will never be able to rise above this view of life. It is still more humiliating to discover how a large number of people living today, who cannot but see that this religion is not tenable, nevertheless try to defend it piece by piece in a series of pitiful rearguard actions. One would like to mix among the ranks of the believers in order to meet these philosophers, who think they can rescue the God of religion by replacing him by an impersonal shadowy and abstract principle, and to address them with the warning words: "Thou shalt not take the name of the Lord thy God in vain!" And if some of the great men of the past acted in the same way, no appeal can be made to their example: we know why they were obliged to.

[Freud, Sigmund. *Das Unbehagen in der Kultur (Civilization and Its Discontents)*. Vienna: Internationaler Psychoanalytischer Verlag, 1930. Available online. Chrysoma Associates Ltd. URL: http://lightoftheimagination.com/Freud-Civil-Disc.pdf. Accessed June 28, 2011.]

Hume, David (1711–1776)   *Scottish philosopher who rejected the design argument, saying that we had no good basis for thinking that the analogy of a designer could be inferred since we had no other universes to compare ours with. The passage below is from his work* Dialogues Concerning Natural Religion.

What I chiefly scruple in this subject, said Philo, is not so much, that all religious arguments are by Cleanthes reduced to experience, as that they appear not to be even the most certain and irrefragable of that inferior kind. That a stone will fall, that fire will burn, that the earth has solidity, we have observed a thousand and a thousand times; and when any new instance of this nature is presented, we draw without hesitation the accustomed inference. The exact similarity of the cases gives us a perfect assurance of a similar event; and a stronger evidence is never desired nor sought after. But whenever you depart, in the least, from the similarity of the cases, you diminish proportionably the evidence; and may at last bring it to a very weak *analogy,* which is confessedly liable to error and uncertainty. After having experienced the circulation of the blood in human creatures, we make no doubt that it takes place in Titus and Maevius: But from its circulation in frogs and fishes, it is only a presumption, though a strong one, from analogy, that it takes place in men and other animals. The analogical reasoning is much weaker, when we infer the circulation of the sap in vegetables from our experience that the blood circulates in animals; and those, who hastily followed that imperfect analogy, are found, by more accurate experiments, to have been mistaken.

If we see a house, Cleanthes, we conclude, with the greatest certainty, that it had an architect or builder, because this is precisely that species of *effect,* which we have experienced to proceed from that species of cause. But surely you will not affirm, that the universe bears such a resemblance to a house, that we can with the same certainty infer a similar cause, or that the analogy is here entire and perfect. The dissimilitude is so striking, that the utmost you can here pretend to is a guess, a conjecture, a presumption concerning a similar cause; and how that pretension will be received in the world, I leave you to consider.

Were a man to abstract from everything which he knows or has seen, he would be altogether incapable, merely from his own ideas, to determine what kind of scene the universe must be, or to give the preference to one state or situation of things above another. For as nothing, which he clearly conceives, could be esteemed impossible or implying footing; nor could he assign any just reason, why he adheres to one idea or system, and rejects the others, which are equally possible.

Again, after he opens his eyes, and contemplates the world, as it really is, it would be impossible for him, at first, to assign the cause of any one event, much less, of the whole of things or of the universe. He might set his fancy a rambling; and she might bring him in an infinite variety of reports and representations. These would all be possible; but being all equally possible, he would never, of himself, give a satisfactory account for his preferring one of them to the rest. Experience alone can point out to him the true cause of any phenomenon.

[Hume, David. *Dialogues Concerning Natural Religion*. Edited by Norman Kemp Smith. Indianapolis, Ind.: Bobbs-Merrill, 1947.]

Kant, Immanuel (1724–1804) *German philosopher who made what he called the philosophical "Copernican revolution," arguing that objects conform to our knowledge, rather than knowledge conforming to objects; he believed that the mind structures experience according to certain categories. While Kant rejected the usual philosophical arguments for God's existence (namely, the ontological, cosmological, and design arguments), he did support a moral argument for God's existence, that is, that morality required God as a standard. The following passage is from his work* Critique of Pure Reason.

Happiness is the condition of a rational being in the world, in whose existence everything goes according to wish and will. It thus rests on the harmony of nature with his entire end and with the essential determining ground of his will . . . Still, the acting rational being in the world is not at the same time the cause of the world and of nature itself. Hence there is not the slightest ground in the moral law for a necessary connection between the morality and proportionate happiness of a being which belongs to the world as one of its parts and as thus dependent on it . . . Nevertheless, in the practical task of pure reason, i.e., in the necessary endeavor after the highest good, such a connection is postulated as necessary: we should seek to further the highest good (which therefore must be at least possible). Therefore also the existence is postulated of a cause of the whole of nature, itself distinct from nature, which contains the ground of the exact coincidence of happiness with morality . . . Therefore, the highest good is possible in the world only on the supposition of a supreme cause of nature which has a causality corresponding to the moral intention . . . Therefore, the supreme cause of nature, in so far as it must be presupposed for the highest good, is a being which is the cause (and consequently the author) of nature through understanding and will, i.e., God . . . Therefore, it is morally necessary to assume the existence of God.

[Kant, Immanuel. *Critique of Pure Reason*. 2nd rev. ed. Translated by F. Max Mueller. New York: Macmillan, 1922.]

Kierkegaard, Søren (1813–1855)   *Danish philosopher considered one of the founding figures of existentialism. A Christian, Kierkegaard believed that Christianity involved a leap of faith and a passionate commitment. The following selection is from his book* Concluding Unscientific Postscript to Philosophical Fragments.

The object of faith is the reality of another, and the relationship is one of infinite interest. The object of faith is not a doctrine, for then the relationship would be intellectual, and it would be of importance not to botch it, but to realize the maximum intellectual relationship. The object of faith is not a teacher with a doctrine; for when a teacher has a doctrine, the doctrine is *eo ipso* more important than the teacher, and the relationship is again intellectual, and it again becomes important not to botch it, but to realize the maximum intellectual relationship. The object of faith is the reality of the teacher, that the teacher really exists. The answer of faith is therefore unconditionally yes or no. For it does not concern a doctrine, as to whether the doctrine is true or not; it is the answer to a question concerning a fact: "Do you or do you not suppose that he has really existed?" And the answer, it must be noted, is to lay so great and infinite a stress on the question whether he has existed or not. If the object of faith is a human being, therefore, the whole proposal is the vagary of a stupid person, who had not even understood the spirit of the intellectual and the aesthetic. The object of faith is hence the reality of the God-man in the sense of his existence. But existence involves first and foremost particularity, and this is why thought must abstract from existence, because the particular cannot be thought, but only the universal. The object of faith is thus God's reality in existence as a particular individual, the fact that God has existed as an individual human being.

Christianity is no doctrine concerning the unity of the divine and the human, or concerning the identity of subject and object; nor is it any other of the logical transcriptions of Christianity. If Christianity were a doctrine, the relationship to it would not be one of faith, for only an intellectual type of relationship can correspond to a doctrine. Christianity is therefore not a doctrine, but the fact that God existed.

The realm of faith is thus not a class for numskulls in the sphere of the intellectual, or an asylum for the feeble-minded. Faith constitutes a sphere all by itself, and every misunderstanding of Christianity may at once be recognized by its transforming it into a doctrine, transferring it to the sphere of the intellectual. The maximum of attainment within the sphere of the intellectual, namely, to realize an entire indifference as to the reality of the teacher, is in the sphere of faith at the opposite end of the scale. The maximum of attainment within the sphere of faith is to become infinitely interested in the reality of the teacher.

[Kierkegaard, Søren. *Concluding Unscientific Postscript to Philosophical Fragments*. Edited and translated by Howard V. Hong and Edna H. Hong. Princeton, N.J.: Princeton University Press, 1992.]

Marx, Karl (1818–1883)   *German philosopher and political theorist. Marx was influenced by Hegel but believed that Hegel had neglected the material conditions under which people actually live. Marx advocated dialectical materialism, according to which history unfolds in a developmental way and will ultimately lead to communism. In the selection below he speaks of religion as the opium of the people.*

The basis of irreligious criticism is this: man makes religion; religion does not make man. Religion is indeed man's self-consciousness and self-awareness so long as he has not found himself or has lost himself again. But man is not an abstract being outside the world. Man is the human world, the state, society. This state, this society, produce religion which is an inverted world consciousness, because they are an inverted world . . .

Religious suffering is at the same time an expression of real suffering and a protest against real suffering. Religion is the sigh of the oppressed creature, the sentiment of a heartless world, and the soul of soulless conditions. It is the opium of the people.

The abolition of religion as the illusory happiness of men, is a demand for their real happiness. The call to abandon their illusions about their condition is a call to abandon a condition which requires illusions.

[Marx, Karl. *Critique of Hegel's Philosophy of Right.* Edited by Joseph O'Malley. Translated by Annette Jolin and Joseph O'Malley. Cambridge: Cambridge University Press, 1970.]

Nietzsche, Friedrich (1844–1900) *German philosopher who wrote on topics ranging from aesthetics and ethics to epistemology and the nature of reality. Nietzsche is famous for his pronouncement that God is dead. With the death of God, Nietzsche believed humans needed to create their own values. In the passage below, Nietzsche claims that what is good is power, as opposed to the qualities he negatively associated with Christianity. By power, Nietzsche did not mean power over others (such as political power), but rather the flourishing of oneself, such as with creativity and maximizing one's potential.*

What is good? Everything that heightens the feeling of power in man, the will to power, power itself.

What is bad? Everything that is born of weakness.

What is happiness? The feeling that power is growing, that resistance is overcome. Not contentedness but more power; not peace but war; not virtue but fitness (Renaissance virtue, *virtù*, virtue that is moraline-free).

The weak and the failures shall perish: first principle of our love of man. And they shall even be given every possible assistance.

What is more harmful than any vice? Active pity for all the failures and all the weak: Christianity.

[Nietzche, Friedrich. *The Antichrist.* Translated by H. L. Mencken. New York: Knopf, 1941. Available online. URL: www.gutenberg.org/files/19322/19322-h/ 19322-h.htm. Accessed July 8, 2011.]

Paley, William (1743–1805)   *English theologian who famously argued for the existence of God through his version of the design argument. The selection below, from his book* Natural Theology, *introduces his famous watchmaker analogy.*

In crossing a heath, suppose I pitched my foot against a *stone,* and were asked how the stone came to be there, I might possibly answer, that for anything I knew to the contrary it had lain there for ever, nor would it, perhaps, be very easy to show the absurdity of this answer. But suppose I had found a *watch* upon the ground, and it should be inquired how the watch happened to be in that place, I should hardly think of the answer which I had before given, that for anything I knew the watch might have always been there. Yet why should not this answer serve for the watch as well as for the stone; why is it not as admissible in the second case as in the first? For this reason, and for no other, namely, that when we come to inspect the watch, we perceive—what we could not discover in the stone—that its several parts are framed and put together for a purpose, e.g., that they are so formed and adjusted as to produce motion, and that motion so regulated as to point out the hour of the day; that if the different parts had been differently shaped from what they are, or placed after any other manner or in any other order than that in which they are placed, either no motion at all would have been carried on in the machine, or none which would have answered the use that is now served by it.

This mechanism being observed—it requires indeed an examination of the instrument, and perhaps some previous knowledge of the subject, to perceive and understand it; but being once, as we have said, observed and understood, the inference we think is inevitable, that the watch must have had a maker—that there must have existed, at some time and at some place or other, an artificer or artificers who formed it for the purpose which, we find it actually to answer, who comprehended its construction and designed its use.

Were there no example in the world of contrivance except that of the eye, it would be alone sufficient to support the conclusion which we draw from it, as to the necessity of an intelligent Creator. It could never be got rid of, because it could not be accounted for by any other supposition which did not contradict all the principles we possess of knowledge—the principles according to which things do, as often as they can be brought to the test of experience, turn out to be true or false . . .

The argument is cumulative, in the fullest sense of that term. The eye proves it without the ear, the ear without the eye. The proof in each example is complete, for when the design of the part, and the conduciveness of its structure to that design is shown, the mind may set itself at rest; no future consideration can detract any thing from the force of the example.

[Paley, William. *Natural Theology*. Albany, N.Y.: Daniel & Samuel Whiting, 1803. Available online. URL: http://www.scribd.com/doc/2063397/William-Paley-Natural-Theology-Teleological-Argument. Accessed July 8, 2011.]

Plantinga, Alvin   (1932–)   *American philosopher who has written extensively on religious epistemology and on the ontological argument. In the passage below, Plantinga argues that the possibility of there being a perfect being (God) entails that there is such a being.*

(1) It is possible that there is a greatest possible being.
(2) Therefore, there is a possible being that in some world W' or other has a maximum degree of greatness—a degree of greatness that is nowhere exceeded.
(3) A being B has the maximum degree of greatness in a given possible world W only if B *exists in every possible world*.

(1) and (2) are the premises of this argument; and what follows is that if W' had been actual, B would have existed in every possible world . . . But logical possibilities and impossibilities do not vary from world to world . . . Accordingly, B's not existence is impossible in every possible world; hence it is impossible in *this* world; hence B exists and exists necessarily.

[Plantinga, Alvin. *God, Freedom, and Evil*. Grand Rapids, Mich.: William B. Eerdmans, 1974.]

Thomas Aquinas (1225–1274)   *Italian medieval philosopher often considered one of the most important thinkers of the Middle Ages. Much of his life's work involved attempts to blend and reconcile teachings of the Catholic Church with the writings of Aristotle. In his most famous work,* Summa Theologia, *he offered what has come to be known as the Five Ways of proving God's existence. The passage below presents two of those ways; both are versions of the cosmological argument.*

The second way is from the nature of efficient cause. In the world of sensible things we find there is an order of efficient causes. There is no case known (neither is it, indeed, possible) in which a thing is found to be the efficient cause of itself; for so it would be prior to itself, which is impossible. Now in efficient causes it is not possible to go on to infinity, because in all efficient causes following in order, the first is the cause of the intermediate cause, and the intermediate is the cause of the ultimate cause, whether the intermediate cause be several, or one only. Now to take away the cause is to take away the effect. Therefore, if there be no first cause among the efficient causes, there will be no ultimate, nor any intermediate, cause. But if in efficient causes it is possible to go on to infinity, there will be no first efficient cause, neither will there be an ultimate effect, nor any intermediate efficient causes; all of which is plainly false. Therefore it is necessary to admit a first efficient cause, to which everyone gives the name of God.

The third way is taken from possibility and necessity, and runs thus. We find in nature things that are possible to be and not to be, since they are found to be generated, and to be corrupted, and consequently, it is possible for them to be and not to be. But it is impossible for these always to exist, for that which can non-be at some time is not. Therefore, if everything can not-be, then at one time there was nothing in existence. Now if this were true, even now there would be nothing in existence, because that which does not exist begins to exist only through something already existing. Therefore, if at one time nothing was in existence, it would have been impossible for anything to have begun to exist; and thus even now nothing would be in existence—which is absurd. Therefore, not all being are merely

194 REALITY, RELIGION, AND THE MIND

possible, but there must exist something the existence of which is necessary. But every necessary thing either has its necessity caused by another, or not. Now it is impossible to go on to infinity in necessary things which have their necessity caused by another, as has already been proved in regard to efficient causes. Therefore we cannot but admit the existence of some being having of itself its own necessity, and not receiving it from another, but rather causing in others their necessity. This all men speak of as God.

[Thomas Aquinas. *Summa Theologia*. In *The Library of Original Sources*, edited by Oliver J. Thatcher. Vol. 5: *The Early Medieval World*, 359–363. Milwaukee: University Research Extension Co., 1907).]

PART III
Philosophy of Mind

Introductory Discussion Questions

1. Do you ever know for sure what another person is thinking or feeling? If yes, how? If not, why not?
2. Could something have a mind if it does not have a brain? Why or why not?
3. If you looked into a brain, you would not see thoughts, feelings, or consciousness. Does this mean that there must be more to the mind than the brain? Why or why not?
4. A human egg that has just been fertilized does not seem to be conscious, but a newborn baby does. At what point does consciousness arise?
5. Are there any computers that have minds? Could a computer *ever* have a mind? Why or why not?
6. Does a pet dog or cat have a mind? How could you tell?

What Is Philosophy of Mind?

Most people would say that some things, such as normal adult human beings, clearly have minds. They think, perceive, and feel. Other things, such as bricks, clearly do not. But in between there are cases that are less clear: Perhaps a frog has a mind, and perhaps a computer capable of carrying on a conversation with a human has a mind. But it is not obvious. Just because something responds to the environment, as a frog does, does not mean that it has a mind: An automatic thermostat responds to the environment by turning on and off the furnace according to the environmental temperature, but an automatic thermostat does not have a mind. What *does* it mean to have a mind? Philosophers of mind ask philosophical questions about mind; this is just one of them. Many of the fundamental questions in the philosophy of mind are metaphysical. That is, they are about the nature of mind and features of mind. For instance, is mind physical? What sorts of things can have minds? Could a computer ever have a mind? What are the basic features of mind? And what is the nature of those features? For instance, adult humans have consciousness. But what does it mean to have consciousness?

One important topic in the philosophy of mind is the mind/body problem. This is the issue of how to understand the relation between the mind and the body. It is called a problem because it has been difficult to give an adequate description of that relation; there is no universally accepted answer to the mind/body problem. Consider what appear to be some basic facts about the mind and the body. The body, of course, is physical, and it has physical properties: It can be weighed, it has a certain color, and it is located in space. The mind, however, is not obviously physical. One's thoughts do not seem to be the kinds of things that can be weighed or have a certain color. Yet there is clearly a close connection between the mind and the body. First, our mind seems to cause our body to move: When you want to walk away from reading this text, it seems that your desire to walk away will cause you to walk away. Moreover, what happens to the body seems to have an effect on the mind: Drinking hot chocolate, for instance, might cause you to feel warmth and pleasure. When the brain is damaged, the mind is damaged also; when a drug affects a person's brain, a person's mind is also affected. How can we explain the apparent differences between the mind and the body, and how can we account for the apparent close connection between the mind and the body? This is the mind/body problem.

One answer to the mind/body problem is dualism. According to dualism, the mind and the body are different in the sense that mind is nonphysical and the body is physical. In one version of dualism, famously defended by the 17th-century philosopher René Descartes (1596–1650), mind is a nonphysical substance and body is a physical substance. In another version of dualism, property dualism, the mind consists of nonphysical properties (the body, of course, has physical properties). Dualism has been widely criticized. There are many reasons why philosophers have rejected dualism, but among the most significant is that dualism cannot account for mind/body interaction. Mental states, such as thinking and wishing, have an effect on bodily states, as when we physically carry out our plans and act on our desires. Bodily states, such as states of pain, have an effect on mental states, as when we feel the sensation of cold when jumping into a pool. An objection to dualism is that it is not clear how such interaction is possible if mind is nonphysical (how could a nonphysical mind cause a physical body to move?). In addition, some philosophers have pointed out that if mental events do cause bodily events, this would violate the well-established scientific law of the conservation of energy (this is because mental events would, by causing bodily events, introduce energy into the universe, energy that would not have previously existed).

According to physicalist views of the mind, the mind is physical. So, for at least some of these views, to explain the mind, we would not ever need to refer to anything nonphysical: A complete explanation of all the relevant physical facts would be enough to account for mind. According to identity theory, the mind is identical to the brain, or as the point is usually made, mental states are identical to brain states. This view has the advantage of explaining why there would be a very close relation between what goes on in our minds and what goes on in our brains: States of the mind just *are* states of the brain. However, identity theory also suggests that only things that have brains can have minds. This would rule out machines. Yet it has seemed to many philosophers that it should not be necessary to have a brain in the human sense (a carbon-based brain, for instance) in order to have a mind. That is, it has seemed at least possible that other beings could have minds even if they did not have human-type brains.

Inspired in part by this reasoning, functionalist views of mind focus on what a brain *does* instead of what it is made of. According to functionalism, mental states are to be identified with functional roles—that is, roughly, with what mental states *do* (their functions). For example, the mental state of pain plays a certain role. It is caused by certain things, such as illness and injury. It causes certain behavior, such as seeking pain medicine and rest. It is also related to other mental states; for instance, the feeling of pain might make a person feel irritable. According to functionalism, whatever internal state plays the role of being caused by illness or injury, causing behavior such as seeking rest, and causing other mental states such as irritability counts as the mental state of pain. In humans, a particular state of the brain (and nervous system) play that role. But in another kind of being, a being made of different kind of stuff and without a brain, another sort of inner state might play that role. Most functionalists believe that such inner states are always physical states; that is, most functionalists are physicalists about mind. Although functionalism is currently the most prominent view about the nature of mind, functionalism faces a number of serious objections. Perhaps the central project in philosophy of mind today is to give a physicalist account of mind that escapes key objections, many of which involve features of mind described below.

Qualia are *feels* that we experience in our mental lives—for example, the sensation of seeing red, the taste of rhubarb, the emotion of joy, and the mood of restlessness. Philosophers debate the precise nature of qualia. In addition, it is not clear how qualia fit into physicalist views about mind. To illustrate this point, some philosophers have described particular thought experiments meant to show that there is more to mind than what is physical. For example, suppose a scientist comes to learn all the physical facts about color but never sees any color; she lives all her life in a room in which everything she sees is black, white, or a shade of gray. Now suppose she emerges from that room and sees the color red for the first time. According to this thought experiment (proposed by Australian philosopher Frank Jackson [1943–]), the scientist would have learned something new about color: She would have learned what it was like to see red. If, however, she learned something new, then there is more to our mental lives than the physical facts. To put the point another way, there is something that it is *like* to see red, and all the physical facts about color do not capture this fact. So, according to the argument, physicalist views about mind are wrong.

Another important topic in the philosophy of mind is consciousness. Philosophers question what it means to be conscious. Consciousness is not, for example, just being awake. This is because one can be conscious of something even while sleeping, as when one is conscious of the contents of one's dreams. Nor is consciousness just awareness of one's environment. An amoeba responds to stimuli and is aware of its environment in that sense, but it seems unlikely that an amoeba is conscious. One way of characterizing consciousness is to say that a creature is conscious if there is something that it is like to be that creature. There seems to be something that it is like to be a bat, something involving being nocturnal, flying, and eating insects. By contrast, there does not seem to be anything that it is like to be a brick. Although this is a starting point for what counts as consciousness, philosophers discuss other features of consciousness and whether consciousness serves a function. In addition, as with qualia, it is controversial whether consciousness can be fully explained in physical terms. The American philosopher Thomas Nagel (1937–) famously argued that knowing all the physical facts about a bat would not tell us what it is like to be a bat. If this is true, then it suggests that there is more to consciousness than the physical facts. This line of reasoning continues to be much discussed.

Intentionality is another issue in the philosophy of mind. Intentionality is "aboutness." Minds are commonly thought to have intentionality. This is because mental states such as thoughts, desires, and beliefs are about something; one does not just have a desire, for instance, one has a desire *about* something or another (say, about visiting Norway). So some states of mind (some mental states) are about something, and those states of mind are said to be intentional. In philosophy, *intentional* is a technical term; it does not mean having an intention or a goal, as it does ordinarily. However, some mental states in the technical sense (being about something) do involve intentions in the ordinary sense (having an intention). For instance, having the intention to visit Paris is a mental state that is intentional in the technical sense because it is about Paris. Not all intentional states in the technical sense have to do with intentions, however. The belief that turtles are reptiles is intentional in the technical sense, for example (it is about turtles), but just having this belief does not mean having an intention to do anything.

The German psychologist Franz Brentano (1838–1917) suggested that intentionality was the mark of the mental: that is, that all mental states have intentionality, and that only mental states have intentionality. This claim, known as Brentano's thesis, has been the subject of much discussion. Some philosophers dispute that all mental states have intentionality, and others dispute that *only* mental states have intentionality.

In addition, as with qualia and consciousness, it is not obvious how physicalist accounts of the mind can adequately account for intentionality. If the mind is physical, then intentionality must be explained in physical terms as well. Yet it is not clear how anything that is merely physical could be *about* something. Consider a lamp, for example: A lamp does not seem to be about anything. Somewhat in the same way, it is not clear how physical items such as brain cells could be about anything, even though mental states are about something.

Artificial intelligence, a discipline that studies the possibility of intelligence in computers, is also relevant in the philosophy of mind. This is because artificial intelligence might shed light on the nature of thought: If computers could be capable of genuine thought, that would seem to tell us something about the nature of thought. Some philosophers believe that humans think in ways analogous to how a computer performs operations, therefore using models of thought in computers could be used to understand thought in human beings.

The Mind/Body Problem, Dualism, and Monism

Dualism and monism are two different ways of addressing the mind/body problem, a core issue in the philosophy of mind. So it is worth saying something about the mind/body problem, the problem of how to make sense of the relationship between the mind and the body, especially the brain. It is because we have minds that we can have mental experiences—that we are able to think, believe, feel, perceive, and so on. But is the mind physical, like the body? Could the mind even be identical with the brain? If the mind is not physical, then what exactly is it? The mind/body problem is a philosophical *problem* in the sense that its answer is far from clear: There is no widespread agreement about how to understand the relationship between the mind and the body.

One one hand, there appear to be some basic differences between the mind and the brain (a part of the body). For instance, the brain has a certain weight and color. But a person's thoughts do not seem to have weight or color; if you are thinking right now that you would like to eat lunch, for instance, plausibly that thought is not blue or purple or any other color. In addition, your thought is also about something, namely about eating lunch. But your brain does not seem to be *about* anything—it is just a brain. Another way that the mind seems to be different from the brain is that you can know what you are thinking just by looking inward at yourself. But you cannot know about your brain just by looking inward; for instance, looking inward does not tell you which parts of your brain are active at any particular moment. These apparent differences between the mind and the body suggest that the mind is not the same thing as the brain. These differences might even suggest that the mind is not physical.

On the other hand, science has shown that the mind and the brain are very closely connected. For example, certain drugs that affect the brain also cause mental activity, such as hallucinations and euphoria. Stimulating the brain in certain ways causes people to have particular mental experiences—for example, to remember childhood events. In addition, when people experience brain damage, their minds are also affected; in severe cases, brain-damaged people might lose consciousness completely for the rest of their lives. These facts suggest that the mind is physical. After all, why else would changes in a *physical* brain cause changes in a person's mind? At the least, any account of the mind must explain why the mind and the brain are so closely connected.

Views about the mind can be said to fall within two broad divisions: dualism and monism. Dualism states that the mind is nonphysical, unlike the body, which is physical. Dualists hold that creatures with minds, such as humans, have a *dual* nature, in the sense that they are both physical and nonphysical: What is bodied about them is physical, but what is mental about them is nonphysical. This view is consistent with some common assumptions about the mind and the body, such as that the mind and body are fundamentally different and that humans are not *just* very sophisticated collections of physical matter (there is something nonphysical about them); it is also consistent with the view that humans have an immaterial soul. The word *monism* derives from the Greek word *monos,* meaning "single," and according to monism, mind and matter are of essentially the same kind of stuff. In other words, there is a single category of stuff to which mind and matter both belong. One version of monism is idealism, according to which reality is fundamentally mental: In this view, ordinary objects such as one's body, houses, and trees are really mental in character, even if they seem to be physical (these objects really do exist, according to many idealists—it is just that they are in some sense mental objects rather than physical objects). Another version of monism states that both mind and matter are essentially material, or physical. On this view, there is nothing more to the mind and all mental experiences (thoughts, feelings, sensations, etc.) than physical stuff and physical processes. Materialists agree that people have minds and mental experiences, but they explain these in material, scientific terms only. One version of materialist monism is logical behaviorism, which understands mind in terms of how people observably behave. Another materialist view about the mind is identity theory. According to identity theory, mental states are identical with brain states. Science has shown that there is a correlation between mental states and brain states: That is, whenever something is going on in your mind, something is going on in your brain. So whenever you are thinking, for instance, your brain is active in a particular way (some brain cells are active, and others are not). Suppose, then, you are thinking right now about going to the beach. At the same time, your brain is in a particular state. On identity theory, your thought about going to the beach is identical to that brain state. In general, in this view, every mental state a person has is identical to some brain state. A third materialist view is functionalism. Functionalism focuses on what the brain *does*; that is, it focuses on the *function* of the brain. According to functionalists, if something has something that functions like a brain, that thing can be said to have a mind (whether it is a human, an alien, a cat, a computer, or something else). More is said about these versions of materialism in later chapters.

Two varieties of dualism are substance dualism and property dualism. According to substance dualism, the mind and body are two different kinds of substances, or, roughly speaking, two different basic kinds of stuff. Body is physical stuff with physical features, or properties, and mind is nonphysical stuff with nonphysical properties. For example, the body has extension, which is just a way of saying it occupies (extends into) space—it is possible to bump into someone, for instance, because a person's body takes up space. On substance dualism, mind is nonphysical stuff without extension; it cannot be touched or located anywhere in physical space. According to property dualism, mind is not a substance but instead consists of nonphysical properties. To illustrate, note that the brain has physical properties, such as having a certain weight, color, and structure. Some property dualists believe that the brain also has nonphysical properties, such as consciousness. These properties cannot properly be understood in terms of the brain's physical properties, according to property dualism, because they are not physical. In interactionist dualist theories, the mind and the body interact. That is, the mind has causal effects on the body and vice versa. For example, suppose someone wants to get out of bed and does so; in an interactionist view, the mental desire to get out of bed causes the body's motions of getting out of bed.

One of the most prominent advocates of dualism was the 17th-century philosopher René Descartes. Descartes gave various arguments in favor of dualism. One of these arguments emerged from his efforts to establish what, if anything, he *knew*—not just what he believed, or what he thought was probably true, but what he knew with absolute certainty. Descartes's method for establishing certain knowledge was to begin by doubting. What he could doubt, Descartes did not consider knowledge (at least, at the beginning phases of his project). On the other hand, he thought that if he could find something it was *not* possible to doubt, then he would have found something he did in fact know. Descartes believed he could doubt a great many things, but he concluded that what he could not doubt was his own existence. This was because he could not doubt that he was *thinking*. And if he was thinking, Descartes reasoned, then he must exist, because there must be *something* that is thinking.

The Latin phrase *Cogito, ergo sum,* used by Descartes in one of his works and meaning "I think, therefore I am," expresses Descartes's line of reasoning. As the phrase suggests, Descartes believed that he was fundamentally a *thinking* thing, as distinct in his view from a physical thing. Moreover, he could not doubt that he was thinking, but he could doubt that he had a body (for all Descartes knew, he thought, he could be merely dreaming that he had a body, or a powerful, evil demon might be making him think that he had a body). What this implies, for Descartes, is that mind and body must be distinct. In this argument, Descartes relied on a principle that later became known as Leibniz's law, which states that for any two things, those two things are identical if, and only if, they have exactly the same properties. So, if two things have different properties, they cannot be identical. For example, one apple cannot be identical to another if one apple is red and the other is green or one apple is in one place and the other apple is in another place. In this case, the property in question is the property of being doubtable: If Descartes could doubt that his body existed but could not doubt that his mind existed (that he was a thinking thing), then his mind must be distinct from the body.

Engraving of René Descartes walking along the streets of Amsterdam

One criticism of Descartes's argument is that simply because one thing can be doubted and something else cannot, it does not mean that the things in question must be distinct. By way of analogy, consider lightning and electrical discharge in the atmosphere. Science now tells us that lightning just *is* electrical discharge in the atmosphere—the terms *lightning* and *electrical discharge in the atmosphere* are just two ways of referring to the same phenomenon. A child who does not fully understand electricity might be incapable of doubting that sometimes there are flashes of light in the sky during thunderstorms (that there is lightning), having seen such flashes in the past. However, she might be capable of doubting that there was electrical discharge in the atmosphere during thunderstorms. Now, following Descartes's reasoning, this suggests that certain flashes of light in the sky (lightning) must be distinct from electrical discharge in the atmosphere. After all, it is possible to doubt that the latter sometimes occurs during thunderstorms, but not that the former occurs. Yet this reasoning is plainly flawed. In fact, lightning (certain flashes of light in the sky) is identical to electrical discharge in the atmosphere; it is just that the child does not understand this, and it is her lack of understanding that leads to her inability to doubt in one case and not in another. Similarly, one could argue that Descartes's inability to doubt that he had a mind and his ability to doubt that he has a body do not necessarily imply that mind and body are two different things. It might simply be Descartes's lack of understanding of the mind and the body that leads to his inability to doubt in one case and not in another. None of this is to say that Leibniz's law is wrong in all cases. But it does suggest that the law does not work if it takes the property in question to be the ability to be doubted.

Descartes gave other arguments in favor of dualism. Below is one of the most famous:

1. The body can be divided.
2. The mind cannot be divided.
3. Therefore, the mind is distinct from the body (body is physical, and mind is not).

In this argument from divisibility, Descartes again relied on Leibniz's law: If the body can be divided but the mind cannot, then body and mind must be distinct. In particular, Descartes believed mind and body are different substances. Why would anyone think the body can be divided? Well, it can be separated or cut into pieces, as when a person loses a limb. Why would anyone think the mind cannot be divided? On one account, the mind seems to consist of a single, unified thing; it is not as if one part of the mind believes, another part desires, and another part perceives, for example. Descartes used this argument to settle the issue, but it has been criticized. Some philosophers argue that the mind is not unified and that it can be divided. In addition, scientific research regarding the brain might seem to suggest as much. For instance, people who sustain brain damage in certain areas of the brain sometimes lose very particular mental functioning (such as the ability to use language), but not all mental functioning.

Many other arguments for dualism follow the same pattern of the argument from divisibility. That is, such arguments name some property that mind has and that body supposedly does not, concluding that mind and body must be distinct (and mind is nonphysical). Some of these arguments were also given by Descartes. For example, Descartes argued that he could come to know about the contents of his mind—what he believed, desired, hoped for, and so on—just through introspection. Roughly, introspection is metaphorically looking inward toward one's self. According to Descartes, he could know what he was thinking, for instance, just by looking inward at his own mind. In contrast, it seems that very often one cannot know about one's physical states just through introspection—for instance, a person cannot know which of her brain cells are active just by metaphorically looking inward.

Of the various properties that have been said to distinguish the mind from the body, two particularly important properties are intentionality and qualia. Intentionality, in the philosophical sense, is the quality of being about something (it does not have to do with having an intention or a purpose). For instance, when a person has a belief, her belief is always about *something*—school, one's pets, free speech, and so on. In one view, mind has intentionality, but the body does not. One's mind has intentionality in the sense that its beliefs, desires, hopes, and so on are about something. But, according to one argument, the body is not *about* anything. Consider a physical item such as a spoon. A spoon does not seem to be about anything; it is just a spoon. In the same way, one argument is that the body and its physical parts (including the brain) are not about anything. So, if the body lacks intentionality, then the body must be distinct from the mind. Qualia are the feels or sensations of experience, such as the sharp pain of hitting one's funny bone or the warmth of a bonfire. Some philosophers have argued that mind experiences qualia, but that the body does not, and therefore mind is distinct from the body. Finally, another important consideration regarding dualism is consciousness. The nature of consciousness is controversial, but some philosophers have argued that consciousness cannot be physical (and therefore that mind is distinct from the body).

Against dualism, a common criticism by materialists is that dualism does little to explain the mind, while it does introduce unnecessary complications in a theory of mind. One of these complications is how to explain how the mind and body interact: If the mind and body are two different substances, then how can the mind have any effect on the body or the body any effect on the mind? In addition, as noted, scientific research on the brain and on consciousness suggests that there is a very close relationship between mind and body. This suggests, in turn, that the mind can be explained in physical terms alone. If the mind can be explained just in physical terms, then there seems to be no reason to claim that mind is nonphysical. In fact, there is a reason for *not* doing so: A theory of mind that explains the mind just in physical terms is a simpler theory than one that does not. In the view of many philosophers and scientists, if two theories are equally good in other respects, a simpler theory is better than a more complex one.

Solipsism and the Problem of Other Minds

One traditional question in the philosophy of mind is known as the problem of other minds. This is the problem of knowing how (or whether) creatures other than one's self have minds. One can know from one's own case whether one has a mind because one has direct access to one's own mind; one has direct access to one's own thoughts, feelings, and perceptions. One can simply, metaphorically look inward to know that one is thirsty, happy, thinking about visiting a friend, or desiring to read a particular book. Philosophers call this ability to look inward and metaphorically see the contents of one's own mind introspection. But introspection applies only to one's self; one cannot use introspection to see the contents of anyone else's mind. In general, outside science fiction, one does not have direct access to anyone else's thoughts, feelings, perceptions, or other mental states. Of course, sometimes you might believe you have a pretty good idea of what others are thinking or feeling. When the dog scratches at the door and whines after having been inside all day, you might infer that the dog wants to go outside. When a friend says she will meet you at noon, you are likely to infer that the friend plans to meet you at noon. But in neither case can you directly access another's mind; you cannot directly access the dog's desires or the friend's plans. Given that this is the case, how can you *know* that others (whether they are human beings, animals, computers, or some other sort of thing) also have minds? After all, just because another person *behaves* as if she had a mind does not necessarily mean she has a mind; an android without consciousness at all, for instance, might act as if it had a mind. So, even if one's friends and family laugh in response to jokes, yelp when touching extremely hot water, and say they'll meet you at noon, this does not seem to establish that in fact they have minds—that they think, experience pain and pleasure, make plans, and so on. And this is the problem of other minds: Since we know directly only our own minds, it is not clear how one can ever know that anyone or anything else really has a mind. One response to this problem is solipsism, the view that nothing has a mind except oneself. Solipsism, however, is not very attractive to many thinkers; it is difficult to believe that one is the only thinking, feeling thing in the entire universe.

One proposed solution to the problem of other minds is an argument from analogy. The basic idea is to conclude that other beings have minds on the basis of their behavior *and* the similarity of other beings to oneself. Consider other human beings. They are like oneself in important ways: They have the same genetic structure, for instance, and they have a brain and a nervous system. Now one knows from one's own case that when one has certain mental experiences, one behaves in certain ways. One knows when one is in pain, one winces or utters an ouch, and when one hears a funny joke, one smiles and laughs. Now, by analogy, if other human beings behave like this—if they laugh and smile upon hearing a funny joke or wince or say ouch when pricked by a needle—these other people also have the mental experiences of pain and finding something funny. After all, if other people have a brain and nervous system, it seems to stand to reason that their brains and nervous systems function in the same way as one's own and are similarly related to mental experiences. Add to this the fact that other people behave in similar ways in similar situations and, according to the argument, one can reasonably conclude that other people think, feel, perceive, and so on—in short, that they have minds.

The argument by analogy is an inductive argument. An inductive argument draws a general conclusion on the basis of one or more cases. For example, one might reason inductively that all crows are black after observing a number of crows. The more cases observed, the stronger the inductive argument. Observing several thousand crows, for instance, provides stronger evidence for the conclusion that all crows are black than observing just 10. The argument by analogy has been criticized for basing a broad conclusion (people who have brains and nervous systems and behave in certain ways have minds) on the basis of just a single case—oneself. According to the criticism, this is rather like arguing that all crows are black after observing a single crow. Now just as that reasoning is very weak, so is the reasoning that others like oneself in certain ways also have minds. In other words, the concern is that the argument by analogy relies on very weak evidence.

Another argument for the existence of other minds notes that people are often very good at successfully predicting human behavior, relying on beliefs about what others are thinking and feeling. For example, when someone yelps after stubbing her toe, supposing that she feels pain explains the yelp; supposing she feels pain also helps one predict that she will stop walking momentarily and maybe rub her toe. Similarly, suppose someone claims to enjoy skiing and smiles broadly while she skis. To suppose that she likes skiing explains her behavior, as well as allows one to predict that she will ski again if given the right opportunity. According to this argument, the reason these explanations and predictions are so often successful is because people *do* have beliefs and feelings—in short, they do have minds, even if we have no direct access to them. Put another way, the claim is that the explanatory and predictive success of supposing that others have minds is good evidence that others do in fact have minds. This kind of reasoning is somewhat like the reasoning given in science about entities that cannot directly be observed. Supposing that there are such entities helps explain phenomena.

A third approach to the problem of other minds, given by Ludwig Wittgenstein (1889–1951), relies on claims about the nature of language. Wittgenstein believed that how we use language is governed by rules, somewhat in the way that games are governed by rules. In order to play a game, there must be some rules to make the game possible (imagine playing baseball without knowing how many outs a team gets or how many players a team may have). Similarly, communication via language requires that people use language in common ways, according to rules (imagine trying to have a conversation without knowing what words are supposed to mean or how to construct a grammatical sentence). Even more basic, for Wittgenstein, is that we could not even learn language without it being rule-governed, without having words retain their meaning over time and across different speakers. A consequence of this view is that there are no private languages. By saying that there are no private languages, Wittgenstein meant that there are no languages that in principle could be known only to one person (that is, privately). Of course, someone could make up a secret language or code, but that language or code would have to have some structure and rules; otherwise, it could not function. And if there were a structure and rules, it would, in principle, be knowable by others (even if no one else actually came to know the language). At its core, then, language is social.

What this suggests is that the very existence of language establishes that other minds exist. This is because language simply could not arise except in a social context. That is, language cannot arise except when there are multiple speakers of a language and these speakers have minds. Wittgenstein's arguments about the impossibility of a private language have attracted much discussion, and there is no consensus on whether his argument settles the problem of other minds.

Mental Causation
and Parallelism

From a commonsense view, what goes on in one's mind has an effect on what goes on with one's body. The usual philosophical way of putting this is that mental events can cause bodily events. (Mental phenomena such as beliefs, sensations, thoughts, desires, etc., are often understood as *events,* as opposed to objects; they are *mental* events because they occur within the mind.) For example, suppose the water in one's shower suddenly turns ice-cold. It is likely that a person would yelp in discomfort and move quickly to turn off the water. So, the bodily event of the cold water striking one's skin seems to cause the mental event of the sensation of pain. Also, the mental event of a person desiring to pet her cat seems to cause the bodily event of the person actually petting the cat. Similarly, a belief that it will snow can cause someone to get out her sled, and the sensation of pain might cause a person to yelp. Another way of putting this point is that there seems to be mental causation, causes that are mental.

The concept of cause is fundamental not only to philosophy and to science but to everyday life. We take it for granted that when something happens, there is a cause (or set of causes) for it happening, even if we do not know what the cause(s) might be. We even take it for granted that when something does *not* happen, there must be some cause for that. However, the basic concept of cause is still unclear. When we say that A causes B, one conception is that A is a necessary condition for B. In other words, in order for B to happen, A *must* happen; if A did not happen, then

B could not happen. However, we commonly speak of one thing causing another, even if it is not a necessary condition. For example, we might say that smoking causes lung cancer. But some people contract lung cancer even though they do not smoke (or even inhale secondhand smoke). Another suggestion to explain the concept of cause is that if A causes B, then A is a sufficient condition for B. In other words, if A happens, that is all it takes for B to happen; perhaps some other things might bring about B, but it is enough that A does. However, once again, this notion of sufficient condition does not match common claims about cause. Again, we say that smoking causes lung cancer, but it does not always cause lung cancer. Some people who smoke do not get lung cancer, so, apparently, smoking is not a sufficient condition for lung cancer.

If the concept of cause raises complex issues, this is no less true of mental causation in particular. We normally think of causation as being a physical interaction between things. However, if the mind is nonphysical, as dualists claim, it is difficult to understand how it can cause the body to do anything. When one ball strikes another in a game of pool, for instance, the second ball moves as a result; physicists can explain this in terms of physical forces. But, for the dualist, no such explanation is available for how the mind causes bodily movement. This is because if the mind is nonphysical, it cannot touch the body or exert any physical force on the body. So, how could it cause the body to move? In addition, dualism seems to have trouble explaining how bodily events can cause mental events, as it seems they sometimes do. For instance, if the water in someone's shower suddenly turns ice-cold, it is likely that she will suddenly feel discomfort: In this case, the cold water striking her skin seems to cause the mental event of pain. If the mind and body are fundamentally different, one nonphysical and one physical, it is not obvious how such mind/body interactions are possible. For the substance dualist, mental causation is one aspect of the interaction problem, the problem of accounting for mind/body interaction.

Many philosophers reject dualism in its various forms because they believe it cannot adequately account for mental causation. For materialist views of mind, what we call mental causation is really just physical causation, because what is mental is physical. For instance, if the mind is just the brain, then mental causation is physical causation simply because the brain is a physical organ.

Parallelism

One dualist way of responding to the interaction problem is parallelism. According to parallelism, it is a mistake to think that mental events cause any bodily events or that bodily events cause any mental events. Rather, mental and bodily events are parallel: They simply occur at the same time (or about the same time). But neither causes the other. Gottfried Leibniz gave the following analogy. If two clocks are set to show the same time, then throughout the day, the clocks will show the same time: They are parallel to each other. But neither clock causes the other clock to show a certain time. In the same way, according to parallelism, mental events and bodily events are parallel, but neither causes the other. It is as if the mind and the body were both set at the same time. Why are mental events and bodily events parallel? The usual answer is that God has arranged it this way. So, there is a pre-established harmony between mental events and bodily events.

Because parallelism denies that mental events and bodily events can have any effect on each other, the view escapes the difficulty of having to explain how two different substances (substance dualism) or two different kinds of properties (property dualism) interact. Moreover, because there is no mental causation on this view, there is no problem of mental causation violating the law of the conservation of energy. However, parallelism faces difficulties of its own. First, few philosophers believe there is an adequate explanation for why mental and bodily events would be parallel. Second, if parallelism is true, then nothing that we think, believe, feel, or want has any effect on anything we physically do; moreover, nothing that happens to our bodies has any effect on what we think or feel. Many philosophers find this too far-fetched to accept.

Epiphenomenalism and Emergentism

Epiphenomenalism

Dualist positions face the issue of how a nonphysical mind could interact with a physical body. One dualist response to this challenge is just to deny that mind does have any such effect on the body. This view is epiphenomenalism. Historically, epiphenomenalism has been associated with substance dualism, the view that mind is a nonphysical substance and the body is a physical substance. More recently, discussion of epiphenomenalism has been connected to property dualism, according to which mental properties are not physical properties. According to epiphenomenalism, the body can affect the mind, but the mind cannot affect the body, or in other words, mental events can be caused by physical events, but mental events cannot cause physical events. In an epiphenomenalist view, mental events are somewhat like shadows. Shadows have physical causes (they are cast by physical objects positioned in light), but shadows have no causal effect on the objects that cast them. Analogously, mental events are caused by physical processes, but they are not themselves the cause of anything.

Unlike versions of dualism that hold that there is mental causation (that mental events can be causes, in particular of physical events), epiphenomenalism does not need to explain how a nonphysical mind can cause physical events. That is because, according to epiphenomenalism, it does not. Epiphenomenalism is also consistent with science in a way that interactionist dualism arguably is not. A common criticism of the latter is that if mental events cause physical events, this would violate the law of the conservation of energy. This law states that the energy in a closed system remains constant; energy is neither created nor destroyed. Yet if mental events caused physical events, they would seem to be introducing new energy that did not exist before (this is because physical events, in order to occur, require energy, and that energy would have to come from somewhere, presumably from what caused the event in the first place). By denying that mental events cause physical events, epiphenomenalism avoids this objection. However, it does so at the cost of denying that one's desires, beliefs, decisions, and so on have any effect on our physical behavior. Many thinkers find this unlikely.

Emergentism

Associated with philosophers such as C. D. Broad (1887–1971), one view is that there are (or could be) emergent properties; in philosophy of mind, some philosophers regard mental properties in particular as emergent properties. Very roughly, an emergent property is a property that emerges from its parts but is not the same as its parts and cannot be understood just by studying its parts. As an example, the harmony of a piece of music might be said to be an emergent property. It emerges from its various parts—the individual notes—and the relations between them. But it is not the same thing as those parts, and it cannot be understood just by studying its parts—just studying each individual note, for instance, would not allow you to understand harmony itself. As another example, salt has properties that its individual components, sodium and chlorine, lack. For instance, sodium and chlorine have different chemical reactions than does salt, even though salt is composed of sodium and chlorine. More precisely, an emergent property is a property that is not reducible to its parts and cannot be predicted beforehand. For example, perhaps no one could have predicted how salt would react chemically with other substances, even knowing how sodium and chlorine react with other substances.

Similarly, according to emergentism, mental properties such as consciousness are emergent properties. They emerge when matter is appropriately arranged and complex; in particular, somehow mental properties emerge from the brain. No one could reasonably have predicted beforehand that they would do so. Of course people can predict that a baby will be conscious when it is born or that it will become conscious; people can predict this on the basis of past experience (other infants were conscious or became conscious). However, prior to consciousness having ever arisen from matter in the first place (from humans, say), no one could have predicted that it would arise on the basis of the physical composition and structure of the brain. Knowing all the physical facts about the brain will not tell you that consciousness (or any other emergent property) will or will not emerge. Emergent properties are also said to be nonreducible in an epistemic sense. To make sense of this, it is worth saying something about reduction as philosophers use it.

Usually when people think of reduction or reducing, they think of something getting smaller. In philosophy, the notion of reduction is a special sense of something getting smaller. It is not the notion that some particular thing actually gets smaller, but rather it is the notion that a concept refers to something simpler. For example, philosophers (and people in general) say that water just is H_2O, or that heat just is molecules in motion. Philosophers speak of this as saying that the concept of water is reduced to the concept of H_2O, or that the concept of heat is reduced to the concept of molecules in motion. Reductionism is the view that more complex things can be reduced to simpler, less complex things.

One kind of reduction is ontological reduction. This simply means that one thing, or kind of thing, really just is a simpler thing, or kind of thing. So, again, water (one kind of thing) is said really just to be H_2O (another kind of thing). By saying that water is one kind of thing and H_2O is another (simpler) kind of thing, what is meant is that water is a complex thing, with various features or properties, such as being wet, quenching people's thirst, having some color or taste or smell. H_2O, on the other hand, in another kind of thing, namely, a molecule composed of different atoms bonded together in a certain way, also with various features or properties. But given what we have learned from science, we now say that water just is H_2O; it is not anything other than H_2O. Take away the hydrogen and the oxygen, and there is nothing left of water.

A second kind of reduction is epistemological reduction (or, sometimes, theoretical reduction). This sense of reduction has to do, not with the physical features or nature of things, but with how we understand and explain things. For example, in physics, physicists say that Newton's theory can be reduced to Einstein's theory. What this means is that Einstein's theory can explain everything that Newton's theory can and even more (but not the reverse; that is, Newton's theory cannot explain everything that Einstein's theory can). Another example is that many scientists, but not all, claim that—at least, in theory—psychology can be reduced to biology. What this means is that anything that psychology can explain could, in principle, be explained by biology, because, after all, people are biological organisms and if we just knew enough about biology we could ultimately explain all human actions (including mental and cognitive actions) biologically. In effect, then, psychology would just be part of biology; it would be reduced to biology. The laws and models and theories that biology uses to explain things could ultimately be used to explain everything that psychology now explains (and more). Just as water really just is H_2O, so, too, psychology really just is biology; this is the view of epistemological (or theoretic) reduction.

To return to the view that mental properties are emergent properties, then, emergent properties are said to be nonreducible in the epistemological sense. That is, mental properties cannot be explained just by explaining everything about the physical stuff from which mental properties emerge. So, according to emergentism, the mind is not reducible to the body. (Sometimes emergent properties are also taken to be nonreducible in an ontological sense, but they do not need to be taken in this way.) Some emergentists regard the emergence of mental properties as not calling for further explanation. The phrase is that such emergence is simply a brute fact. Consciousness, for instance, emerges from the brain just because that is the way it is. The stimulation of the body in certain ways leads to certain sensations (pain, ticklishness, the sensation of warmth, etc.), because that is just how things are. On this view, there is really nothing to be explained. Asking for an explanation of why consciousness emerges from the brain might be something like asking why the force of gravity is exactly what it is; arguably, that the force of gravity is what it is (rather than, say, being slightly stronger or slightly weaker) is not something to be explained. It just is, a brute fact that cannot itself be explained.

However, some philosophers have not found this account of consciousness and other mental properties very satisfying. Typically, we look for explanations for natural phenomena, that is, phenomena that occur in the natural world. It is common to assume that there are such explanations, even if we do not always know what they are. Scientific theories account for many phenomena today that once seemed inexplicable—earthquakes, fire, magnetism, even the origin of life on Earth. Natural phenomena seem to happen for *some* reason or another, and these reasons have very often fit (eventually) comfortably into a scientific account. Some earthquakes, for example, occur because of the stress of colliding continental plates, and at one level they can be explained in terms of laws of physics (laws that tell us what must happen when objects with certain physical properties collide with each other in certain ways and with certain degrees of force). Scientists even offer explanations for fundamental laws such as the law of gravity; there is no consensus regarding such explanations, but some thinkers believe that there *is* some explanation, even if we do not yet know what it is. Arguably, perhaps consciousness should not be any different. To suppose that consciousness simply emerges from the brain and that no explanation is to be had for its emergence suggests that consciousness is somehow uniquely different from other natural phenomena in being beyond explanation. But, for critics of emergentism, why this should be the case is not obvious.

Another issue closely related to emergentism is that of downward causation. According to emergentism, mental properties can have causal effects on the physical realm, causing physical events. But this seems problematic. It is problematic because it implies that some physical events (such as smiling, picking up a brownie, running a marathon) cannot be explained in physical terms alone. They cannot be explained in physical terms alone because, according to emergentism, mental properties are not reducible to physical properties. So, any explanation of certain physical events must make reference to mental properties. The problem is that this conclusion is inconsistent with the claim that the physical world is causally closed—that is, that every physical event has a physical cause and can be explained in physical terms only. This principle, called the causal closure principle of the physical world, is a fundamental presupposition in contemporary science. So, according to critics, insofar as emergentism runs counter to this principle, emergentism is mistaken.

Idealism, Behaviorism, and Identity Theory

Idealism

In philosophy, the term *idealism* does not refer to idealism as it is often understood. In a nonphilosophical sense, idealism means having lofty ideals. However, in philosophy, idealism is the view that reality is in some way dependent on the mind (about ideas, not ideals). Idealism is often contrasted with realism about the objects of ordinary, everyday experience (such as trees and computers), which holds that these objects are not dependent on the mind. Idealism is a form of monism, the view that there is only one basic kind of real stuff. Idealists hold that the character of that stuff is mental, as opposed to physicalism, which holds that the one kind of real stuff is physical. Sometimes idealism is also used to refer to views according to which what is most real is not physical. In this sense, the ancient Greek philosopher Plato (ca. 428–348 B.C.E.) is an idealist: He believed that what is most real are nonphysical things called Ideas. When he spoke of Ideas, he meant not some thought in someone's mind but whatever it is that matches the correct definition of something that was being defined. However, Plato held that the ideas exist independently of the mind. So, he was not an idealist in the first philosophical sense of the term described here.

The modern philosopher George Berkeley (1685–1753) was the first major idealist in this sense. (Berkeley himself called his view immaterialism.) A devout Christian, Berkeley disliked the common view of his time that the physical world operated mechanistically, as though the physical world and the physical objects within were complex machines. He was also eager to defend belief in God and in an immaterial soul. According to Berkeley, reality consists of minds and ideas. So, Berkeley denied the existence of matter. This did not mean that he denied that the objects of our everyday, ordinary experience are real, such as tables and trees and cups of coffee. Berkeley agreed such ordinary objects are real, but he believed that they were not physical. Rather, they are mental; specifically, they are collections of ideas.

Berkeley's reasoning depends on certain beliefs common to the philosophers of his time. First, Berkeley understood ideas broadly. An idea for him is not just a thought, as when a person trying to solve a problem suddenly says he has an idea. Sensations are also considered ideas, as are images. The image of a horse as a person imagines one, the sensation of heat, the idea that philosophy is fun: All of these are ideas. Second, Berkeley believed that we experience only ideas: We do not directly experience anything outside of our own ideas. That is, we do not experience directly objects that exist independently of ourselves. Suppose, for instance, a person looks at a gray horse and suppose that the horse is physical. According to John Locke (1632–1704) (whose views greatly influenced Berkeley), the horse would produce in a person who saw it ideas such as the idea of gray and the idea of a certain shape (the shape of the horse). But a person would not experience the horse directly; rather, she would experience ideas that the horse causes her to have. Locke also distinguished between primary and secondary qualities. Primary qualities are qualities of an object that are in the object itself—for example, the solidity of a horse really is in the horse, not just in one's mind. Secondary qualities are qualities that are not in an object itself. The color of a horse, for instance, is not in the color itself, although the horse produces in a person who sees the horse the idea of that color (to see why color would not be in the object itself, consider that the color an object appears to be varies according to circumstances; for instance, a white snowball would look pink under a red light).

Berkeley agreed with Locke that we experience only ideas. But he departed from Locke in claiming that there are no physical objects at all. Berkeley thought that Locke's claim that there are material objects that exist independently of being perceived leads to skepticism. (After all, if we never experience anything but our own ideas, how do we know that our ideas in any way match up with an independently existing reality? It appears that we *cannot* know.) Insofar as skepticism should be rejected—and Berkeley thought that it should—the idea that physical objects cause ideas should be rejected. In addition, Berkeley thought, if we experience only ideas and not objects that exist independently of our minds, then we have no reason to suppose that such objects exist in the first place. The ordinary objects of experience just *are* ideas or, more precisely, collections of ideas. When a person perceives a gray horse, there would be no physical horse that is the cause of the idea of a gray, horse-shaped figure. Instead, the gray horse would *be* the idea of a gray, horse-shaped figure. More precisely, for Berkeley, the horse would consist of a collection of such ideas (grayness, a certain shape, a certain horsey smell, a certain horsey feel, and so on). That is *all* apparently material objects are—collections of ideas in the mind.

According to Berkeley, *all* the qualities of the objects we perceive—qualities such as shape, size, solidity, taste, smell, and so on—are mind-dependent. In other words, Berkeley rejected the primary/secondary qualities distinction. Secondary qualities are not in the objects themselves and therefore depend on a perceiver. But, Berkeley argued, it was impossible to conceive of a sensible object (object perceived through the senses) without thinking of it as having secondary qualities. So, if secondary qualities depend for their existence on the perceiver, so, too, do primary qualities—and this is just to say that objects themselves depend on the mind.

Because apparently physical objects are just collections of ideas and ideas exist only when a mind has them, Berkeley argued that to *be* is to be perceived or, in Latin, *esse est percipi*. In other words, in order for such objects to exist, a mind must perceive them. (In addition, the question of how it is possible to know that our ideas match up with independently existing objects does not arise. That is because there are no such independently existing objects.) None of this means that sensible objects (objects perceived through the senses) are not real. Rather, it just means that their existence is mind-dependent. In response to Berkeley, Samuel Johnson famously said, "I refute Berkeley thus" and kicked a rock. Presumably Johnson meant that his ability to kick the rock proved that the rock was physical, thus refuting Berkeley's claim that there are no physical objects.

Painting of Samuel Johnson, 1775 *(Painting by Joshua Reynolds)*

But this was not really a refutation of Berkeley. This is because Berkeley never denied that a person could kick a rock. In general, he never denied that we can act on the ordinary objects of experience or, for that matter that we can be acted upon by the ordinary objects of experience (as when falling snowflakes make a person feel cold and wet). For Berkeley, the sensation of resistance that is felt when a person kicks a rock is an idea in the person's head—of course it is real, but it is not physical in nature. Similarly, the perception of the rock moving away from oneself after being kicked is also an idea. Berkeley never denied that one could have such experiences. He just denied that these experiences are best explained by supposing such objects are physical. A person can successfully kick all the rocks she wants—but neither she nor the rock is physical. One can also ride a horse, burn oneself on a hot stove, and go hiking through a desert landscape. But in each case, for Berkeley, the experiences would involve ideas and collections of ideas—they would not involve matter.

   If all that is real are minds and ideas, and ideas depend for their existence on minds, then it must be the case that when an idea is not had by any mind, the idea does not exist. This seems to suggest that objects go in and out of existence depending on whether someone perceives them. However, Berkeley thought that ordinary objects typically do not go out of existence, for the reason that they are ideas in God's mind (as long as God has those ideas, they exist). In other words, the ordinary objects of experience continue to exist, even when no person or animal perceives them, because God perceives them. In general, sensible ideas are ideas in the mind of God. In addition, Berkeley thought that God himself is the cause of our ideas. To see why this is so, Berkeley noted that some of our ideas are involuntary; it is not up to us whether we have them (for instance, one cannot decide to see an apple just because one wants to). Yet they must have some cause. Berkeley thought that that cause must be another mind, specifically the mind of God.

It might sound strange to believe that only ideas and minds exist and material objects do not. Berkeley believed, however, that his view was actually consistent with common sense, because what we ordinarily talk about and have beliefs in are objects of experience. Once prominent, idealism finds less favor in philosophy today. However, idealism is not dead. Few philosophers deny with Berkeley that matter exists, but it is more common to agree that the mind somehow organizes experience—in other words, that what is real might be mind-dependent in the sense that what we experience depends at least in part on how our minds structure experience. What we know of reality would seem to depend in part on how the mind works; it is difficult to make sense of the reality of anything that is wholly beyond our ability to grasp mentally.

Introduction to Physicalism

Most (but not all) contemporary philosophers are physicalists or materialists about mind. That is, they view the mind as being essentially material; when they explain the mind, they do not talk about nonphysical substances or nonphysical properties. Although materialism is the dominant view in philosophy of mind today, it is not confined to contemporary thinkers. For example, Thomas Hobbes (1588–1679), a contemporary of the dualist Descartes, subscribed to materialism, describing what is real as matter in motion, including mental activities. In other words, thinking, feeling, planning, hoping, etc., for Hobbes consisted of certain matter moving about in particular ways (and,

Hobbes thought, moving about mechanically). Julien Offray de La Mettrie (1709–51) was another famous materialist who believed that mind can be explained only in physical terms.

One motivation for materialism is the desire to understand the mind in a scientific way, insofar as scientific practice invokes only what is material or physical in its explanations of natural phenomena. Such scientific practice has made great advancements over the centuries, and scientists have been able to explain phenomena that once seemed quite beyond the reach of scientific explanation. For example, people once thought that explaining life—explaining what it is that makes living creatures alive—was beyond the reach of science, but now scientists comfortably answer this question just in terms of the natural sciences (such as through biology). On a materialist view, it makes sense to suppose that mind, too, can be explained within a scientific framework, without appealing to nonmaterial substances or properties.

However, materialist views are often thought to have difficulty accounting for certain key aspects of the mind. One of these aspects is intentionality, the property of being about something. At least some mental states are about something—a desire to fly is a desire *about flying,* and a belief about clouds is a belief *about clouds.* One concern regarding materialist theories of mind is simply that it is difficult to make sense how something merely material—such as a brain state— could be *about* anything. A person's belief that cows chew cud is a belief about cows, for instance; but could a group of brain cells be about a cow? Another major concern regarding materialist theories of mind is qualia, the felt aspects of experience, such as sensations and feelings. It has often been argued that materialism cannot adequately account for qualia. For example, suppose the mind is identical to the brain. If this is the case, then the mental state of perceiving a yellow lemon is identical to a certain brain state. Arguably, however, knowing everything there is to know about that brain state—and even knowing all the physical facts about color and the perception of color—does not tell us what it is *like* to see a yellow lemon. If this is so, critics charge, perhaps there is more to perception (and therefore more to mind) than the brain. Similar arguments have been given about the ability of materialist theories of mind to explain consciousness.

Another issue in materialist views of mind is the status of what is called folk psychology. Psychology is, roughly, the scientific study of the mind. So folk psychology is our everyday, commonsense view about the mind—a view that ordinary folk believe in—as distinguished from a scientific view of the mind. In the philosophy of mind, folk psychology is often understood as consisting of ordinary concepts related to the mind, such as the concepts of thought, belief, desire, feeling, and even the concept of mind itself. It is commonly agreed that these concepts help us predict and explain human behavior. Suppose, for instance, someone peers out the window, frowns at the gathering gray clouds, and picks up her umbrella before she goes out the door. A likely explanation for her behavior is that she *believes* it will rain and she *wants* to stay dry. This explanation involves the concepts of belief and desire, concepts of folk psychology. Similarly, it is reasonable to predict that once she is outside, she will actually use the umbrella if it starts to rain. Why predict that she will do so? Because it appears that she wants to stay dry. So predicting how this person will behave relies on folk psychology, specifically on the concept of desire.

Merely because folk psychology is useful for explaining and predicting, however, does not necessarily mean folk psychology is true. For instance, do we really have beliefs, desires, and feelings? Do we really have mental processes such as thinking? Perhaps we behave the way we do because our brains function in a certain way, not because we have beliefs and desires. According to some views in the philosophy of mind, folk psychology is more or less true (even if it is not perfect). But according to one version of materialism, eliminative materialism, folk psychology is false. In eliminative materialism, folk psychology is rather like outdated historical theories that have turned out to be false. For example, people used to believe that the Earth was the center of the universe. On the basis of this belief, people were often able to predict successfully where planets would appear in the night sky. So in this sense, the view that the Earth was the center of the universe was useful. Yet it turned out to be false, as scientists later showed. In the same way, according to eliminative materialism, scientists will show that folk psychology is false also. The idea is that when scientists understand the brain and the nervous system more fully, we will see that we do not have beliefs, desires, or other such mental states. So eliminative materialism *eliminates* references to mind, beliefs, desires, and other concepts of folk psychology. Many philosophers disagree with eliminative materialism, however, including many materialists.

Materialism: Behaviorism

Logical behaviorism, also known as philosophical behaviorism, is a view about mental terms, that is, terms that describe mental states such as anger, hope, belief, and the like. Logical behaviorism is a view about the meaning of certain words. Yet it is relevant to philosophy of mind. This is because knowledge about the meanings of mental terms goes hand in hand with knowledge about the natures of mental states. Knowing the meaning of *tree* entails knowing something about trees; in the same way knowing the meaning of *desire,* for instance, entails knowing something about the mental state of desire. So knowing the meanings of *all* mental terms involves knowing what it means to have a mind.

A rough statement of logical behaviorism is that it is the view that mental terms are to be defined in terms of behavior. For instance, *happy* is to be defined in terms of behavior (such as smiling and laughing) and not in terms of what a person is feeling. A more precise statement of logical behaviorism is that it is the view that mental terms are to be defined in terms of dispositions to behavior. In other words, a definition of a mental term gives a description of how a person is *disposed* to behave in certain circumstances. For instance, consider the belief that chocolate is tasty. To say that someone believes that chocolate is tasty is to say something about how she is disposed to behave in certain circumstances. If offered some chocolate, for example, she would accept it; if asked whether she thought chocolate was tasty, she would say yes. So, to say "Ellen believes chocolate is tasty" is equivalent to saying "if Ellen were offered some chocolate, she would accept it, and if she were asked whether she thought chocolate was tasty, she would say yes." Of course, this is a very simple example, and no doubt there is a lot more that Ellen would do if she believed that chocolate was tasty. The point is that for a logical behaviorist mental terms are understood in terms of dispositions to behavior. A full description of such dispositions to behavior might be rather long, but a complete description would tell us the meaning of the relevant mental term. An important aspect of this view is that, for logical behaviorism, behavior means publicly observable behavior: It refers to what a person does that others can observe. A person's private, inner sensations—such as the pleasure she gets in eating chocolate—are not publicly observable. So, they are not involved in definitions of mental terms. Behavior can include a person's mouth watering or a person lick-ing her lips, because this behavior can be observed by others (scientists can measure the saliva in a person's mouth, and of course people can just see someone licking her lips).

One motivation for logical behaviorism is to escape some of the difficulties of the view called dualism, especially substance dualism. Substance dualism is the view that mind is a nonphysical substance. A problem with this view is how to account for the apparent fact that mind influences the body—to take a simple example, it seems that a person's desire to walk down the street causes her body to move in such a way that she walks down the street. However, it is not clear how a nonphysical mind could cause a physical body to move. Logical behav-iorists avoid this problem because they eliminate any reference to any nonphysical mind; by defining mental terms in terms of dispositions for behavior, they regard mental states just in terms of behavior.

The British philosopher Gilbert Ryle (1900–76), often associated with logical behaviorism, described—and criticized—the notion that there is a nonphysical mind inhabiting a physical body by calling it a "ghost in the machine" view. In Ryle's analogy, a nonphysical mind is the ghost and the machine is the body. The idea of a ghost living inside a machine and making the machine function seems a bit silly, and Ryle's phrase "ghost in the machine" suggests that substance dualism is mistaken. According to Ryle, substance dualism is based on a category mistake. A category mistake is the mistake of thinking that something has a particular characteristic, when in fact that characteristic applies only to things that belong to a different category. For example, it would be a mistake to say that a microwave has reached puberty. Only livings things reach puberty. Because microwaves are not the sorts of things that can reach puberty, they belong to a different category than things such as humans, who can. So it is a category mistake to use the term *puberty* for a microwave. Dualism, according to Ryle, is based on a category mistake. This is because dualists suppose that mental events (events such as thinking, believing, and desiring) must be nonphysical events that take place inside us. But mental events do not belong to a category of things that must be nonphysical and take place inside us. Rather, according to Ryle, we can understand mental events in terms of behavior.

A second advantage to defining mental terms in terms of publicly observable behavior is that such behavior is, by definition, observable by others. A common view in versions of behaviorism is that theories based on what can be publicly observed are more objective than those based on inner mental activities. A person's private thoughts, sensations, and feelings are just that—private. Someone outside that perspective does not have access to them, so according to some behaviorists, those private experiences cannot be studied scientifically. Somewhat similarly, it would seem strange in physics to base a theory on something only one person could experience, for there would be no way to test the theory independently.

In addition, because inner mental states are private, according to some philosophers it is not clear how they can play any role in the meanings of mental terms. Ludwig Wittgenstein gave this analogy: Suppose everyone had a little box, and no one could look inside another person's box. You might have a beetle in yours, but no one could ever know this; nor could you ever know what is in anyone else's box. A person's inner sensations are rather like the beetle in a box: No one but oneself has access to them. But if no one else has access to inner sensations, then these inner sensations do not seem relevant for communication. After all, only the person having a given sensation has access to that particular sensation. For instance, consider the word *pain* and the sensation of pain. On this reasoning, you know what the word *pain* means, not because it is associated with a sensation (after all, you cannot observe the sensation in another person, any more than you can see inside someone else's box), but at least in part because of how people behave.

In spite of these apparent advantages of logical behaviorism, most contemporary philosophers believe logical behaviorism fails to give an adequate account of mental states. There are at least three serious objections to the view. The first is that logical behaviorism cannot define mental terms without referring to other mental states. This is a problem because logical behaviorists seek to define mental terms just in terms of behavior—not in terms of other mental states. However, according to the objection, it is not possible to eliminate references to other mental states, because mental states are related to other mental states. For example, consider again the sentence "Ellen believes chocolate is tasty." We saw that the logical behaviorist would understand this sentence as

meaning something about how Ellen would behave in certain circumstances—that she would, for example, accept some chocolate if it were
offered. However, Ellen would accept the chocolate if offered only if she
believed the chocolate was safe and only if she did not *feel* too full. Similarly, she would answer, yes to the question "do you believe chocolate is
tasty?" only if she *wanted* to answer truthfully. So, it looks as if "Ellen
believes that chocolate is tasty" means "Ellen would accept some chocolate if offered" (if she did not feel too full and she believed the chocolate
was safe). If she were asked whether she thought chocolate was tasty,
she would say yes, provided that she wanted to answer truthfully. With
its references to what Ellen believes, feels, and wants, it is clear that this
definition involves much more than just behavior.

A second objection to behaviorism is that it wrongly ignores how
some mental states *feel*. That is, logical behaviorism ignores qualia.
Qualia are the feels or particular sensations—for example, the particular sweet taste of chocolate, the sensation of seeing red, and the feel of
a feather tickling one's feet. According to the objection, because some
mental states involve qualia, there is more to some mental states than
behavior. For instance, there is more to the mental state of pain than the
disposition to behave in certain ways in certain circumstances: Pain has
a particular feel to it, and behaviorism ignores this feeling.

Third, some philosophers have also argued that, rather than mental states being identical to behavior (or dispositions to behavior), they
seem rather to be *causes* of behavior. A person who often chooses to eat
chocolate and smiles with pleasure while doing so, for instance, does
those things *because* she likes chocolate, not because dispositions to do
those things are identical to liking chocolate.

Materialism: Identity Theory

Identity theory is another materialist view of the mind, according to
which mind is wholly material, consisting of material stuff with material properties. To illustrate the key idea of identity theory, consider that
what goes on in our brains seems to change with what goes on in our
minds. That is, there is a correlation between mental states and brain
states. (Mental states are states of one's mental life, such as the state of
believing, hoping, feeling pain, and so on.) When a person recalls a
fond memory, her brain is in a certain state; it has particular physical

and chemical properties or characteristics. If she were startled by a loud noise, she would feel surprised, and her brain would undergo chemical and physical changes (it would be in a different state). According to identity theory, however, there is not just a correlation between a person's mental states and her brain states. Rather, mental states, such as beliefs, hopes, desires, sensations, and so on, are identical to brain states; they just *are* brain states.

There are two main versions of identity theory: token identity theory and type identity theory. A token is a particular, individual thing—for example, a particular donkey named Guinness. A type is a *kind* of thing, such as the species donkey. So, Guinness is a token of the type donkey: He is an individual that belongs to a certain kind of thing (the kind donkey). According to token identity theory, tokens of mental states are identical to tokens of brain states. On this view, for instance, a person's individual belief that donkeys are friendly is identical to a particular brain state. According to type identity theory, types of mental states are identical to types of brain states. For instance, the belief that donkeys are friendly is a kind of mental state and identical with a kind of brain state.

One argument for identity theory is that it explains mind-body interaction. To illustrate, consider first an opposing view of mind, dualism. According to dualism, mind is nonphysical. But if mind is nonphysical, it is difficult to explain how a nonphysical mind can have an effect on a physical body, or vice versa. Yet a commonsense view is that what goes on in one's mind can have an effect on the body, and vice versa. For instance, a desire to eat chocolate can cause a person's hand to put a piece of chocolate in her mouth; stubbing one's toe seems to cause the mental experience of pain. If, as dualists claim, mind is nonphysical, how can it interact with the body in such ways? It has seemed to many philosophers that dualists cannot account for mind-body interaction. In contrast, identity theory addresses the issue by identifying mental states with brain states. Because brain states are physical, mental states (such as the desire for chocolate) would seem to have no difficulty in causing physical motion (such as putting chocolate in one's mouth). Physical causes have physical effects, as when raking a leaf-strewn yard causes leaves to move into a pile; on identity theory, mental states can be one kind of physical causes.

Another argument in favor of identity theory is that compared to nonmaterialist views of the mind such as dualism, identity theory is simpler. That is, it explains mind in a simpler way than dualism does, and in that respect identity theory is a better view. To illustrate, consider two explanations for the fact that every time one turned the key in the ignition of a car, the car started. One explanation for this is that turning the key in the ignition awakens a tiny elf, who then sets into motion a physical process in the engine. Another explanation is that the key directly sets into motion a physical process in the engine. Both of these explanations explain why the car starts when the key turns in the ignition. However, the second explanation is simpler. The view that there is an elf involved raises questions that the second explanation does not (where does the elf live in the car? why do we never see the elf?). Moreover, there seems to be no need to suppose there is an elf in the first place, because the second explanation gives an adequate account of why the car starts. Dualism is often regarded as rather like the explanation involving the elf: It raises a lot of questions that identity theory does not (how can a nonphysical mind interact with a physical body?) and introduces a nonphysical mind when there is no need to do so. There is no need to do so, according to proponents of identity theory, because identity theory gives a sufficient account of mind. In addition, science has shown that there is a very close relation between the mind and brain, and identity theory explains this very close relation.

Often the identification of mental states with brain states is compared to well-known identifications in science. For example, lightning is identical to electrical discharge in the atmosphere. People did not always know, of course, that lightning is identical to electrical discharge in the atmosphere, but eventually scientists discovered that it was. In the same way, according to identity theorists, over time science will fully explain the identification of mental states with brain states. This point is important because it might be tempting to argue against identity theory this way: We know about our mental states just by looking inward, through introspection; one knows that one is happy, for instance, just by looking inward. But a person does not know what physical and chemical properties her brain has just by looking inward. If mental states are identical to physical states, how can this be? In answer, consider that people could not tell just through everyday observation that lightning is electrical discharge. That discovery took scientific research. In the same way, the identity theorist might argue, scientific research is needed to learn all about our mental states (looking inward is not enough).

There are various objections against identity theory. Some objections point to apparent differences between mental states and brain states. These objections are based on the idea that if mental states are different than brain states, they cannot be identical. One important objection to identity theory concerns intentionality. Intentionality in the philosophical sense has to do with being *about* something. A person's beliefs, for instance, are about something. One criticism of identity theory is that brain states do not seem to be *about* anything. If you observed the physical and chemical properties of a person's brain, those properties do not seem to be about donkeys or anything else; they just seem to be physical properties. But if mental states *are* about something (and we know that they are), then mental states cannot be identical to brain states. Another objection is that identity theory cannot account for qualia, the particular feels of things, such as the sensation of seeing red.

Perhaps the most significant objection to identity theory is the multiple realizability argument introduced by Hilary Putnam. Human brains are made of a certain kind of physical stuff and are structured in particular ways. But, according to the objection, it is possible that something could have mental states without having a physical composition and structure just like a human's. Aliens, for instance, might have beliefs and desires even if aliens are physically very different than humans. Yet identity theory denies such a possibility: If types of mental states are identical to types of *brain* states, and if aliens do not have brains, then according to type identity theory, such aliens could not have mental states. This aspect of type identity theory has seemed wrong to many philosophers. The idea here is that mind can be made of many different kinds of physical stuff (it can be multiply realized), and type identity theory mistakenly ignores this fact.

This objection does not apply to token identity theory. A token identity theorist could just say that a human's particular mental states are identical to particular brain states, and an alien's particular mental states are identical to some particular physical states of the alien (call them, say, "schmain" states). However, token identity theory has been criticized on the grounds that it does not adequately explain the nature of mental states. Analogously, consider money. Money comes in many forms—dollars, yen, pesos, and euros (and more). But just to say that money is identical to dollars, yen, pesos, or euros does not seem to explain the nature of money. What is needed to understand money is an understanding of what these different forms of money have in common. In the same way, an objection to token identity theory is that just saying that mental states are identical to brain states or schmain states does not explain the nature of mental states. What is needed is an account of what makes all such states uniquely mental. In part because of the multiple realizability argument, some philosophers have turned to functionalism, another materialist view of mind.

Consciousness, Qualia, and Materialism

Any account of mind must give some account of consciousness. Philosophers use the word *consciousness* both to talk about creatures and to talk about mental states. That is, we say some creatures (such as normal, functioning humans) have consciousness and that some mental states are conscious states. A mental state is just a state of mental activity—for example, the state of believing that whales are mammals, the state of feeling pain, and the state of seeing a redwood forest. In addition, consciousness is not the same as just being awake. This is because one can be conscious while dreaming, for example, in the sense that one has feelings and desires during the dream. Inspired by the philosopher Thomas Nagel, one very common way of describing consciousness is to say that if a creature is conscious then there is something that it is like to be that creature. There does not seem to be anything that it is like to be a rock, for instance—a rock lacks consciousness. But, arguably, there is something that it is like to be a bat (something involving being nocturnal and finding food through echolocation). Similarly, there seems to be something that it is like to experience pain. So, states that exhibit consciousness are states that there is something it is like to be in those states.

In spite of this rough characterization of consciousness, there are various additional questions. One question is simply what things have it or even what things *could* have it. Some things clearly have consciousness, such as most adult human beings; some things clearly do not, such as rocks. Other cases, however, are less clear. Spiders, for instance (unlike rocks) seem to be aware at some level, mending their webs and capturing prey: If they were not aware in some way that a web was damaged, presumably they would not mend it, and if they were not aware at some level that insects have blundered into their webs, spiders would not capture them. But it is not clear that spiders have consciousness. Computers perform very complex calculations, but it is not obvious that any computer (no matter how sophisticated) could ever have consciousness.

Another issue related to consciousness is the issue of what consciousness is for. What function (if any) does consciousness serve? Many philosophers believe that humans are the result of a physical, evolutionary process. However, it is not clear why consciousness would have evolved: It seems that humans could have survived and reproduced without ever coming to have consciousness. Some philosophers argue that though consciousness is indeed the result of evolution, it still serves no evolutionary function. In this view, a person's beliefs do not affect behavior.

Third, although the conception that there is something that it is like to be a conscious creature or have a conscious state says something about the nature of consciousness, what additional features there are of consciousness is controversial. Three features often thought to characterize consciousness are worth mentioning. The first is that a feature of some conscious states is intentionality, or aboutness. That is, some conscious states are *about* something. One's belief that whales are mammals, for instance, is about whales (and mammals). A second feature of consciousness has to do with the privileged access a conscious creature has to its own consciousness. To say one has privileged access to one's consciousness is just to say that one can know the content of one's consciousness (what one believes and feels, for example) in a way that others cannot. Only the person who is angry, for instance, has direct access to her anger (others might believe an angry person is angry because they see her slam the door, say, but they cannot perceive her actual sensation of anger).

Third, many states of consciousness have distinctive feels to them; they feel a certain way. Philosophers sometimes call such felt qualities of experience phenomenal qualities or, more commonly, qualia. A feature of some conscious states is that they have qualia. The notion of feeling here does not just involve physical contact; it includes other bodily sensations as well, such as the sensations of seeing purple clouds, hearing a flute, and tasting popcorn. Other qualia include the feelings associated with emotions. When a person feels a surge of anger, for example, her mental state of anger has a quale (it feels a certain way). Even a mood has a quale—the mood of boredom, for example, has a different feel than the mood of melancholy. It is usually thought that not all conscious states have qualia. For example, most philosophers think that the experience of having a belief does not have a quale. There does not seem to be something it is like to believe that whales are mammals, for instance; having this belief does not feel a particular way.

As with other mental phenomena, a major issue in the philosophy of mind is whether consciousness can be explained in physical terms only or, put another way, whether a materialist account of consciousness is or could be correct. Of particular concern is the relation between consciousness and the brain. On the surface, conscious mental states seem to be rather different than brain states. A brain has various features, such as having a certain shape and weight. However, a person's thoughts do not seem to have a shape or weigh anything. In addition, sensations such as joy are features of some conscious mental states but are not obviously features of the brain: It seems unlikely that a careful examination of the brain would uncover the sensation of joy. In part because the mind and the body do seem different, some philosophers have advocated dualist views of consciousness, according to which consciousness is nonphysical. Most (but not all) contemporary philosophers reject dualism. They seek to explain consciousness in physical terms only. It is apparent that there is a close relation between the brain and consciousness. For example, a person who is brain-dead lacks consciousness, and some drugs that affect the brain also seem to cause conscious mental states, such as hallucinations. Such facts suggest that consciousness can be explained in physical terms alone; perhaps if we knew everything there is to know about the brain and how it works, we would understand consciousness. Perhaps consciousness just *is* a matter of processes in the brain. If this were so, it would explain the very close relation between consciousness and the brain. Some views in the philosophy of mind, such as identity theory and functionalism, attempt to explain consciousness just in physical terms.

However, *how* to account for consciousness just in physical terms has proven difficult. There is often said to be an explanatory gap when it comes to consciousness. The idea is that we are unable to explain the connection between physical states and consciousness. Just examining the physical properties of the human brain would not seem to tell us why a human would be conscious. We know that there is a close relation between the mind and the brain, but it is difficult to see why there is such a relation. Often this point is made about qualia. Humans feel pain when certain physical fibers in the human body (C-fibers) are stimulated. But why should stimulating C-fibers cause pain and not some other sensation, such as heat? There seems to be no explanation for why certain physical states should be related to certain conscious states.

In addition, at least on the surface, it is difficult to understand qualia in materialist theories of mind. A famous thought experiment illustrates one difficulty with such theories. Suppose there was a scientist, Mary, who studies color and who has always lived in a room in which everything is black and white. Except for these colors, she sees no colors at all. Mary comes to know all the physical facts about color while in this room. Now suppose, upon leaving the room, she sees colors for the first time—green grass, the blue sky, a red apple. "Ah," she exclaims upon seeing the apple, "so that is what it is like to see red!" It appears that Mary has learned something new about red: what it is like to see red. This is a problem for materialist theories of mind because, according to the materialist, Mary should already have known everything there was to know about color (including red): After all, before leaving her black-and-white room, she knew all the physical facts about color. So, if Mary learned something about red upon seeing red for the first time, this suggests that there is more to our conscious experiences than physical facts. This suggests, in turn, that a theory of mind that attempts to explain consciousness just in terms of physical facts leaves something out. So, according to the objection, materialist theories of mind are wrong. This line of argument is often called the knowledge argument.

A related thought experiment was given in 1974 by the philosopher Thomas Nagel in an essay called "What It Is Like to Be a Bat?" Like Frank Jackson's imaginary case of Mary, the color scientist, Nagel's essay posed a challenge for accounting for consciousness in strictly physical, scientific terms. Nagel directed his challenge specifically toward reductionist and eliminativist views about mind. So, it is worth looking first at some of these views.

Views of consciousness that explain consciousness in physical terms only are called reductionist views: They are reductionist in the sense that they reduce the mind to the physical, that is, physical matter and physical properties. According to these views, much of what we ordinarily say about the mind and mental activity is true: It is true, for example, to say that what a person wants to do often affects what she does (the desire to swim, for instance, might cause a person to dive into a pool). Other philosophers believe there is (or will be) no need to talk about the mind at all: Just knowing about the brain (or some other physical stuff) eliminates any need to talk about a mind. On these views, much of what we ordinarily say about the mind and mental activities—such as believing, desiring, hoping, and so on—is misleading. Such talk is rather like an outdated scientific theory, somewhat like the old theory that living beings had something called a vital force that explained their ability to live. The notion of vital force was discarded as scientists came to understand biology and physiology more fully. Somewhat in the same way, according to eliminativist views about the mind, as we come to have a fuller scientific understanding of the brain, we can eliminate the notion of the mind and mental activities such as beliefs and desires.

Nagel's essay pointed out an apparent problem with reductionist and eliminativist views of consciousness. It seems that a bat is conscious and has experiences. So, Nagel supposed, there is something that it is like to be a bat (presumably this involves things such as flying and locating objects through echolocation). Nagel argued that knowing all the physical facts about a bat—all about the bat brain, say—will not tell us what it is like to *be* a bat. The point is that conscious experience is experienced from a particular perspective. In this case, it is the bat's perspective in question. We seem unable to know what it is like, from the bat's perspective, to be a bat. Nagel agrees, of course, that we can imagine some aspects of what it is like to be a bat: We can imagine what it is like to hang upside down, for example, and what it is like to fly. According to Nagel, however, this is just imagining what it is like for *us* to have batlike experiences and that is not the same thing as imagining what it is like for a *bat* to have bat experiences. Humans view the bat's experiences from a third-person perspective, that is, from outside the bat's

Photograph of a bat hanging upside down *(Photograph by H. Crepin; used under a Creative Commons license)*

perspective; we cannot experience what the bat itself experiences. The challenge for reductionist or eliminativist views about consciousness is this: If they are correct, then it seems that knowing all the physical facts about a bat should be enough to tell us all about a bat's consciousness. But, according to Nagel, it does not. What is missing from a strictly physical, scientific account is knowledge of what it is like to *be* a bat. Scientific knowledge is knowledge from a third-person perspective; it does not include knowledge from a first-person perspective, the perspective of the bat itself.

Nagel himself did not claim that his essay showed that reductionist and eliminativist views about mind are false. However, the essay presents a serious challenge for these views. One response can go, rather roughly, something like this: Perhaps the scientist who knows all the physical facts about a bat does know all about the bat's consciousness, but she learns about the bat's consciousness in a different way than the bat itself does. To illustrate, there are two ways of coming to know about Venus. Venus is visible in the sky in the early morning, as well as at night. One way of knowing about Venus is seeing Venus in the morning. Another way of knowing about Venus is seeing Venus at night. Similarly, perhaps one way of coming to know about consciousness is by learning all the physical facts about the conscious creature (the third-person perspective). But perhaps another way of coming to know about consciousness is by actually having the experience of being a bat (the first-person perspective). If this is so, then the scientist who knows all the physical facts about the bat is not missing any facts about the bat's consciousness; she has just learned about the bat's consciousness one way rather than another. However, this is a very rough response, and the issue continues to be controversial. In general, there is currently no consensus about whether (or how) materialist theories of mind can adequately account for consciousness.

Anomalous Monism and Functionalism

Anomalous Monism

Another account of mind that takes mind to be nonreducible to the physical is a view called anomalous monism. Anomalous monism is a version of monism in the sense that, according to it, mental events are physical events. Anomalous monism is anomalous in the sense that, according to it, mental events are anomalous, meaning that there are no strict scientific laws that govern the relation between mental events and physical events. The American philosopher Donald Davidson (1917–2003) has been the most prominent defender of anomalous monism, and this discussion will focus on his version of the view.

Most philosophers, when they write about mental phenomena, discuss those phenomena in terms of mental states (such as the state of seeing a red sunset, the state of feeling hungry, and so on). Davidson preferred to talk instead of mental events (as well as physical events). His reasons for this are complex and beyond our present scope. Still, it is worth saying something about mental and physical events. Suppose someone looks at an orange sunset. That experience of perceiving the sunset can be understood as an event—it is caused by certain things (such as the sun setting, the light reflecting in certain ways off the clouds, and the eye and the brain interpreting the visual information it receives), and it has a beginning and an end. Similarly, the experience of thinking things—that, say, it would be nice to take a walk in the woods—can be understood as an event. Something caused the thought (say, the memory of a past hike), which prompted the thought to form, and at some point the thought ends (say, as a person starts thinking about lunch instead). At the same time a person is having such mental experiences (perceptions, thoughts, feelings), there are physical changes that take place in a person's brain. Certain brain cells become active, and then their activity changes as another mental phenomenon occurs. These changes can also be understood as events, the result of certain causes, occurring for a given period of time, and then coming to an end.

With an event framework in place, Davidson makes three basic claims: First, that some mental events interact with physical events; second, that causation is governed by strict laws; and third, that there are no strict psychophysical laws, that is, strict laws governing the relation between mental events and physical events. Let us consider these claims in sequence. To say that some mental events interact causally with physical events is to say that some mental events cause physical events, and physical events cause some mental events. For an illustration of the first case, think of a person's desire to answer the phone, causing her to pick up the phone and answer it. For an example of the second case, think of the phone ringing as causing a person to desire to answer the phone. Regarding Davidson's claim that causation involves strict laws, a rough way of putting this point is that certain kinds of events cause other kinds of events, because those events are governed by strict scientific laws. For example, when a comet passes by the Earth, the Earth exerts a certain gravitational force on the comet, according to the law of gravity. In this instance, an event of one kind (a comet passing close to Earth) causes an event of another kind (the Earth exerting a gravitational force on the comet), because a strict scientific law governs those events. Insofar as two such events occur, they will occur according to such laws: Whenever a comet passes near the Earth, it simply must be the case that the Earth exerts a particular gravitational force. To return to the causal interaction between mental and physical events, according to Davidson, if mental events cause physical events and vice versa, then they must do so according to strict scientific laws.

We now turn to Davidson's third claim, that there are no strict laws governing the relation between physical events and mental events (that there are no psychophysical laws). Davidson's defense of this claim relies on his view of how people make sense of what other people are thinking, hoping, feeling, wishing, and so on. In brief, Davidson's claim is that we do so according to the principle of rationality: We try to understand another person in such a way that the person can be considered rational. Consider a person who says, "I'm just not myself today." One way of understanding this remark is to suppose that the speaker believes she is literally not herself—she is not identical with herself. But this is contradictory; it would be strange for a person really to mean and believe that she is not the same as herself when she says that. So, one is not likely to suppose that that is what she believes; one will cast about for a more sensible interpretation, on which the speaker appears to be more rational. One such interpretation is that the speaker means that she is behaving in ways that she normally does not, and more likely than not, that is what the speaker believes—not the contradictory belief that she is not the same as herself. What this illustrates is that when we try to make sense of what people believe, we proceed on the assumption (as much as we are able) that the speaker is rational. We avoid attributing to someone beliefs that are obviously false and beliefs that are plainly inconsistent. For instance, if someone seems to believe that there is a blizzard going on, we are less likely to think that she believes she will be comfortable in shirtsleeves if she goes outside (unless there are some rather odd circumstances that might make this latter belief rational). In short, when we attribute beliefs to others, we normally attempt to do so in such a way that the person seems rational. Similar remarks apply to how we make sense of what people desire, hope, value, and so on; for example, we are not likely to suppose that at the same time a person hopes to sail around the world she also desires never to leave her hometown.

Making sense of mental events, then—events such as a person's beliefs, intentions, desires, and so on—requires the principle of rationality. However—and this is a key difference—making sense of physical events does not require the principle of rationality. Making sense of why the brain is active in certain ways in response to certain stimuli, for instance, does not require the principle of rationality. Rather, we understand the relations between physical events in terms of strict scientific laws. Davidson's claim, in other words, is that whereas we understand mentality (believing, thinking, wishing, hoping, etc.) in terms of rationality, we understand the physical world in terms of strict scientific laws. It is this difference between the realm of the mental and the realm of the physical that, for Davidson, implies that there are no strict psychophysical laws. That is, this difference implies that there are no strict laws that govern the relation between mental events and physical events. In that sense, mental events are anomalous—unlike physical events, they cannot be explained or predicted according to strict scientific laws.

For Davidson, this also implies that when mental events cause physical events, they must do so in virtue of some feature other than a mental property. This is because strict scientific laws apply to physical events, not mental events. For Davidson, mental events are *identical* to physical events. One way of understanding this is that mental events, because they are physical events, have physical properties in virtue of which they can cause physical events. As an example, suppose someone's belief that the phone is ringing causes her to pick up the phone. The mental event (the belief) must have some physical property that causes the physical event (picking up the phone). For Davidson, in general, *every* individual mental event is identical to some individual physical event. That event can be described in different ways. It can be given a description in terms of mental activity, such as she's thinking she'd like to take a walk in the woods. But it can also be given a description in physical terms, a description that would presumably involve describing the activity of brain cells. Davidson believed that mental events *supervene* on physical events. That is, although mental events cannot be explained just in terms of physical events (mental events are not reducible to physical events), there could be no two physical events that are exactly alike yet have different mental properties.

An important point is that if Davidson is correct that there are no psychophysical laws, then there are no laws that govern what a person believes, desires, hopes, intends, or so on. Not only are there no such laws, but it is also impossible to predict what a person believes, desires, hopes, or intends on the basis of physical events in a person's brain. Knowing all there is to know about the brain will not allow us to predict that someone will want to wear orange socks, believe that there is intelligent life on other planets, or hope that a particular rock band will release another album. Moreover, knowing all the physical facts about the brain will not explain any of these mental events, nor any mental event. All of this, in turn, implies that humans have free will in the sense that our beliefs, desires, goals, and so on are not determined by past physical events. (Davidson also thinks they are not determined by past mental events.)

Anomalous monism, like other views in philosophy of mind, has attracted its share of attention and debate. One criticism commonly charged of anomalous monism is that it really amounts to an epiphenomalist view. That is, according to the criticism, anomalous monism cannot account for mental causation, for the apparent fact that mental events cause physical events. Instead, according to the criticism, anomalous monism implies that mental events are caused by physical events but cannot themselves cause physical events. To see why this might be so, suppose mental event M causes physical event P. Because mental events are identical to physical events (according to Davidson), and there are no strict laws governing the relations between mental events and physical events, this means that none of M's mental properties could have caused P. After all, if M caused P in virtue of M's mental properties, then it looks as if by Davidson's lights there would be laws governing how mental events are related to physical events. (This is because causation involves strict laws, according to Davidson.) But Davidson denied this. So, if M really did cause P, then it must have done so in virtue of physical properties. Notice, however, that there then seems to be no work for M's mental properties to do—M's *physical* properties are doing all the work to cause P. But then it appears that M's mental properties are really not involved in causing P at all—in short, it appears that they are epiphenomenal. As an illustration, suppose that M is the desire to eat pizza, and P is the event of taking a bite of a slice of pizza. M has physical properties—say, a certain pattern of brain cell activity. It is those physical properties that cause P, the taking a bite of a slice of pizza. But then it seems that the mental properties of M—the desiring part of M—are irrelevant to P after all. It is the physical properties that are doing all the causal work. Various versions of this objection have been raised against anomalous monism, and defenders of anomalous monism have given equally varied replies. As with so much in philosophy of mind, there is no broad consensus about the issue.

Functionalism

In the philosophy of mind, functionalism is the view that mental states (states such as thinking, perceiving, and feeling) should be defined in terms of their functions—in terms of what they *do*. It does not matter what mental states are made of, according to functionalism, as long as they perform certain functions. Analogously, a camera can be made of many different kinds of materials, such as plastic, metal, wood, and even paper. For something to be a camera, what matters is just that it functions a certain way (that it can take pictures), not what it is made of. Similarly, what matters for being in a mental state is to be in a state that functions in a certain way, not to be in a state made of any particular kind of stuff.

A function of a camera is to take pictures. But what is the function of a mental state? Functionalists typically understand the function of a mental state in terms of a mental state's causal relations—in other words, in terms of what causes a mental state and what the mental state causes. Consider, for instance, the mental state of pain. Pain is caused by certain things (such as injury or illness), and in turn, it causes certain behavior (for example, groaning and taking pain medication). In addition, pain is causally related to a person's other mental states; pain might cause a person to plan to see a doctor, for example, or cause a feeling of grumpiness. A way of talking about the various things that pain causes and is caused by is to say that pain has a causal role. This role is related to three things: stimuli (for example, injury), behavior (such as wincing), and other mental states (planning to see a doctor, for instance). According to functionalism, all mental states should be defined in terms of their causal roles. Causal roles, in turn, are understood in terms of stimuli, behavior, and other mental states.

Now cameras, although they are defined functionally, are made of something. Similarly, mental states are made of something too. In philosophy, this point is often made by saying that mental states are *realized*. For instance, humans are made of certain kinds of physical stuff and have a certain physical structure. States of this physical stuff play the causal role of pain. When a person burns herself on a hot stove, for example, certain fibers in the human body are stimulated and particular signals are sent to the brain, resulting in the feeling of pain. This state of the brain and nervous system play the causal role of pain; functionally speaking, this state of the brain and nervous system (together with this state's causal relations to other mental states) *is* pain. Of course, there are other animals that are physically quite different than humans, such as the octopus. As long as there is a state in the octopus that plays the causal role of pain, according to the functionalist, the octopus can experience the mental state of pain. It is even possible that aliens, computers, and assortments of tin cans and other trinkets could have mental states, as long as they have the appropriate functional organization. For instance, some internal state of the computer—a state likely involving circuit boards and microchips—could play the causal role of pain: It would be caused by things such as injury, cause certain behavior such as trying to avoid pain, and be related in certain ways to other mental states. Note that this is another way of saying that it is at least theoretically possible that aliens, computers, and organizations of tin cans could have minds. Most functionalists are materialists about mind; that is, they believe mind is material. (Strictly speaking, however, one can be both a functionalist and a dualist. To do so, one would agree that to be a mental state is just to function in a certain way *and* claim that at least some mental states are made of something nonphysical.)

Today functionalism is often seen as the most widely accepted view of mental states and, therefore, of mind. This is in part because functionalism avoids key objections faced by two other views of the mind. For example, according to identity theory, mental states are identical with brain states (of human structure and composition). An objection to this view is that it seems to suggest, falsely, that only beings with humanlike brains could have mental states; functionalism avoids this objection. In addition, according to behaviorism, mental states are identical with behavior; for instance, pain is identical to wincing, groaning, seeking pain relief, and so on. A problem with behaviorism is that it seems possible for a person to be in pain even if she does not exhibit these behaviors (a person in pain might show no sign of it, tightly controlling her behavior). Because functionalism views mental states as *causes* of behavior (not identical with behavior), functionalism avoids this objection too.

However, functionalism faces a number of objections of its own. Some philosophers have questioned whether having a certain functional organization is enough to have mental states. One standard objection is the inverted spectrum argument. Imagine that there is a person, Mona, who sees the color spectrum in an inverted way, relative to the vision of a normal person. That is, Mona sees red things as green, green things as red, yellow things as blue, and so on. For instance, when she looks at grass, she experiences the sensation of red (not green), although she calls grass green. According to the objection, the problem for functionalism is that this person seems to be functionally equivalent to a person with normal vision (call him Tom). Remember that the functional role of a mental state is its causal role: Mental states play a causal role regarding stimuli, behavior, and other mental states. Mona's mental state of seeing grass seems to be the same, functionally speaking, as Tom's mental state of seeing grass. It is the result of the same stimuli (the sight of grass), it produces the same behavior (for instance, calling grass green), and it is related in the same way to other mental states (for example, both believe that grass is roughly the same color that limes are). Yet Mona and Tom's mental states seem to be different: When Mona sees grass, she has the sensation of seeing red, and when Tom sees grass, he has the sensation of seeing green. If Mona and Tom are functionally equivalent, but their mental states are different, this must mean that there is more to being a mental state than functioning a certain way. So (according to the objection), functionalism is wrong.

A general concern illustrated by the inverted spectrum argument is that functionalism does not adequately address the issue of qualia. Qualia are sensations, or feels of things: for example, the tickly feel of a feather when it is brushed lightly against the skin or the sensation of seeing red (in the inverted spectrum objection, Mona and Tom experience different qualia). A related objection to functionalism regards *absent* qualia. Here the idea is that there could be something that would seem to have mental states, according to functionalism, yet lack qualia. For example, one philosopher imagines a robot controlled by the residents of a very populous nation, such as China. Each resident would receive information (say, via satellite) about stimuli presented to the robot, and in turn each resident would send a signal to the robot, who would then move in particular ways as a result. According to the story, the functional structure of the robot and the robot-controllers could be the same as the functional structure of the human body and the human brain (think of each person as corresponding to a human brain cell). If functionalism is true, then it would appear that the robot had mental states. For instance, there would be a certain state of the robot caused by injury that would cause the robot to try to avoid future injury and also relate in the right way to other mental states. So, the robot would experience pain. But, according to the objection, it is plain that the robot would not feel pain at all; it is just a robot. The qualia (the sensation of pain) would be absent. If this is so, then it looks as if there must be more to having some mental states than having states that play certain causal roles.

Another objection to functionalism is that it does not adequately account for cognition—how thought and understanding work. Of particular interest here are computers and whether it is possible for computers to think. Functionalism holds that they can, at least in principle (that need not mean, of course, that there are currently computers that think). Before considering the question further, it is worth considering the nature of cognition and two competing views regarding cognition: computationalism and connectionism.

Cognition, Artificial Intelligence, and the Chinese Room Argument

Cognition

A central question in the philosophy of mind is the nature of mind, and one aspect of mind is cognition. Knowing the nature of cognitive processes can tell us something about the nature of mind. Cognitive processes can be understood as processes for gaining knowledge. One way of considering cognition is by contrasting it with mental processes that do not seem to require conscious thought. For example, perceiving the warmth of sunlight on one's skin does not, by itself, seem to require thought; deciding to put on sunscreen to prevent sunburn does. Believing, reasoning, deciding, planning—these are all examples of cognition, or to put the point another way, these are all cognitive processes. However, there also seem to be cognitive processes we use that we are not consciously aware of. For instance, most people are capable of recognizing a great number of human faces, and most of the time such recognition does not involve conscious thought: Usually one does not, for example, consciously compare a person's face with a memory of that face, asking oneself questions such as is his nose long enough or are the eyebrows bushy? Rather, without consciously thinking about *how* we recognize a face, we just recognize that face. What this suggests is that not all cognition occurs consciously; facial recognition is one example of nonconscious cognition.

In cognitive science, as well as in some versions of functionalism, a popular view of human cognition is that it is computational. The basic idea is that the mind is like a computer. First, what matters for something to be a mind is how it is organized and what it does, not what it is made of physically. Just as software can be installed on computers made of different physical stuff, a mind could run on something other than a carbon-based brain. Second, as a computer performs computations, a mind performs computations. According to computationalism, then, cognition consists of performing computations. A computation is the manipulation of symbols to deliver a particular result (or output). Simple arithmetic, for instance, is computational. When a child adds 100 to 200, for example, she performs an operation of addition on symbols that represent the numbers 100 and 200, with the result that she comes up with the sum 300. According to computationalism, thinking in general involves manipulating symbols. Computers function by manipulating symbols in the forms of strings of 0s and 1s.

One way of illustrating this is with a Turing machine. A Turing machine, named after British mathematician Alan Turing (1912–54), who had the idea for such a machine, is a theoretical machine that

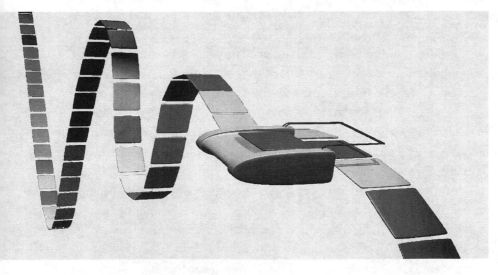

A graphic representation of the Turing machine

represents how a computer functions. Imagine a machine that has a scanner and can scan an infinitely long strip of paper (or tape) that is divided into squares. On each square of the paper is a symbol, a 0 or 1. The symbols themselves represent information. As the machine scans a particular square with the symbol on that square, it will either print a new symbol on that square (erasing the symbol that was already there) or move on to the next square and scan the symbol there. What the machine does in response to a given square depends on the state of the Turing machine at that moment, the particular symbol or symbols it scans, and its instructions; the machine is programmed to do certain things in response to some symbols. So, what the Turing machine does is take a certain input (the symbol on a square) and yield a certain output (writing a new symbol or moving on to the next symbol) according to rules. It does this in a step-by-step way. Although this sounds simple, the Turing machine is an accurate representation of how computers today actually function.

Somewhat in the same way, according to computationalism, the brain performs cognitive processes by manipulating symbols in the brain. (These symbols are not 0s and 1s but symbols particular to brains. Nor is this necessarily a conscious process; it is not as if we are consciously aware that our brains are manipulating symbols.) The symbols themselves represent information: for example, that bananas are nutritious, that in the formula $E = MC^2$, E stands for energy, and so on. When the brain manipulates inner symbols, it does so according to algorithms. This just means that it manipulates symbols in step-by-step processes (first the mind does one thing, and then it does another) and that it follows strict rules. As a result of following such processes, the mind delivers certain outputs. For instance, one recognizes one's teacher from the third grade, decides to have a banana with one's lunch, or comes to understand what the formula $E = MC^2$ means.

Important questions about cognition are whether *any* cognition is computational and whether *all* cognition is computational. A person's thought processes as she works out a mathematical proof seem to be rather a different sort of cognition than one's cognitive processes in recognizing 100 faces (the first processes are conscious, and the others are usually not; the first processes seem to occur in steps, but this is not obviously the case with the second processes). Does a computational view of cognition really account for each of these forms of cognition equally well? What about other forms of cognition, such as language use? Can all cognition really involve following strict rules? What about uses of intuition? These questions and similar ones are much debated. One alternative to computational views of mind is the view that cognition is embodied. According to this view, human cognition is a result of the facts that we have bodies and that we interact with our environment (with objects, other people, weather, and so on). So, it is a mistake to try to explain cognition in terms of computations, because computations alone make no reference to these basic facts. In part because of concerns about the classic view of computationalism, other thinkers argue that connectionism better describes human thought processes.

Connectionism

Connectionism is an area of cognitive science and artificial intelligence that, according to its advocates, might help answer the question of how people think by providing a model for how the human brain works. In contrast to a computational system that operates in a step-by-step process according to specific rules, a connectionist system need not operate according to specific rules. In addition, in a connectionist system, a network of units (parts) process information. So, connectionist systems need not just operate in a step-by-step fashion. Because each unit processes information simultaneously, connectionist systems are often called systems of parallel distributed processing: The processing of information is distributed (it occurs in different parts of the network) and it is parallel (it occurs in different parts at the same time). On the opposite page is an illustration of a simple connectionist network.

In this illustration, the input units are activated by stimuli from outside the system—for example, if the system were designed to detect a human face, the appearance of a human would activate the input units. When input units are activated, they transmit information to the hidden units. The hidden units, in turn, transmit information to the output units. So, what the connectionist system ultimately does in response to a stimulus depends on what all the units in the network do. What individual units do is a matter of what they decide to do in response to the information given to them by other units to which they are connected. ("Decide" is a metaphor; the unit does not make a decision in the sense of consciously thinking about the best thing to do.) Connections

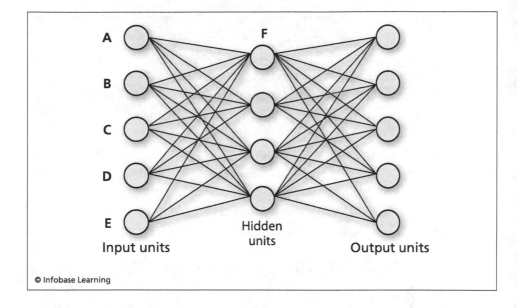

Input units | Hidden units | Output units

© Infobase Learning

between units are of different strengths: Connections between some units are stronger than connections between other units. The strength of a connection is called a weight. Specifically, the information transmitted is information about the activation level of the given unit—that is, information about how active that unit is. If a unit A is very active, for example, it communicates to other units that it is very active; if it is only mildly active, it communicates to other units that it is only mildly active. Unit F, for example, receives information from units A, B, C, D, and E. Suppose units A, B, C, D, and E each have a different level of activation—some are very active, some are mildly active, and some are not active at all. Unit F must evaluate all this information and decide how active to be in response to the information it has been given. What the entire system does in response to some stimulus, then, is a result of individual decisions by units.

We can think of a connectionist system as a model for the human brain. In the brain, nerve cells called neurons transmit information by transmitting nerve impulses. These nerve impulses travel via synapses, the junctions between neurons. So, in a connectionist network, the individual units of the system are analogous to neurons, and the weights between units are analogous to synapses. If the brain functions like a connectionist system, then human thinking is not a matter of following rules. Instead, thinking is a matter of different parts of the brain simultaneously processing information; also, neurons respond to the information they are given by other neurons. In addition, some neurons will be more strongly connected to each other than others.

One apparent advantage to connectionism over the classical view of cognition is that the human brain does not seem to function just in terms of rules. For example, there seems to be no rules for recognizing faces. However, it is controversial whether the brain is really more like a connectionist system rather than a digital computer. Perhaps the strongest objection to the view that the brain functions like a connectionist system is that connectionist systems do not account for the systematic nature of human thought. The idea here is that there is something systematic about some ways that human think, and connectionism does not adequately account for that. Often this systematic nature is linked to the human ability to understand and use language. For example, a person who understands the sentence "The cat saw the mouse" is very likely to understand the sentence "The mouse saw the cat" even if she has never encountered it before. This makes sense if there are rules governing language and humans understand these rules and follow them as they use language. What this suggests is that the human brain operates systematically in a way that connectionist systems do not. But if this is true, connectionism provides an inadequate model for the human brain. However, it is controversial whether this objection is a good one, and philosophers and cognitive scientists continue to have lively debates about how closely (or not) the brain functions like a connectionist system.

Artificial Intelligence

Connectionism and the classical view of cognition associated with computationalism provide different models for how cognition works. Some researchers build computers that are connectionist systems; others build computers that operate according to algorithms. However, whether it could *ever* be possible for a computer actually to think and understand, either in a connectionist way or in the algorithmic way described by classical computationalism, is a question that is central to artificial intelligence. Artificial intelligence is a discipline that investigates (and tries to create) intelligence and intelligent-acting behavior in computers. Certainly some computers are capable of striking feats. In

1997, for example, a computer named Deep Blue defeated Gary Kasparov, the reigning world champion, in a game of chess. But does this show that Deep Blue was intelligent? By investigating the possibility of intelligence in computers, artificial intelligence raises philosophical questions such as what is it to think, to be intelligent. By trying to answer such questions, it is possible that researchers in artificial intelligence will help us better understand the nature of intelligence and thought—and, by extension, the nature of mind.

One influential idea in artificial intelligence has been the Turing test, also named after Alan Turing. Instead of asking can machines think, Turing thought it was better to ask can machines perform certain tasks as well as a human. The idea behind this is that we say someone (or something) is intelligent on the basis of what it can *do*. For instance, we are likely to attribute intelligence to humans who can solve problems and carry on a conversation (having intelligence here means something along the lines of being capable of genuine thought, reason-

Statue of Alan Turing, logician who developed the Turing machine, in Bletchley Park, England *(Statue by Stephen Kettle; photograph by Jon Callas)*

ing, and problem-solving). In the same way, if computers can perform such tasks as well as humans, that seems to be a reason for attributing intelligence to those computers. Turing applied this idea specifically to using language. Suppose a human and a computer were communicating via typed messages, never seeing the other. If the human could not tell if she was communicating with a computer, then the computer would have passed the Turing test and could be considered intelligent. (Turing's test as he originally described it is more complicated than this description, but the basic idea is the same.) Influenced by Turing, many researchers in artificial intelligence have tried to build computers that can perform other tasks as well as humans, such as playing chess and recognizing faces.

In classical artificial intelligence, computers operate according to step-by-step instructions, doing first one thing and then another, according to specific rules (in connectionism systems, in contrast, computers operate by performing several processes at once). However, there are difficulties associated with artificial intelligence understood in this strict, rule-governed way. One problem has been that computers lack common sense. Humans acquire a great deal of knowledge just by living in the world. Since computers lack this life experience, they are likely to make mistakes a human would never make. For example, a person encountering the sentence "Sally deposited her paycheck in a bank" would assume that *bank* means a financial institution (not a riverbank), because she would know that people generally deposit paychecks in financial institutions, not riverbanks. A computer would lack such knowledge, however, unless it was supplied with rules regarding when *bank* means riverbank and when it means financial institution. However, common sense is not easily given in terms of rules. So, it is difficult to program common sense into computers that operate by following step-by-step rules. To take a simple example, suppose a computer followed the rule that *bank* means financial institution when it appears in a sentence involving money. According to this rule, "Sally buried her money in the bank" would mean that Sally buried her money in a financial institution. But this is a strange interpretation: Except in very unusual circumstances, people do not bury money in financial institutions. So to choose the correct meaning of *bank*, the computer would also need rules about *bury*. These rules, in turn, would have to take into account the unusual circumstances in which a person would in fact bury money in a financial institution. There are so many possible unusual circumstances, it seems unlikely that they could be described in advance by listing rules.

In addition, one important objection to classical artificial intelligence is that human behavior is not just a matter of following rules. Sometimes people use intuition instead. For example, when a person plays chess, she is not simply following rules. She follows hunches about her opponent's likely tactics and sometimes makes moves based on her feelings about how effective they are likely to be. Because intuition is not a matter of following rules, it could not be programmed into a computer that operated according to rules. The upshot of this objection is that computers could not have the intelligence of a human.

The Chinese Room Argument

The Chinese room argument is a famous argument given by the American philosopher John Searle (1932–   ) against the view that computers could ever have minds. A computer might be able to act *as if* it had a mind—for example, computers can solve complex mathematical problems and defeat world champion chess players. However, according to Searle, in such cases the computer does not actually think or understand anything. Such computers are sophisticated, but they do not have minds. Searle's argument is important for the question of what it is to have a mind in the first place; if computers cannot have minds but people can, then that seems to tell us something about the nature of mind itself. In part for these reasons, the Chinese room argument has generated much discussion in the philosophy of mind.

In Searle's imaginary situation, he is locked inside a room. While in this room, he is handed pieces of paper with Chinese symbols written on them. In response, Searle hands back other pieces of paper that also have Chinese symbols on them. Searle knows which Chinese symbols to hand back because he is following a rule book, and this rule book (written in English) tells him which symbols to hand back when he receives such and such symbols. Now Searle speaks English, but he does not know Chinese at all. So he does not know what any of the Chinese symbols mean. All he knows, in this scenario, is that when he receives symbols that have a certain shape, he is supposed to hand back symbols that have a certain shape. So Searle is not choosing Chinese symbols to hand back on the basis of what those symbols mean. Rather, he is choosing symbols to hand back on the basis of how the symbols look. In this imaginary situation, the symbols handed to Searle are questions (written in Chinese, of course), although he does not know this. Nor does Searle know that the symbols he hands back are answers to those questions (also written in Chinese). Now consider the person handing Searle the Chinese questions and getting the Chinese answers in return. Suppose this person knows Chinese. From her perspective, it would appear that Searle understands Chinese. This is just because the Chinese answers that Searle gives in response to the Chinese questions makes perfect sense: They are appropriate answers to the questions. But of course Searle does not understand Chinese: All he is doing is matching up symbols according to their shapes.

This imaginary situation is related to computers because Searle believes that, if he were locked in a Chinese room matching symbols with symbols, he would be functioning like a computer. This is because computers function by doing things with symbols (for instance, symbols in a machine language) according to specific instructions. A computer program, for instance, is just a set of instructions; Searle's rule book for matching Chinese symbols is like a computer program. The point is this: If Searle is functioning like a computer but does not understand Chinese, there must be more to understanding than functioning like a computer. Otherwise, in the Chinese room, Searle would understand Chinese—but he does not. If there is more to understanding than functioning like a computer, then computers lack understanding. Searle argues that true understanding involves knowing what the symbols *mean*. But computers have no idea what symbols mean. As Searle puts it, computers have syntax—that is, they have rules about how to match up symbols and combine them. But computers have no semantics—that is, no meanings associated with those symbols.

If Searle's argument is successful, it demonstrates at least two major points. The first is that computers (insofar as they function just by doing things with symbols according to rules) cannot have minds. They are incapable of real thinking, believing, or other mental activity. Second, if it is successful, Searle's argument shows that the human brain cannot be understood simply as a kind of computer. This is because computers lack understanding. But humans do have understanding—so, our brain is not just like a computer. Searle himself specifically argues that hav-

John Searle teaching a class. Searle presented the Chinese room argument as a way to differentiate between computers and the human mind. *(Photograph by Matthew Breindel)*

ing a mind is dependent on having a brain (and computers, of course, lack brains). Mind might function like a computer in some ways, but its capacity for understanding does not rest on those functions.

However, there is much disagreement about whether the Chinese room argument is successful. There have also been many responses to the argument. One common response is called the systems reply. According to this response, it is true that Searle, if he were locked in the Chinese room, would not understand Chinese. Rather, the whole system—Searle, the room, the rule book, the pencil and paper Searle uses—understands Chinese. It might sound strange to suppose that the entire Chinese room system in this sense understands Chinese. However, the idea here is that the Chinese room system is supposed to function like a computer. And it is not likely that one would say that a part of a computer understands—rather, one would say the computer *as a whole* (as an entire system) understands. For example, a computer named Deep Blue defeated a world chess champion. But if this computer understands chess, it is not as if one circuit board in the computer understands chess; rather, the *whole* of Deep Blue understands chess. Similarly, according to the systems response, it would be a mistake to suppose that Searle in the Chinese room understands Chinese. After all, he is only one part of a system, somewhat like an individual circuit board is only part of Deep Blue. But it is not a mistake to think that the whole system of the Chinese room understands Chinese, in the same way one might think that a very sophisticated computer *as a whole*, such as Deep Blue, understands chess. Searle believes the systems reply (and others) is flawed, and the Chinese room argument continues to be controversial.

Mysterianism and Extended Mind

Mysterianism

Although many contemporary philosophers are materialists about mind, it is difficult to account for certain features of the mind in physical terms, especially intentionality (the fact that some mental states are about something or another, as a belief might be about volcanoes, guitars, happiness, etc.) and qualia (feelings or sensations, such as sadness and the sensation of seeing red). There have been many materialist accounts, but none currently enjoys widespread agreement. Some philosophers, in response, have turned to versions of dualism to explain consciousness, regarding mind as nonphysical in some way. An alternative approach to the hard problem of consciousness—the problem of explaining how consciousness has risen from matter and physical processes—has been called mysterianism. The basic idea of mysterianism is that humans cannot understand consciousness.

Among its proponents is the contemporary British philosopher Colin McGinn (1950–   ). For McGinn, it is impossible for humans ever to understand consciousness; it is simply beyond our conceptual abilities. McGinn himself is a materialist; he believes that consciousness has in fact arisen from physical processes, and that there is some property (or properties) of the brain that give rise to consciousness. But what those properties are and how they have given rise to consciousness are questions whose answers are forever beyond our reach. By way of analogy, McGinn notes that a chimpanzee cannot ever understand theoretical physics; it just lacks the conceptual abilities ever to do so. Similarly, humans cannot ever understand consciousness; doing so is simply beyond our conceptual abilities. Consciousness is a mystery.

In defense of this conclusion, McGinn notes that how we have access to consciousness is very different from how we have access to the brain. Unlike the brain, consciousness cannot be perceived through the five senses. It cannot be seen, weighed, touched, or measured. If somehow one were to gaze at a living person's brain, all one would see is a brain, not consciousness. That person might be experiencing all kinds of mental activity—she might feel a little cold, be thinking that it is odd for anyone to be looking at her brain, and hoping to have some lunch soon. But none of these mental experiences would be visible just by looking at a brain. Of course, scientists might tell us that certain parts of the brain are more active than others at any given moment. But that is not the same thing as perceiving the mental experience itself; witnessing brain cells fire does not seem to be the same thing as perceiving a person's consciousness. Consciousness, McGinn writes, is "radically and intrinsically" unobservable. In other words, by its very nature consciousness is fundamentally unavailable for observation via the five senses. Instead, one has access to consciousness only through introspection. It is difficult to define introspection, but it is a sort of metaphorically looking inward at oneself (so, a person has direct access only to her *own* consciousness—outside science fiction stories, no one experiences any consciousness but her own). One knows that one is happy, for instance, or what one is thinking just by looking inward at one's own mind. One knows one has consciousness at all just through inspection. In contrast, the brain is not perceivable through introspection. A person cannot know how much her brain weighs, its color, or which brain cells are firing just by looking inward. In short, we have access to consciousness only through perception, and we have access to the brain only through our five senses.

For McGinn, this fundamental difference about how we come to know about consciousness and the brain points to the fact that we cannot ever come to know how the brain gives rise to consciousness. If we cannot ever have access to consciousness except through introspection and we cannot ever have access to the brain except through perception, then it is impossible for us to understand the connection between them. We cannot, McGinn wrote, "derive the imperceptible from the perceptible." What is imperceptible here is consciousness, and what is perceptible is the brain. So we cannot ever see how consciousness derives from the brain. McGinn's way of putting this point is to say that we are "cognitively closed" with respect to consciousness: An explanation for consciousness is "closed" to us because we are not conceptually equipped to understand such an explanation.

Critics have responded to this view in various ways. Some philosophers argue that there is no reason to suppose that our knowledge of consciousness through introspection, combined with our knowledge of the brain through perception, cannot together account for consciousness (that is, explain how the brain has given rise to consciousness). True, we cannot access consciousness via perception, and we cannot access the brain through introspection. But, some critics ask, why can we not take the different information we have received through perception and introspection, consider it together, and so use all of it to explain consciousness? Another response to McGinn is simply the point that just because we are (apparently) now incapable of explaining consciousness does not mean that we will forever be incapable of explaining consciousness. Perhaps McGinn is overly pessimistic, taking our current inability to explain consciousness for a permanent inability to explain consciousness. Yet another response to mysterianism is the claim that consciousness is a brute fact. In this view, there is nothing to explain regarding how the brain gives rise to consciousness: It simply does. Not all philosophers are satisfied with these various responses, and mysterianism continues to be controversial.

The Extended Mind Hypothesis

Another alternative to traditional views of mind is the view of extended mind. When a person thinks of the mind, what typically does she think of? If she is a dualist, she might think of something nonphysical. A materialist is likely to think of the brain. In either case, the view of mind is typically that mind is internal to a person, usually thought of as somehow inseparable from the brain. (Even Descartes, who defended dualism, believed that the nonphysical mind was somehow closely tied to a person's body, even if it was not identical to any part of the body.)

One way of putting this point is to say that the mind, whatever it is, does not lie outside one's skin: It is internal to oneself.

The view of extended mind departs from this traditional view. For defenders of an extended mind view, mind is extended in the sense that it is not confined to the brain, or even to a person's body. In particular, mind is extended in the sense that it incorporates objects in a person's external environment. This view, defended by the contemporary philosophers Andy Clark (1957–) and David J. Chalmers (1966–), makes this point by discussing cognitive processes in particular (that is, processes related to cognition, such as thinking and remembering). They illustrate with the following imaginary scenario: Suppose two people, Inga and Otto, each want to go to a particular museum. (They do not know each other, so they make their plans separately.) Now Inga simply remembers where the museum is and successfully makes her way to the museum on the basis of that memory. Otto, on the other hand, suffers from Alzheimer's disease, and his memory is faulty. To make up for his faulty memory, Otto keeps a notebook in which he writes down information. In this particular instance, Otto does not remember where the museum is. So before he starts off on his trip, he consults his notebook, in which he has written the location of the museum; he finds the location written there and goes to the museum.

Now for proponents of the extended mind, Otto's mind extends to his notebook. It is not just that Otto uses his notebook to do things like get to the museum; it is that his notebook is really *part* of his mind in the sense that it is part of his cognitive system. The notebook is part of how Otto actually cognizes, how he actually thinks, remembers, and reasons. Put another way, we can consider the notebook and Otto's brain as a coupled cognitive system. Because Otto's cognitive system includes the notebook, it would be a mistake to suppose that Otto's mind is just his brain. One way we can think of this is in terms of beliefs. Inga's belief that the museum is located at such and such streets is in her head. Otto's belief that the museum is located at such and such streets is in his notebook. Otto's notebook functions like Inga's memory does, and just as Inga's belief (in her brain) is part of Inga's mind, Otto's belief (in his notebook) is part of Otto's mind. Not all cognitive processes are in the head.

In general, according to the extended mind thesis, the environment is not passive in our cognitive processes. Other thinkers have pointed to the use of other external objects to help a person think, plan, remember, or so on. For example, people use pencil and paper to perform mathematical equations. Scrabble players move tiles around in an effort to see what different words those tiles might form. Others write when they think. In all these cases, the use of objects such as pencils, paper, tiles, and computers are part of cognitive processes, and the mind extends to them.

Animal Minds

Animals sometimes behave in surprising and impressive ways. Vervet monkeys give warning calls to alert other monkeys of predators, using a different call for each kind of predator. Carrier pigeons find their way home across hundreds of miles of unfamiliar territory. Honey bees dance to inform other bees of the location of food. Such behavior seems complex and sophisticated, but it is not clear what it tells us about the mental lives of animals. Do animals think? Can they reason, and do they experience emotions? Are animals conscious? These are questions basic to philosophical work on animal minds. They are significant not only for theories of consciousness but also for animal ethics: If animals are conscious, then it would appear that we ought to consider their interests and well-being, so we cannot treat them any way we like.

In one commonsense view, it seems obvious that at least some animals reason. Most people who have pets believe that some animals are both aware and capable of feeling and thought. For instance, if a person praises the family dog for staying off the furniture, it is usually on the assumption that the dog understands praise, desires it, and will modify its behavior to get it. However, a machine might also behave according to changes in its environment: Pressing a button on a toaster can cause the toast to toast lighter or darker, without the toaster having any thoughts about toasting (or anything else). In one important historical view, the view of the 17th-century philosopher René Descartes, animals are more like toasters than they are like people. According to Descartes, animals are not capable of feeling, thought, or reason; they are mechanisms, mindless machines made of flesh and blood. So, when a dog refrains from jumping on the furniture, it is not because it has learned that that is what people want it to do. Its behavior is purely mechanical, much in the same way that the toaster's behavior is purely mechanical. Descartes believed that animals lack minds because he believed that they could not reason (specifically, that they could not use problem-solving skills in a wide range of situations) and because they could not use language. Differences in human-animal anatomy (such as the shape of the mouth and tongue) did not explain the lack of language in animals, Descartes thought. After all, many humans physically incapable of speaking could nonetheless learn to write or use sign language. What did explain the lack of language, Descartes believed, was lack of thought. (The utterances of words by parrots and the like Descartes regarded as mere thoughtless imitation, not as true use of language.)

Few philosophers today believe that animals are mechanisms lacking any sensations or awareness. Most (but not all) philosophers agree that some animals are sentient—that is, able to experience positive and negative experiences, such as pleasure and pain. However, some contemporary philosophers have continued to link language to thought, denying that thought can exist independently of language and therefore also denying that animals can think. (Language here includes written and sign language; it does not just refer to spoken language.) The most prominent of these philosophers is Donald Davidson. Davidson's reasoning is complex, but at the heart of his reasoning is the claim that to have a belief it is necessary to have the concept of belief. So, if a creature does not have the concept of belief, it cannot have beliefs (which, for the purpose of this discussion, is another way of saying it cannot have thoughts). This is related to language because, according to Davidson, one acquires the concept of belief through interpreting speech; if one does not have language, one cannot interpret speech. As animals do not have language, they do not interpret speech and therefore do not acquire the concept of belief. So, Davidson reasons, insofar as animals lack language, they lack thought. (An interesting consequence of Davidson's argument is that young children who have not yet acquired language also lack thought.) Davidson's argument has been criticized on various grounds; some philosophers deny that having a belief requires having the concept of a belief. Even if Davidson is right that thought requires language, there is some question regarding whether this establishes that animals cannot think. Some empirical studies involving chimpanzees (as well as the case of an African gray parrot named Alex) are suggestive of the view that some animals are capable of learning language to an extent. However, many linguists deny that the animals in these studies genuinely learned a language, and their significance remains controversial.

Another important issue related to animal minds is animal consciousness. The nature of human consciousness is the subject of much discussion in philosophy of mind, and currently there is no single accepted account. In addition, the word *consciousness* is used in a multitude of ways. Most philosophers agree that there are some animals that are conscious in the sense that they are aware of their environments and respond to them, as when, say, a zebra spots a lion and flees. More controversial is whether animals are conscious in the sense that there is a *feel* to their experiences. In his essay "What Is It Like to Be a Bat?" Thomas Nagel assumed that there is something that it is like to be a bat; the experiences of a bat have a certain qualitative feel to them. To see what this might mean, consider a person's experience of skiing—the experience *feels* like something, including perhaps the sensations of speed, wind on one's face, and exhilaration. The kind of consciousness that involves a distinct feel to one's experiences is phenomenal consciousness, and philosophers and others have variously argued for and against the view that (at least some) animals have this kind of consciousness. Donald Griffin has argued that animals are conscious on the basis of field studies of animals in their natural environments (a discipline called cognitive ethology). Griffin's claims have been criticized for being anthropomorphic (wrongly attributing human characteristics to animals), but this criticism has itself been criticized.

One reason for thinking that some animals are phenomenally conscious is simply that there are significant similarities between people and animals. For example, humans share anatomical and physiological structures with many mammals. Animal behavior is also often strikingly similar to human behavior. Animals tend to avoid things that cause them pain, for instance, and they often react to apparent pain by grimacing, writhing, and vocalizing (responses shared by humans). One might argue that the best explanation for such similarities is that animals that share them with humans are conscious, even as humans are conscious. In addition, these considerations might gain strength through the supposition that humans and animals are products of the same evolutionary processes. If this is the case, it seems reasonable that there is no sharp division between humans and other animals; if consciousness is a product of evolution, then there seems to be no reason why it would not have developed in animals in addition to humans. However, there are objections to this reasoning. Even if animals *could* have developed consciousness, this does not mean they did. In addition, animal-human similarities need not imply that animals (like humans) are conscious. For instance, a robot could react to pain in the same way a person does, but this would not show that the robot is conscious.

Two other issues related to consciousness are worth mentioning. The first is the idea of a theory of mind. When we attribute thoughts and beliefs to other beings, we can be said to have a theory of mind; in other words, we have beliefs about someone (or something) else's beliefs, and sometimes we act on the basis of our beliefs. For example, a spy might communicate a message in a secret code because she believes that another person knows the code and that their enemies do not. Whether animals have a theory of mind about other animals (or humans) is another important and controversial topic. Some philosophers have argued that animals do not, arguing (roughly) that because they do not, animals do not have phenomenal consciousness either. A second important issue is consciousness of self. Studies of chimpanzees and dolphins have suggested that these animals recognize themselves in the mirror, and some thinkers argue that this is evidence that these animals are self-aware. However, this issue also continues to be controversial.

Concluding Discussion Questions

1. Why does explaining mental causation pose a problem for substance dualism? How does parallelism respond to this problem? How does epiphenomenalism? Do you think these are good accounts of mental causation? Why or why not? If not, do you think any materialist account of mind does a better job of explaining mental causation?

2. Suppose an alien came to Earth. It carries on conversations, laughs at jokes, and winces when it is pricked with a needle. What would a logical behaviorist say about whether it has a mind? What would an identity theorist say? What would a functionalist say?

3. According to Berkeley, what does reality consist of? If you kicked a rock, why does that not refute Berkeley? Is there any way to show that Berkeley is wrong?

4. What is the argument by analogy for the existence of other minds? What does it mean to say it is an inductive argument? Do you think the argument is a good argument? Why or why not?

5. What is consciousness, as described by Thomas Nagel? How does his claim that we cannot ever know what it is like to be a bat challenge materialist views of mind? Do you think his claim

shows that materialist views of mind must be wrong? Why or why not?

6. What is the computational view of cognition? Do you think humans really think computationally? If not, what are some ways in which they do not?

Further Reading

Berkeley, George. *Principles of Human Knowledge and Three Dialogues.* Edited by Howard Robinson. Oxford: Oxford University Press, 2009.

Blackmore, Susan. *Consciousness: An Introduction.* Oxford: Oxford University Press, 2004.

Boden, M. A. *The Philosophy of Artificial Intelligence.* Oxford: Oxford University Press, 1990.

Churchland, Paul M. *Matter and Consciousness.* Rev. ed. Cambridge, Mass.: MIT Press, 1996.

Clark, Andy. *Mindware: An Introduction to the Philosophy of Cognitive Science.* Oxford: Oxford University Press, 2000.

Descartes, René. *Meditations on First Philosophy.* Indianapolis: Hacket, 1993.

Feser, Edward. *Philosophy of Mind: A Short Introduction.* Oxford: Oneworld, 2005.

Heil, John. *Philosophy of Mind: A Contemporary Introduction.* New York: Routledge University Press, 2004.

Lowe, E. J. *An Introduction to the Philosophy of Mind.* Cambridge: Cambridge University Press, 2000.

Ludlow, Peter, Yujin, Nagasawa, and Daniel Stoljar. *There's Something about Mary: Essays on Phenomenal Consciousness and Frank Jackson's Knowledge Argument.* Cambridge, Mass.: MIT Press, 2004.

Lycan, William G. *Mind and Cognition.* Malden: Blackwell, 1999.

Preston, John, and Mark Bishop. *Views into the Chinese Room.* Oxford: Oxford University Press, 2002.

Ryle, Gilbert. *The Concept of Mind.* Introduction by Daniel Dennett. Chicago: Chicago University Press, 2000.

Wynne, Clive D. L. *Animal Cognition—The Mental Lives of Animals.* New York: Palgrave, 2001.

Glossary

anomalous monism   the view that mental events are identical to physical events, mental events sometimes cause physical events and vice versa, and there are no strict laws governing the relation between mental events and physical events.

artificial intelligence   a discipline that investigates and tries to create intelligent and/or intelligent-acting computers; in this way, it can shed light on the nature of thought (and, by extension, mind).

computationalism   the view that the mind functions like a computer, by processing information, represented by symbols, according to step-by-step rules.

connectionism   an area in philosophy of mind and artificial intelligence that models cognitive processes as though they take place through the activity of multiple connected units that simultaneously process information.

dualism   in philosophy of mind, the view that mind is nonphysical and the body is physical. Substance dualism holds that mind is a nonphysical substance, body is a physical substance, and that neither is reducible to the other. Property dualism holds that mind consists of, or has, nonphysical properties, and body has physical properties, and that neither mental properties nor physical properties are reducible to the other.

eliminative materialism   a materialist view of the mind according to which ordinary concepts related to the mind, such as the concepts of beliefs, desires, and feelings, will be eliminated in a complete, scientific understanding of the mind.

emergentism   the view that mental properties emerge from what is physical, such as the brain, but that they cannot be reduced to what is physical, nor predicted from their physical origin.

epiphenomenalism   the view that mental events do not cause physical events, although mental events can be caused by physical events. According to this view, some mental events (or phenomena) are the result of physical events, but they have no causal effects on the physical world.

extended mind hypothesis   the hypothesis that mind does not exist just within the confines of a person's brain or body but can extend to include objects in a person's external environment.

folk psychology   our ordinary understanding of and concepts regarding the mind, such as the concepts of beliefs, intentions, desires, and feelings.

functionalism   the view that mind is best characterized functionally—to have a mental state, for example, is to have inner states that play particular causal roles (they cause some behavior, are caused by some events, and are related in certain ways to other inner states).

idealism   the view that reality is essentially mental; George Berkeley's idealism holds that only minds and ideas exist and that physical matter does not. His idealism is monistic in the sense that it holds that only what is mental is real.

identity theory   the materialist view that mental states are identical to brain states. According to token identity theory, individual mental states are identical to individual brain states. According to type identity theory, certain kinds (types) of mental states are identical to certain kinds of brain states.

intentionality   a term for a feature of some mental states; a mental state is said to have intentionality if it is about something (the belief that cats like catnip, for instance, is about cats and catnip; such a belief has intentionality). Some mental states, such as the state of pain, are commonly thought to lack intentionality.

logical behaviorism   the view that terms for mental states should be understood as saying something about how one is disposed to behave in publicly observable ways; no reference is made to inner sensations, thoughts, feelings, etc.

materialism/physicalism   in philosophy of mind, the view that mind is physical or material.

monism   in philosophy of mind, the view that mind and body are made of the same stuff; two versions of monism are idealism and materialism.

mysterianism the view that humans are conceptually incapable of understanding consciousness, particularly the relation between consciousness and the brain.

parallelism the view that mental events and physical events have no effect on each other; mental events do not cause physical events, and physical events do not cause physical events. Rather, a person's mental events are parallel to the physical, bodily events.

qualia the felt aspects of experience, such as emotions (e.g., joy) and sensations (e.g., ticklishness, the sensation of seeing yellow, the scent of roses).

reductionism the view that a thing, concept, or theory can be reduced to a more basic thing, concept, or theory. In ontological reduction, a thing is thought to reduce to something else that is more basic (for instance, water can be reduced to H_2O; that is all there is to water). In epistemological reduction, some concept or theory can be reduced to a more basic concept or theory (the more basic concept or theory explains all there is to explain about the other concept or theory). For example, some philosophers believe that the concept of mind can be reduced to (be explained entirely by) the concept of the brain.

solipsism the view that only oneself exists; for solipsists, there are no other minds.

Turing machine a hypothetical machine that illustrates how a computer functions. Turing machines function by scanning symbols printed on an infinitely long strip of paper and either replacing those symbols with new ones or scanning a different symbol on the paper, depending on the machine's internal state, the symbol it scans, and the set of instructions it follows.

Turing test a test proposed by English mathematician Alan Turing for determining whether a machine counts as intelligent. For a machine (such as a computer) to pass the Turing test, it must pass itself off in conversation with a person as another person; in such tests, the person would not see the machine, and conversation might proceed through devices such as keyboards rather than through speaking out loud. The ability to pass the Turing test, some believe, is a sign of intelligence.

Key People

Berkeley, George (1685–1753)   *Irish philosopher who defended idealism, arguing that reality consists of ideas and minds; Berkeley denied the existence of matter.*

In the passage below, Berkeley acknowledges that ordinary objects (such as tables) exist but argues that they are nothing but ideas and therefore dependent for their existence on a perceiving mind.

> The table I write on I say exists that is, I see and feel it; and if I were out of my study I should say it existed—meaning thereby that if I was in my study I might perceive it, or that some other spirit actually does perceive it. There was an odor, that is, it was smelled; there was a sound, that is to say, it was heard; a color or figure, and it was perceived by sight or touch. This is all that I can understand by these and the like expressions. For as to what is said of the absolute existence of unthinking things without any relation to their being perceived, that seems perfectly unintelligible. Their *esse* is *percipi,* nor is it possible they should have any existence out of the minds or thinking things which perceive them.
>
> . . . It is indeed an opinion strangely prevailing amongst men that houses, mountains, rivers, and, in a word, all sensible objects have an existence, natural or real, distinct from their being perceived by the understanding. But with how great an assurance and acquiescence soever this principle may be entertained in the world, yet whoever shall find in his heart to call it in question may, if I mistake not, perceive it to involve a manifest contradiction. For what are the forementioned objects but the things we perceive by sense? And what do we perceive besides our own ideas or sensations? And is it not plainly repugnant that any one of these, or any combination of should exist unperceived?

[Berkeley, George. *A Treatise Concerning the Principles of Human Knowledge.* In *Works*, vol. 2. Edinburgh: Thomas Nelson, 1710.]

Broad, C. D. **(1887–1971)** *British philosopher who formulated a thesis that there could be emergent properties, properties that cannot be reduced to nor predicted from the parts from which they emerge.*

In this passage Broad offers a characterization of the theory of emergence.

> On the first form of the theory the characteristic behaviour of the whole *could* not, even in theory, be deduced from the most complete knowledge of the behaviour of its components, taken separately or in other combinations, and of their proportions and arrangements in this whole. This alternative, which I have roughly outlined and shall soon discuss in detail, is what I understand by the "Theory of Emergence" . . . there is no doubt, as I hope to show, that it is a logically possible view with a good deal in its favour.

> [Broad, C. D. *The Mind and Its Place in Nature*. London: Routledge & Kegan Paul, 1925.]

Davidson, Donald **(1917–2003)** *American philosopher who defended anomalous monism, the view that mental events are identical to physical events, mental events causally interact with physical events, but that there are no strict laws that govern the relation between mental events and physical events.*

In the passage below, Davidson explains why, in his view, there can be no explanation of mental events in general in terms of physical laws.

> Mental events as a class cannot be explained by physical science . . . the explanations of mental events in which we are typically interested relate them to other mental events and conditions. We explain a man's free actions . . . by appeal to his desires, habits, knowledge and perceptions. Such accounts of intentional behavior operate in a conceptual framework removed from the direct reach of physical law by describing both cause and effect, reason and action, as aspects of a portrait of a human agent. The anomalism of the mental is . . . a necessary condition for viewing action as autonomous.

> [Davidson, Donald. "Mental Events." In *Essays on Actions & Events*. Oxford: Clarendon, 1980.]

Descartes, René (1596–1650)   *Often called the father of modern philosophy, Descartes was a French philosopher who defended substance dualism, the view that mind is a nonphysical substance and the body is a physical substance.*

Descartes claims in the following selection that, because he can clearly distinguish the mind from the body, the mind and body must be distinct.

> And, firstly, because I know that all which I clearly and distinctly conceive can be produced by God exactly as I conceive it, it is sufficient that I am able clearly and distinctly to conceive one thing apart from another, in order to be certain that the one is different from the other, seeing they may at least be made to exist separately, by the omnipotence of God; and it matters not by what power this separation is made, in order to be compelled to judge them different; and, therefore, merely because I know with certitude that I exist, and because, in the meantime, I do not observe that aught necessarily belongs to my nature or essence beyond my being a thinking thing, I rightly conclude that my essence consists only in my being a thinking thing [or a substance whose whole essence or nature is merely thinking]. And although I may, or rather, as I will shortly say, although I certainly do possess a body with which I am very closely conjoined; nevertheless, because, on the one hand, I have a clear and distinct idea of myself, in as far as I am only a thinking and unextended thing, and as, on the other hand, I possess a distinct idea of body, in as far as it is only an extended and unthinking thing, it is certain that I, [that is, my mind, by which I am what I am], is entirely and truly distinct from my body, and may exist without it.

[Descartes, René. *Meditations* (Meditation VI). In *The Method, Meditations and Philosophy of Descartes, Translated from the Original Texts, with a New Introductory Essay, Historical and Critical by John Veitch and a Special Introduction by Frank Sewall.* Washington: M. Walter Dunne, 1901.]

Hobbes, Thomas (1588–1679)   *English philosopher who argued for materialism, claiming that all mental activity can be understood in terms of movement of matter (matter in motion).*

Hobbes here describes the functioning of animals (including humans) as matter in motion: Just as physical processes such as digestion are to be understood in terms of the motion of physical matter, mental activities (such as desiring) are to be accounted for in terms of the motion of physical matter.

There be in animals, two sorts of *motions* peculiar to them: one called *vital;* begun in generation, and continued without interruption through their whole life; such as are the *course* of the *blood,* the *pulse,* the *breathing,* the *concoction, nutrition, excretion,* &c. . . . the other is *animal motion,* otherwise called *voluntary motion;* as to *go,* to *speak,* to *move* any of our limbs, in such manner as is first fancied in our minds. That sense is *motion* in the organs and interior parts of man's body, caused by the action of the things we see, hear, &c.; and that fancy is but the relics of the same *motion,* remaining after sense, has been already said in the first and second chapters. And because *going, speaking,* and the like voluntary *motions,* depend always upon a precedent thought of *whither, which way,* and *what;* it is evident, that the imagination is the first internal beginning of all voluntary *motion.* And although unstudied men do not conceive any *motion* at all to be there, where the thing moved is invisible; or the space it is moved in is, for the shortness of it, insensible; yet that doth not hinder, but that such *motions* are. For let a space be never so little, that which is moved over a greater space, whereof that little one is part, must first be moved over that. These small beginnings of *motion,* within the body of man, before they appear in walking, speaking, striking, and other visible actions, are commonly called endeavour . . . This endeavour, when it is toward something which causes it, is called appetite, or desire; the latter, being the general name; and the other oftentimes restrained to signify the desire of food, namely *hunger* and *thirst.* And when the endeavour is fromward something, it is generally called aversion.

[Hobbes, Thomas. *The English Works of Thomas Hobbes of Malmesbury; Now First Collected and Edited by Sir William Molesworth, Bart.* 11 vols. Vol. 3. Chapter VI: "Of the Interior Beginnings of Voluntary Motions; Commonly Called the Passions; and the Speeches by Which They Are Expressed." London: Bohn, 1899–45.]

Jackson, Frank (1943–) *Australian philosopher who posed the famous knowledge argument, according to which knowing all the physical facts about color and perception would not tell a person what it is like to see that color; according to the argument, this shows that physicalism is false.*

Below, Frank Jackson gives a very brief summary of the knowledge argument against physicalism; the name "Mary" here refers to a hypothetical color scientist who all her life has been living in a room in which she sees only black, white, and shades of gray.

> Physicalism is not the noncontroversial thesis that the actual world is largely physical, but the challenging thesis that it is entirely physical. This is why physicalists must hold that complete physical knowledge is complete knowledge simpliciter . . . It seems, however, that Mary does not know all there is to know. For when she is let out of the black and white room . . . she will learn what it is like to see something red, say. This is rightly described as *learning* . . . Hence, physicalism is false. This is the knowledge argument against physicalism in one of its manifestations.

> [Jackson, Frank. "What Mary Didn't Know." *Journal of Philosophy* 83, no. 5 (May 1986): 291–295.]

Nagel, Thomas (1937–   ) *American philosopher who asked what is it like to be a bat. In an essay whose title is that question, Nagel argued that humans cannot ever know what it is like to be a bat. Consciousness, he thought, is always from a first-person perspective, and therefore materialist views of mind cannot adequately account for consciousness.*

In the following passage, Nagel summarizes what he sees as a difficulty for any objective account of consciousness.

> It is impossible to exclude the phenomenological features of experience from a reduction in the same way that one excludes the phenomenal features of an ordinary substance from a physical or chemical reduction of it . . . If physicalism is to be defended, the phenomenological features must themselves by given a physical account. But when we examine their subjective character it seems that such a result is impossible. The reason is that every subjective phenomenon

is essentially connected with a single point of view, and it seems inevitable that an objective, physical theory will abandon that point of view.

[Nagel, Thomas. "What Is It Like to Be a Bat?" *Philosophical Review* 83, no. 4 (October 1974): 435–450.]

Putnam, Hilary (1926–) *American philosopher who defended an early version of functionalism, according to which mental states are to be understood in terms of their functions (what they do) rather than what they are made of.*

Putnam argues against the claim that mental states are identical to brain states, in favor of a functionalist account of mental states. He notes that the similarity of behavior among organisms who seem to experience certain mental states (for instance, pain behavior is similar in humans, cattle, and birds) suggests that these organisms share a certain functional organization; in particular, it suggests this more strongly than that these organizations have the same material composition.

I shall argue . . . that pain is not a brain state . . . but another *kind* of state entirely. I propose the hypothesis that pain . . . is a functional state of a whole organism. Turning now to the considerations *for* the functional-state theory . . . we identify organisms as in pain, or hungry, or angry, or in heat, etc., on the basis of their *behavior.* But . . . similarities in the behavior of two systems are . . . a reason to suspect similarities in the functional organization of the two systems . . .

[Putnam, Hilary. "The Nature of Mental States." In *The Nature of Mind*, edited by David M. Rosenthal. Oxford: Oxford University Press, 1991.]

Quine, Willard Van Orman (1908–2000) *American philosopher who defended a version of behaviorism that focused on how we learn language; according to Quine, we do so by observing behavior (including verbal behavior).*

In the passage below, Quine describes behavioral evidence as the only available evidence for someone trying to translate a language with which she is utterly unfamiliar.

The recovery of a man's current language from his currently observed responses is the task of the linguist who, unaided by an interpreter, is out to penetrate and translate a language hitherto unknown. All the objective data he has to go on are the forces that he sees impinging on the native's surfaces and the observable behavior, vocal and otherwise, of the native. Such data evince native "meanings" only of the most objectively empirical or stimulus-linked variety.

[Quine, W. V. O. *Word and Object*. Cambridge, Mass.: MIT Press, 1960.]

Ryle, Gilbert (1900–1976) *British philosopher associated with logical behaviorism, according to which mental terms are to be understood in terms of dispositions to behavior.*

Ryle coined the phrase "ghost in the machine" to describe dualist views inspired by Descartes; he believed such views are due to what he called a category mistake.

I shall often speak of . . . [dualism inspired by Descartes] with deliberate abusiveness, as "the dogma of the Ghost in the Machine." I hope to prove that it is entirely false, and false not in detail but in principle. It is not merely an assemblage of particular mistakes. It is one big mistake and a mistake of a special kind. It is, namely, a category mistake. It represents the facts of mental life as if they belonged to one logical type or category . . . when they actually belong to another. The dogma is therefore a philosopher's myth.

[Ryle, Gilbert. *The Concept of Mind*. London: Hutchinson and Company, 1949.]

Searle, John (1932–) *American philosopher who argued in his famous Chinese room argument against the possibility that computers could ever be capable of genuine thought. Searle believes, as the passage below illustrates, that there must be more to the capacity for understanding than the way a digital computer functions.*

Of course the brain is a digital computer . . . The point is that the brain's causal capacity to produce intentionality cannot consist in its instantiating a computer program, since for any program you like it is possible for something to instantiate that program and still not have any mental states. Whatever it is that the brain does to produce intentionality, it cannot consist in instantiating a program, since no program, by itself, is sufficient for intentionality.

[Searle, John. "Minds, Brains, and Programs." *Behavioral and Brain Sciences* 3, no. 3 (September 1980): 417–424.]

Skinner, B. F. (1904–1990) *Pioneering psychologist who established the school of behaviorism in psychology, according to which psychology should make no references to inner mental states but confine its attention to publicly observable behavior. This view influenced other versions of behaviorism.*

Below Skinner likens the role of environment in influencing human behavior to natural selection in evolution. He suggests that it is the relation between behavior and the environment that explains human behavior, not mental states such as desires and plans.

The environment not only prods or lashes, it selects. Its role is similar to that in natural selection . . . Behavior is shaped and maintained by its consequences . . . Behavior which operates upon the environment to produce consequences . . . can be studied by arranging environments in which specific consequences are contingent upon it. The contingencies under investigation have become steadily more complex, and one by one they are taking over the explanatory functions previously assigned to personalities, states of mind, feelings, traits of character, purposes, and intentions.

[Skinner, B. F. *Beyond Freedom and Dignity*. Indianapolis: Hackett, 1971]

Turing, Alan (1912–1954) *British mathematician who invented both the idea of the Turing machine (a hypothetical machine that represents how a computer works) and proposed the Turing test as a means for testing intelligence. If a computer, unseen by a human, could pass for a human in conversation, it could be said to pass the Turing test and be considered as intelligent.*

Turing suggested replacing the question can machines think with the question of whether machines could succeed in the imitation game, in which a computer is intended to try to pass as a human in conversation.

In the passage below, "the more accurate form of the question" is this second question.

> Consider first the more accurate form of the question. I believe that in about fifty years' time it will be possible to programme computers, with a storage capacity of about 10^9, to make them play the imitation game so well that an average interrogator will not have more than 70 per cent. chance of making the right identification after five minutes of questioning. The original question, "Can machines think?" I believe to be too meaningless to deserve discussion.

> [Turing, Alan. "Computing Machinery and Intelligence." In *The Essential Turing*, edited by B. Jack Copeland, 449. Oxford: Clarendon Press, 2004.]

Wittgenstein, Ludwig (1889–1951)   *Very influential Austrian philosopher who wrote on topics such as language, mind, reality, and the nature of philosophy itself. Wittgenstein argued against the possibility of a private language; some believe his arguments show that the existence of language establishes that other minds must exist.*

Wittgenstein imagines a person, strictly by himself, trying to establish that the meaning of a word is a particular sensation he sometimes has (put another way, trying to establish the connection between the word and the sensation). His claim is that such a connection must follow a rule but that rules are social by nature; there are no criteria of correctness that could apply in principle just to one person.

> A definition surely serves to establish the meaning of a sign.—Well, this is done precisely by the concentrating of my attention; for in this way I impress on myself the connexion between the sign and the sensation.—But "I impress it on myself" can only mean: this process brings it about that I remember the connexion *right* in the future. But in the present case I have no criterion of correctness. One would like to say: whatever is going to seem right to me is right. And that only means that here we can't talk about "right."

> [Wittgenstein, Ludwig. *Philosophical Investigations*. 3rd. ed. Translated by G. E. M. Anscombe. Englewood Cliffs, N.J.: Prentice Hall, 1958.]

INDEX

A

Abelard, Peter 37–39, *38*, 91, 92
abstraction 39
abstract objects 6, 27–30, 61
accident v. essence 10–11
actuality 81
aesthetic life 160
The Age of Reason (Paine) 116
agnosticism 113
air 11, 12, 15
analogy, argument by 213–214
analytic/synthetic 50–51, 56
Anaxagoras 15
Anaximander 12
Anaximenes 12, 15
animal minds 272–275
animal suffering 153–154
anomalous monism 246–250, 279, 283
Anselm 122, 182–183
anthropic principle 142
apeiron 12
a posteriori 51
appearance v. reality 10
a priori 47, 50–51
Aquinas, Thomas. *See* Thomas Aquinas
Aristotle 183–184
  on cause 44
  on change 130–131
  on form and matter 33–35
  on God 130–131, 183–184
  on Ideas 33, 35
  on motion 131

artificial intelligence 203, 260–263, 279
atheism 112–114, 171
atomism 15
Augustine 184
axiology
  and cause 46
  and creationism 141
  and evolution 139
  and religion 111–112
  and theism/atheism 114
Ayer, A. J. 53, 56, 66

B

basic elements. *See* four elements
behaviorism. *See* logical behaviorism
Being, Parmenides on 13
Berkeley, George *19*
  on experience 16, 18–20, 93, 225–227, 282
  on God 18, 20, 228
  idealism of 16, 18–20, 224–228
  on ideas 225–226, 228, 282
  on knowledge 20
  on mind 20, 92–93, 282
  on reality 18, 19
  on skepticism 19, 226
best of all possible worlds 154–156
body. *See* mind/body problem
body continuity view 66–67, 68

brain
    cognitive science on 255–
      258
    connectionism on 258–260,
      259
    and consciousness 71–72,
      241, 268–269
    emergentism on 57–59
    empiricism on 25
    functionalism on 201, 206,
      287
    identity theory on 22–24,
      200–201, 206, 234–238
    and mind 22–24, 45, 200–
      201, 204–205. *See also*
      mind/body problem
brain states 22–24, 71, 201, 206,
    229, 234–238, 287
Brentano, Franz 203
Brentano's thesis 203
Broad, C. D. 57, 220, 283

C
Candide (Voltaire) 116, 156
Carnap, Rudolf 53
categories 16–26, 47–48, 50, 51,
    88
category mistake 232, 288
causal closure of the physical 21,
    60
causality 44–46
causal powers 29
causation, downward 60, 223
cause
    anomalous monism on 247,
      250
    Aristotle on 44
    definition of 88
    efficient 132, 193
    Hume on 42–44, 45, 51–52,
      93–94
    and incompatibilism 75–76
    Kant on 45, 52
    material 21–22
    in mind/body problem 216–
      218, 219–220
Chalmers, David J. 270

change
    Aristotle on 130–131
    Empedocles on 15
    Heraclitus on 13
    Parmenides on 100
    and personal identity 65–66
    Zeno of Elea on 14–15
change v. permanence 10
Chinese room argument 263–266,
    288–289
choice 74, 75–76, 120, 152–153
Christianity. *See also* God
    Kierkegaard on 159–160,
      188–189
    Nietzsche on 173–176, 190
Civilization and Its Discontents
    (Freud) 184–185
Clark, Andy 270
cogito ergo sum 207
cognition 254, 255–258
compatibilism 75, 77
computationalism 256–258, 279
computers. *See* artificial
    intelligence; Chinese room
    argument
conceptualism 30, 37–39, 88
Concluding Unscientific Postscript
    (Kierkegaard) 160, 188–189
concrete objects 27–29
connectionism 258–260, *259*, 279
consciousness 70–72, 239–245
    in animals 274
    and brain 71–72, 241, 268–
      269
    description of 71, 202,
      239–241
    dualism on 71, 241
    emergentism on 57–60, 220–
      221, 222
    function of 240
    Hume on 42
    mysterianism on 267–269
    mysticism on 162
    nonphysical 71, 241
    physical 71–72, 202, 241–245
contingency 81, 124, 125
cosmological argument 117, 121,
    129–130, 143–144, 180

creationism 139–142
creation science 142
Critique of Pure Reason (Kant) 50, 187–188

D

Davidson, Donald 246–250, 273–274, 283
Dawkins, Richard 136
decision theory 165
de dicto possibility 82–83, 84–85, 127
deism 112, 114–116, 180
Democritus *14*, 15
de re possibility 82–83, 85, 127
Descartes, René *208*
    on animals 272–273
    criticism of 208–209
    on knowledge 207
    on mind/body problem 200, 207, 209–210, 284
design argument 134–137
    anthropic principle in 142
    in creationism 140
    definition of 111, 117, 180
    in deism 115
    description of 121–122, 134, 144
    Paley on 134–137, 144, 191–192
determinism 46, 75–77, 119–120, 145
Dewey, John 61
Dialogues Concerning Natural Religion (Hume) 185–187
divine 109–111
divine command ethics 165–168, 180
divine predestination 146
divisibility 209
Doctrine of Ideas. *See* Ideas (Plato)
doubt 207–209
downward causation 60, 223
dualism
    on consciousness 71, 241
    criticism of 200, 208–209, 210–211, 217, 232, 236, 288

definition of 180, 205, 279
    on mind/body problem 23–24, 200, 206–210, 217, 219–220, 232, 235, 284
    property 200, 206–207, 219
    substance 81, 206, 232, 284

E

earth 11, 12, 15
efficient cause 132, 193
Either/Or (Kierkegaard) 160
eliminative materialism 230, 279
emergentism 57–60, 88, 220–223, 279, 283
emotivism 55
Empedocles 15
empiricism
    of Berkeley 18
    of Hobbes 25
    of Hume 40, 41
    logical. *See* logical positivism
    of William of Ockham 35
Enlightenment, Age of 115
An Enquiry Concerning Human Understanding (Hume) 40
An Enquiry Concerning the Principles of Morals (Hume) 40
epiphenomenalism 219–220, 250, 279–280
epistemic possibility 126
epistemological reduction 221–222
epistemology
    and cause 45–46
    and creationism 141
    evolutionary 139
    and religion 110–111
    religious 121–128
    and theism/atheism 114
esse est percipi 16, 20, 226
ethical life 160
ethics 157–176
    evolutionary 139
    and religion 111, 165–168
Euthyphro (Plato) 166
evil, problem of 119, 152–154, 180, 184

evolution 137–139, 141, 275
evolutionary epistemology 139
evolutionary ethics 139
experience
    anomalous monism on 246–
      247
    Berkeley on 16, 18–20, 93,
      225–227, 282
    Hobbes on 25
    Kant on 17, 47–51, 94–95
    Locke on 18, 225
    logical positivism on 54, 55
    mystical 162–163
    pre-Socratic philosophy on
      10
extended mind hypothesis 269–
  271, 280

F

faith 117–120, 158, 159–160,
  188–189
Fear and Trembling (Kierkegaard)
  161
Fichte, Johann Gottlieb 17
fideism 158, 180
final cause 44
fire 11, 12, 15
First Cause 129–130
Five Ways 130–133, 180, 193–194
flying arrow paradox 14
folk psychology 229–230, 280
foreknowledge, problem of divine
  119–120, 145–146, 180
form and matter 33–35
four elements 11–12, 15
Franklin, Benjamin 116
freedom 72–77
    and choice 46, 74, 75–76
    constraints on 73–74
    Hobbes on 26
    and incompatibilism 75–77
    metaphysical 72–75
    negative 72–73
    political 72
    positive 72–73
    and problem of evil 152–153
Frege, Gottlob 53

Freud, Sigmund 171–172, 172,
  184–185
functionalism
    definition of 280
    on mind 201, 206, 250–254,
      287

G

The Gay Science (Nietzsche) 173
German Idealism 17
God
    Aristotle on 130–131, 183–
      184
    atheism on 113
    axiological aspects of 114
    Berkeley on 18, 20, 228
    cosmological argument on
      117, 121, 129–130, 143–
      144, 180
    deism on 112, 114–116, 180
    design argument on. See
      design argument
    divine command ethics on
      165–168, 180
    epistemological aspects of
      114
    Freud on 171–172
    Kant on 187–188
    Kierkegaard on 159–161,
      188–189
    Leibniz on 78, 154–156
    metaphysical aspects of 114
    modal argument on 127–128
    moral argument on 118,
      187–188
    mysticism on 162–163
    nature of 118–120, 145,
      147–151, 181
    as necessary being 83–84,
      123–125, 127–128, 132,
      181, 193–194
    Nietzsche on 173–176
    ontological argument on 118,
      121–123, 127, 149, 181,
      182–183
    pantheism on 112, 150
    Pascal on 163–165

Plantinga on 127–128, 192
Plato on 166
and problem of evil 119,
152–154, 180, 184
theism on 112–114, 152
Thomas Aquinas on 83–84,
124, 149, 193–194
governance of the world 133
government, and religion 168–169,
181
gradation, proof of 132–133
Griffin, Donald 274

H

Hegel, Georg W. F. 17, 159
Hempel, Carl 53
Heraclitus 12–13
Herbert of Cherbury *115*, 115–116
Hicks, John 153
Hobbes, Thomas 24–26, *25*, 228–
229, 284–285
Hume, David 40–44, *43*
on cause 42–44, 45, 51–52,
93–94
on consciousness 42
on ideas 41
on metaphysics 8
on nature 43, 44
on personal identity 41–42,
67
on religion 185–187
on science 43, 44
on skepticism 40–42

I

idea
Berkeley on 225–226, 228,
282
Hume on 41
idealism 16–18, 224–228. *See also*
German Idealism
of Berkeley 16, 18–20, 224–
228
definition of 88, 280
on reality 16, 205, 224
transcendental 17

Ideas (Plato) 16, 30–33, 34, 100,
224
identity theory 22–24, 200–201,
206, 234–238, 280
images of the world 61–69, 102
immaterialism 20, 224–225
incompatibilism 74–75
inductive argument 213–214
innate ideas 18
intelligent design 142
intentionality 202–203, 210, 229,
237, 280
inverted spectrum argument
252–253

J

Jackson, Frank 63, 202, 242, 286
James, William 162, *163*
Jefferson, Thomas 116, 168–169
Johnson, Samuel 226–227, *227*

K

Kant, Immanuel 46–52, *49*
on cause 45, 52
on experience 17, 46–51,
94–95
on knowledge 17, 46–51,
94–95
on mind 17, 47–48, 95
on morality 187–188
on nature 94–95
on personal identity 48–50
on time and space 17, 47
transcendental idealism of 17
Das Kapital (Marx) 170
Kierkegaard, Søren 158–162, 166,
188–189
knowledge
of abstract objects 29
Berkeley on 20
of concrete objects 29
Descartes on 207
of divine and sacred 110–111
Kant on 17, 46–51, 94–95
logical behaviorism on 231
logical positivism on 53

of nature of God 118–120,
150–151
pre-Socratic philosophy on 10
of the world 40–52

L

La Mettrie, Julien Offray de 229
language
    Davidson on 273–274
    logical positivism on 54–55
    Quine on 287–288
    Wittgenstein on 214–215,
    290
Leibniz, Gottfried 78–81, 79,
95–96, 154–156, 155
Leibniz's law 207, 209
Leucippus 15
Lewes, George 57, 58
Lewis, David 84–85, 96–97
libertarianism 75–77
life, materialism on 22
Locke, John 18, 66, 225
logical behaviorism 206, 231–234,
280, 288
logical empiricism. See logical
    positivism
logical positivism 8, 53, 88,
102–103
logical possibility 82, 125–126
Love, Empedocles on 15

M

manifest image 61, 63, 102
The Manifesto of the Communist
    Party (Marx) 170
many v. the one 10, 11
Marx, Karl 170, 170–171, 189–
190
master morality 175
materialism 21–24. See also
    functionalism; identity theory;
    logical behaviorism; physicalism
    critics of 24
    definition of 21, 88, 180, 280
    dualism compared to 23–24

eliminative 230, 279
of Hobbes 24–26, 228–229,
284–285
on mind/body problem
22–23, 228–238, 284–285
pre-Socratic 21
Mawdudi, Abu'l A'la 169
Mayr, Ernst 137
McGinn, Colin 267–269
Mead, George Herbert 67
meaningfulness 54–56
meaning of life 112
mental causation 45, 216–218
mental events 246–250, 283
mental states
    and body 200
    and brain states 71, 201
    definition of 70
    functionalism on 201, 250–
    254, 287
    identity theory on 22–24,
    201, 206, 234–238
    intentionality of 202–203,
    229
    logical behaviorism on 231–
    234
metaphysical freedom 72–75
metaphysics 1–103. See also
    reality
    and cause 45
    and creationism 140
    definition of 5
    and evolution 139
    importance of 8–9
    rejection of 8, 53–56
    and religion 110
    and theism/atheism 114
    topics in 5–7
Mill, John Stuart 57, 97–99, 98
mind 8–9, 195–290. See also
    cognition; consciousness
    of animals 272–275
    anomalous monism on 246–
    250, 283
    Berkeley on 20, 92–93, 282
    and brain 22–24, 45, 200–
    201, 204–205

emergentism on 59, 220–223

extended 269–271, 280

folk psychology on 230

functionalism on 201, 206, 250–254, 287

Hegel on 17

idealism on 16, 224–228

identity theory on 22–24, 200–201, 206, 234–238

intentionality of 202–203, 210, 229, 237

Kant on 17, 47–48, 95

logical behaviorism on 231–234

materialism on 22–23, 228–238

other, problem of 212–215

physicalism on 200, 201, 203, 205–206, 228–230

qualia experienced by. *See* qualia

theory of 275

mind/body problem 199–200, 204–211

cause in 216–218, 219–220

Descartes on 200, 207, 209–210, 284

dualism on 23–24, 200, 206–210, 217, 219–220, 232, 235, 284

epiphenomenalism on 219–220, 250

Leibniz on 80–81

materialism on 23–24, 205–206, 284–285

monism on 205–206

mind continuity view 66–67, 68

modal argument 127–128

modality 7, 81–84, 89, 125–128

modal realism 84–85, 96–97

monads 78–80, 95–96

monism. *See also* idealism; materialism

anomalous 246–250, 279, 283

definition of 11, 205, 280

on mind/body problem 205–206

pre-Socratic 11–15

moral argument 118, 187–188

morality

Kant on 187–188

Nietzsche on 175

and religion 111, 165–168

motion

Aristotle on 131

Heraclitus on 13

Parmenides on 100

Zeno of Elea on 14–15

multiple realizability argument 237

mysterianism 267–269, 281

mysticism 162–163

N

Nagel, Thomas 71, 202, 239, 242–244, 274, 286–287

naturalism 61, 139

natural religion 140, 143–145, 180. *See also* deism

natural theology 110–111

Natural Theology (Paley) 191–192

nature

complexity of. *See* design argument

creationism on 139–142

evolution in 137–139

Hume on 43, 44

Kant on 94–95

uniformity of 43, 44

necessary being 83–84, 123–125, 127–128, 132, 181, 193–194

necessity and possibility. *See* modality

negative freedom 72–73

Neurath, Otto 53

Nietzsche, Friedrich 173–176, *174*, 190

no continuity view 66, 67

nominalism 30, 35–37, *36*, 89, 99

noumena/phenomena 17, 48
nous 15
numbers 12

O

Ockham, William of 35–37, *36,*
    99, 166
Ockham's razor 35
omnibenevolence 147, 181
omnipotence 147, 149, 181
omniscience 147, 181
On the Genealogy of Morals
    (Nietzsche) 175
On the Plurality of Worlds (Lewis)
    97
ontological argument 118, 121–
    123, 127, 149, 181, 182–183
ontological commitment 89
ontological reduction 221
ontology 5–6, 89
other minds, problem of 212–215
overman. *See* superman

P

Paine, Thomas 116
Paley, William 134–135, 136–137,
    144, 191–192
pantheism 112, 150
paradox of the stone 147–149,
    181
parallelism 80–81, 218, 281
Parmenides 13, 15, 100
particulars 29–30, 39, 89
Pascal, Blaise *164,* 164–165
Pascal's wager 163–165, 181
personal identity (self) 8–9, 63–68
    of animals 275
    and change 65–66
    components of 64–65
    Hume on 41–42, 67
    Kant on 48–50
    views of 66–67, 68
Phaedo (Plato) 100–101
phenomena. *See* noumena/
    phenomena

physical, causal closure of the 21,
    60
physicalism 21, 228–230. *See also*
    materialism
    definition of 280
    on mind 200, 201, 203, 205–
        206, 228–230
physical possibility 82, 125–126
Plantinga, Alvin *126,* 192
Plantinga's modal argument 127–
    128
Plato *31,* 100–101
    on God 166
    on Ideas 16, 30–33, 34, 100,
        224
pluralism 11, 15
political freedom 72
positive freedom 72–73
possibility
    de dicto 82–83, 84–85
    de re 82–83, 85
    logical 82
    physical 82
possible worlds 78–85, 89, 97,
    154–156
prayer 111
predestination, divine 146
pre-Socratic philosophers 9–15, 21
primary qualities 18, 20, 225, 226
primary substance 34
Prime Mover 129–130
properties 33–35
property dualism 200, 206–207,
    219
Proslogium (Anselm) 182–183
psychology 229–230. *See also* folk
    psychology
psychophysical laws 249
Putnam, Hilary 237, 287
Pythagoras 12, *13*

Q

qualia
    and consciousness 240–241
    definition of 281
    dualism on 210

functionalism on 253–254
logical behaviorism on 234
materialism on 201, 229
thought experiment on 63,
    201–202, 242
qualitative sameness 65
qualities 18, 20, 225, 226
quantitative sameness 65
Quine, Willard Van Orman 53,
    56, 83, 127, 287–288

R

rationality, principle of 248–249
realism
    Abelard on 37
    definition of 89
    v. idealism 16, 224
    modal 84–85, 96–97
    Plato on 30–33
    on universals 30
    William of Ockham on 35, 37
reality
    Berkeley on 18, 19
    categories of 16–26
    components of 5–6
    Hegel on 17
    idealism on 16, 205, 224
    Leibniz on 78, 80
    Parmenides on 100
    Plato on 32, 100
    Sellars on 62
reason 48
reductionism 221–222, 243, 281
religion 105–194. See also
    Christianity; faith; God
    axiological aspects of 111–
        112
    characteristics of 109–110
    epistemological aspects of
        110–111
    Freud on 171–172, 184–185
    and government 168–169,
        181
    Hume on 185–187
    Marx on 171, 189–190
    metaphysical aspects of 110

natural 140, 143–145, 180.
    See also deism
Nietzsche on 173–176, 190
revealed 143–146, 181
and science 157–176
religious epistemology 121–128
revealed religion 143–146, 181
revelatory theology 111
Rousseau, Jean-Jacques 116
Russell, Bertrand 53
Ryle, Gilbert 232, 288

S

sacred 109–111
sameness
    qualitative 65
    quantitative 65
Schelling, F. W. J. von 17
Schlick, Moritz 53, 54
science
    on brain 205, 206, 236
    and creationism 140–142
    Hume on 43, 44
    logical positivism on 53–54
    and materialism 21
    and religion 157–176
    Sellars on 62–63
scientific image 61, 63, 102
Searle, John 263–266, 265,
    288–289
secondary qualities 18, 20, 225,
    226
secondary substance 34
self. See personal identity
Sellars, Roy Wood 61
Sellars, Wilfrid 61–63, 62, 102
sensations
    Hobbes on 25
    Kant on 47, 48, 50
    logical positivism on 54, 55
sentences
    contingency of 125
    logical positivism on 54–55
skepticism
    Berkeley on 19, 226
    of Hume 40–42

Skinner, B. F. 289
slave morality 175
social continuity view 66, 67
Socrates 166–167
solipsism 212–215, 281
soul
    dualism on 205
    evil and 153
    Leibniz on 78, 80
space. *See* time and space
Strife, Empedocles on 15
substance
    Aristotle on 33–35
    definition of 89
    Leibniz on 78
    Mill on 97–99
substance dualism 81, 206, 232,
    284
Summa Logicae (Ockham) 99
superman (overman) 173
A System of Logic (Mill) 97–99
systems reply 265–266

T
technological possibility 126
teleological argument. *See* design
    argument
teleology 44
temporal possibility 126
Thales 11, 21
theism 112–114, 152
theocracy 110, 168–169, 181
theodicy 181
theology 110, 143
theoretical entities 61–62
Theseus's ship 68–69
Thomas Aquinas 83, *131, 148*
    Five Ways of 130–133, 180,
        193–194
    on God 83–84, 124, 149,
        193–194
Thus Spoke Zarathustra
    (Nietzsche) 173

time and space
    and abstract and concrete
        objects 28–29
    Kant on 17, 47
token identity theory 22–23, 235,
    237–238
transcendental ego 49–50
transcendental idealism 17
truth 160
Turing, Alan 256–257, 261, *261,*
    289–290
Turing machine *256,* 256–257,
    281, 289
Turing test 261–262, 281, 289
type identity theory 22, 23, 235,
    237

U
universals 29–30, 36–39, 90, 91,
    99
Unmoved Mover 130–131, 132,
    183–184

V
verifiability/verificationism 54–56,
    90
Vienna Circle 53, 102–103
Voltaire 116, 156, *156*

W
Waismann, Friedrich 53
watchmaker argument 134–137,
    144, 191–192
water 11, 12, 15
Whitehead, Alfred North 53
Wittgenstein, Ludwig 55, 214–
    215, 233, 290

Z
Zeno of Elea 14–15